BROTHERS
UNDER THE SKIN

CHRISTOPHER HOPE

BROTHERS UNDER THE SKIN

TRAVELS IN TYRANNY

PICADOR

First published 2003 by Macmillan

This edition published 2013 by Picador
an imprint of Pan Macmillan, a division of Macmillan Publishers Limited
Pan Macmillan, 20 New Wharf Road, London N1 9RR
Basingstoke and Oxford
Associated companies throughout the world
www.panmacmillan.com

ISBN 978-1-4472-5974-9

A CIP catalogue record for this book is available from
the British Library.

Typeset by SX Composing DTP, Rayleigh, Essex

All Pan Macmillan titles are available from www.panmacmillan.com
or from Bookpost by telephoning 01624 677237

To those Zimbabweans I may not name, and in memory of those I cannot forget

Sections of this book first appeared, in a slightly different form, in: the *Guardian*; the *Sunday Times*; BBC Radio 3 and Radio 4; Condé Naste 'Traveller'; *New British Writing*; *Esquire*; the *New Republic* and the *Berliner Wochenpost*.

When he laughed respectable senators burst with laughter,
When he cried the little children died in the streets

W. H. Auden, 'Epitaph for a Tyrant'

ONE

THE GREAT SILENCE

I crossed the Limpopo River at Beit Bridge. Ahead of me Zimbabwe loomed in a shimmer of heat. I'd been passing to and fro across this bridge on South Africa's northern border for decades. The drought had reduced the river to a muddy dribble far below. Now the flood was on the bridge itself, and it was human: a constant stream of travellers desperate to get out of Zimbabwe and into South Africa, the green land fat with promise. Traders, refugees, the hungry, the frightened – and the 'border jumpers' who, if they cannot cross the bridge today, will be back tomorrow at less well-known points, ready to dodge the South African border patrols, to risk the Limpopo and its crocs, and the veld and its lions, to get down south. South was salvation. Only fools, or truckers, or people looking for trouble, headed in the other direction.

The South African border police were surprised to find someone who actually wanted to cross into Zimbabwe. There were two cops, him and her. Why did I want to go there – when there was so little to be had? No soap, no sugar – 'no nothing'. Journalists went to Zimbabwe, but that was a bad idea because they were not allowed there. The country was gearing up for an election, and the year of 2002 was already marked by fear and bloodshed. 'That old man up there is causing so much trouble.' I could feel his quizzical scepticism focus on my car, my baggage. His colleague patted my shoulder: 'Please come back to us, safely.'

I was too old a South African to have anything but mixed feelings about the kindness of constables. It didn't matter that these were the new South African police, or that they were black, but their words worried me as I drove across the ramshackle iron raft that spanned the thin waters of the Limpopo River.

No one today thinks about the name of this bridge, but then in Zimbabwe today no one thinks much about anything, except hunger and politics and fear. That is a pity. Between the grandiose dreams of these hoodlum-tycoons, and the present-day misery of Zimbabwe, there is a link as real as this rusting shaft of steel. The man who gave this bridge its name, a Jewish diamond trader named Alfred Beit, was the man who, together with Cecil John Rhodes, invented – or might be said to have 'floated' – the country across the Limpopo, more or less the way investors float a company. It looked and sounded like a real country, and it was named Rhodesia, in honour of its founder-chairman, but it was, literally, a corporate raid, an armed take-over by men hungry for gold.

All that has gone now. Rhodesia is no more, and the country that succeeded it, Zimbabwe, born in such great hopes, is as sad a place as exists on the planet. Robert Mugabe has been in power for over twenty years and he has decided, in what is perhaps a final spasm of his absolute power, to redress the wrongs of history by seizing back from the white formerly British settlers, all their ill-gotten gains. It is late in the day. Once upon a time there were around a quarter of a million white people in Rhodesia–Zimbabwe.

Since Robert Mugabe took power in 1980, their numbers have dwindled and now stand at around 30,000 – some think the number is lower, no one is counting any more. The remaining 'whites', a hateful description of a tiny remnant, still have some financial importance, but they are of no political standing. That doesn't mean that the Leader's war of extirpation can be relaxed for a moment. As I crossed the border at Beit Bridge they were changing the names of towns and schools, to remove signs of alien contamination. The Leader had grown exasperated: 'Look, we have even more little Englands, new Englands and south Englands here than there are in Britain itself. All these filthy imperial names must go.'

That was the essence of Robert Mugabe's election programme: semantic hygiene, racial cleansing; a new and pure Zimbabwe, scrubbed clean of all foreign pollutants – English names, treacherous blacks in the pay of foreign imperialists, decadent white farmers, 'filthy' British, scheming Jews and prancing, plotting mafias of gay conspirators. In Zimbabwe today all enemies are 'white'; even black enemies undergo this skin transplant and become pale-faced messengers of foreign forces, Caucasian 'teaboys', imitation Englishmen. These pariahs, these enemies of the 'pure', native-born sons of the soil, are to be harried and got rid of by any means possible, hunted by gangs of militia, tracked down by the police and army, or assaulted by 'veterans' of the old liberation army. I go there compulsively because I do not believe what I hear – and when I see it, I still have the greatest difficulty believing it.

Once I had driven across Beit Bridge on to the Zimbabwean side of the river, I waited in a holding area, a bureaucratic limbo, where the dozens of truckers who shunt food and petrol into Zimbabwe from South Africa spend hours waiting to clear customs. Two men in caps and badges directed me to a quiet spot where they offered me the relevant customs forms for a 'fee', pointing out that without these papers it would be dangerous to proceed. The forms were useless, the men were thugs, but it was an offer hard to overlook. These highwaymen were working with increasing desperation since South African tourists had stopped visiting Zimbabwe. I paid up and then went into the passport control office to get my permit, paid again, and went on paying up until finally I reached the old iron gate which the guard opened just wide enough to allow one car at a time to squeeze through. I was in.

The road ran up the hill and into the heat haze. I drove past the steak house, the duty-free shop and the Sexually Transmitted Infections Clinic. I drove past dusty curio stalls where patient hawkers waited beside carved wooden elephants for tourists who never came. The money-changers hoisted their wares – great bricks of near-worthless banknotes. Several men ran into the road: pimps, offering women. Zimbabweans have nothing anyone wants to buy, except themselves.

The first face I had seen on the other side was the Leader's. He looked at me from the fence to which his poster had been wired – just him and me, in the immensity of Africa. The eyes were to follow me across the country. The posters were models of understatement. A small headline said: 'Vote ZANU-PF 2002', and all the other space was given over to presenting the face of the party, the face of the country, the face of the future. As I found out soon enough, the face was everywhere. As I drove into the flat dry fastness of Southern Matabeleland, the image of the Leader had been fastened to the fences in serial displays – posters were planted in clumps like some strange crop, and flowered before me. There were no competing images. One face alone. He raised a clenched fist, a curious gingerly brandishing of the freedom fighter's tight-fingered club – but then there has always been something strangely timid about Mugabe. He is a modest exterior over a deep well of malevolence: green army fatigues and curious pinky glasses – Ozymandias in rose-tinted specs.

What struck me as I travelled across the burning land was the great silence. I'd been this way before many times, but something had altered, the silence had deepened. The country was baked bone dry, aching for rain, food was scarce, but more than that – and nothing prepared me for it – was the sense of vacancy. Overhead the eagles were lifting on the warm air currents, otherwise nothing moved; you had the feeling that this was a country in hiding. The police, however, were everywhere.

The shops were sad bedraggled affairs: bare shelves and rising prices, inflation topping 100 per cent. Zimbabwe had no cooking oil, soap, paraffin, and little maize-meal, the staple food, but it did have one of the highest Aids counts in Africa. People were hungry, unhappy, angry and ill. Zimbabwe, in February 2002, was out of energy, out of luck and a little bit out of its mind.

I drove for about two hours along the road to Bulawayo without seeing a soul – just the occasional wrecked car rusting under the thorn trees and a dead donkey in a ditch, its legs pointing stiffly at the high blue sky. It was a relief then to meet Sam. He was walking, he was very thin, but he was human and I gave him a lift. Sam was on his way to Bulawayo because he'd heard that the president was to speak in a nearby town and Sam was a fan. Sam was on his way to tell the president he would vote for him though the people in his village were hungry and his cousins further north were eating roots. I asked him why food was scarce – did he blame the drought? 'No', said Sam, he blamed, 'the British'. They were working with certain farmers and others 'to keep maize for themselves'.

'British?'

He looked slightly unsure. 'Well – whites,' he said.

I dropped Sam in Bulawayo where I spent the night and next morning I set off deeper into Matabeleland. I had the vague idea of heading towards Victoria Falls, about six hours away, but really I just wanted to wander in the countryside. The best way I knew of getting somewhere was to get gently lost. I wasn't much fussed about where I ended up, though I was a little anxious. 'Best not drive today, not to drive at all between Bulawayo and Vic Falls,' people told me. There were rumours of roadblocks, militias, police. 'Besides,' they said, 'you will stand out.'

I drove along the flat empty road that runs between Bulawayo and Victoria Falls. Again, the eerie silence. An hour went by before I saw another car. It was Saturday, a summer afternoon and the heat was becoming oppressive. More than anything I felt tension. It wasn't the isolated incidents, bloody as they were: someone decapitated, a farmer shot – it was a palpable adulteration of the light, it was like some metallic taste. Zimbabwe was plunging into some peculiar circle of hell far from anything I knew and yet, in a perverse way, the place felt like home. I was scared, yes, but it was a kind of homing fear, a fear I could ride, it made a pathway that took me back to what I knew best, to where I belonged. I had been here before, or in places like it; in a previous life, in several previous lives. I had been travelling in this country for forty years. I was, in a curious way, at home. But here was the odd thing – I didn't really recognize Zimbabwe. It took me back to somewhere I knew far better – South Africa in the Sixties – the same fear, the same reiterated slogans so weird it seemed no one could possibly take them seriously. It came as a shock that you were wrong about that, and those who ran the show believed very passionately in all they said. If you did not see that then you, and not they, were the problem.

Apart from the cows and the warthogs, the occasional elephant – nothing – not the peace of the countryside, but a mute and mutinous, edgy, hateful silence of fear. I could feel it and I could smell it. Africa, in the bush, is not a quiet place. At the very least there is the wind, there are always stirrings of life, if only the cicadas. This strange humped waiting emptiness was something that I'd never encountered before – a hesitant, heightened expectancy. Partly, I knew it was my own internal anxiety that gave this feeling to the great rolling land that stretched away on either side of the road to Victoria Falls; but, partly, it was the spirit of the country that was hushed, it was a country in waiting. Alone in Africa, you know that there are animals which might suddenly veer into your path, but you also know that the predators of the bush are no danger when measured beside the unbearable stupidity and cruelty and malice of modern human beings.

My first roadblock was a modest affair, several stones and

a large tree trunk had been laid across the road, and a group of young men in white T-shirts stood armed with copies of AK47s carved from wood. I knew who they were, they were the youth brigade, the militia, the party White Shirts, and they showed a green legend across their chests that read: 'The Third Chimurenga'. The Chimurenga were notable struggles for freedom in Zimbabwe. The First Chimurenga was the uprising by Shona forces against the occupying British colonialists who had taken away large swathes of their country and made it their own. The First Chimurenga failed but it was remembered with pride. The Second Chimurenga was the bush war against the white regime of Ian Smith in the Seventies. The people of Zimbabwe won the Second Chimurenga and Zimbabwe was born. Now Robert Mugabe had launched the Third Chimurenga. This time the enemy was anyone who opposed him, anyone who did not belong to the ruling party, anyone who did not show sufficient appreciation for the benefits the Leader had brought to his people, anyone who whispered that, after twenty years of absolute power, independence and free-dom, things had been better under the British, things had even been better under Ian Smith. And since it was almost impossible to travel across Zimbabwe without finding people everywhere who believed that, and said so with surprising frankness, the Third Chimurenga had become a war directed by the Leader against his own people.

The young men in the white T-shirts were Mugabe-*Jugend*, the wandering militias. Their job, principally, was to terrify people. They wanted my papers, they wanted me out of the car. They wanted me to open my boot, my baggage, and my glove compartment. I did as I was told. I didn't know what they were looking for, and they didn't know what they were looking for, but they would know it when they found it. When they had searched my car and found nothing, they turned to me and asked what a white man was doing on these roads on a hot afternoon. They had found what they were looking for. I had been singled out because of the colour of my skin. To these young men anyone of my racial type was an enemy, a spy, or both. My colour alone made me a representative of the former colonial power. I was essentially and intrinsically bad – in the words of their Leader: 'The white man is evil.'

That is what I meant when I said I felt entirely at home, and familiar, in Zimbabwe – perhaps, and very nervous, but not for a moment did I fail to see where I was. I was in exactly the same position as many blacks had been in in South Africa, in the days when, in the eyes of whites, your race elevated you or, if you were black, set you apart – as untrustworthy, treacherous, backward. Your skin colour helped to identify you for the devil you were and you had no defence against the charge. These young men, with their angry paranoia, were exactly the same sort of brutal, boring, muscled hoodlums whose delight and duty it was in the old South Africa to hate and harass black people. What was new this time round was that I was on the receiving end. Surrounded by the Mugabe Militia, I was in a position to see the irony of my situation, but it did nothing to relieve the sense I had of the overwhelming, bone-crushing, ele-phantine stupidity of my captors.

Even in the old days, under the regime of Ian Smith, Rhodesia had little of the obsessive, semi-mystical, fatal obsession with race and colour that had been South Africa's tragedy. You went to Zimbabwe to get away from all that; you went there because you did not find terminal tensions.

There was nothing in Zimbabwe of our disease: The sniffing out of 'wrongly' coloured people, the cult of the skin, the measurement of melanin, or the lack of it. The plague had never jumped the border. Until now. In the windless heat of February on that African afternoon, I took note of what I was seeing. When people said later: 'Of course, Zimbabwe was never like that, no one would have been that crazy, that stupid, that diabolical', then I would have my notes.

The young men in the Chimurenga T-shirts tired of me. I had disappointed them; I carried nothing but a suitcase and a notebook. My car was registered in Johannesburg, my passport was Irish. I was not a 'settler', a white farmer, the villain demonized in the Zimbabwean party press for his conspiratorial, murderous ways. They took another look through my suitcase. Nothing. There were other cars coming along and I saw they hoped perhaps they'd catch another, more interesting, victim. I worried a little about my notebook, but the idea of anyone writing anything down was far from the minds of these young men. They handed me back my pen and my notebook as if they were quaint and outworn devices, like ladies' fans, or a snuff box – relics from another era that no one in the modern world had any use for. They may well have been right, but I was glad they didn't look too hard.

I drove on into the hushed immensity of Matabeleland, came over a rise, and hit a second roadblock. This time it was the police, polite and effective, and they searched my car for arms. It is a fact everywhere to be noted in a police state that the police believe they are facing an invisible army of well-armed fighters and so they stop you often, searching for arms. But I had no arms, I was heading towards Victoria

Falls where all foreigners wish to go, and so they waved me on my way.

I'd almost relaxed, and I was driving down a long hill near a place called Lupane, when I saw the third roadblock at the bottom of the slope. It was manned by men in ties and dark glasses, and I knew before they opened their mouths and asked for my passport who they were. I had, within an hour, met with two branches of Mugabe's private army: the youth militias, the uniformed police, and here was the third: his palace guard, his eyes and ears, the secret police, the slim young men of the CIO, the Central Intelligence Organization. They were, with perhaps a shade or two in difference in skin colour, the same secret army of spooks who had once served the old white tyrant, Ian Smith and his government, that amazing combination of preposterous whip-carriers and boastful cranks. When Smith went in 1980, and Mugabe arrived, it has always been one of those cherished legends that he asked the Chief of the CIO, Ken Flower, to stay on. He agreed, stayed on and served, as did numbers of his operatives. This has sometimes been held up as rather desirable, the continuity provided by democratic civil servants who moved between governments without taking sides. It is also nonsense. The old CIO – like the old intelligence organizations in South Africa of which the best known was the Bureau of State Security, or BOSS – was not there to safeguard the security of the country, but to ensure that the regime should stay in power forever, and it did so by eliminating enemies of the state. The CIO was amongst the most vicious and malicious of the secret agencies dedicated to protecting the ruler and his entourage.

As an agency, it has been encouraged to harass and murder anyone designated an 'enemy'. It has done so with eagerness; it has never been held responsible for its actions, not under Ian Smith nor under Robert Mugabe.

The CIO under Ian Smith spent much energy laying plans to assassinate Robert Mugabe: the CIO under Robert Mugabe spent much time planning and carrying out assassinations of his enemies. And the Organization did so safe in the knowledge that its officers would never be called to account. Those who complained that agencies like the secret police were 'beyond the law' missed the point. These professional, well-dressed, softly spoken thugs were entirely within the law. They lived by the only reality that held in Zimbabwe, the only rule that counted: 'Preserve the President and prolong him in power, by all means possible, forever and ever, amen.' When people say to me that these things are 'perfectly normal', when liberals turn Machiavellian, confronted by realities in far-away countries where they do not live, I disagree. No matter how many times I see a tyrant's police in action I am shocked – by their easy assumption of power, by their cynicism, by their sleek, comfortable ordinariness.

I watched the CIO men flagging down the occasional passing truck or taxi; their demeanour was so effortlessly superior that you realized for how many years they had been the untouchable élite, accustomed to obedience, always above the people, the law – above human comprehension. The CIO operatives were urban, middle-class, and this made them even more distinctive in the hot and helplessly poor place that Lupane was. Along the dirt roads that intersected the national road there appeared bus after bus filled with passengers drawn from the surrounding villages.

I also noticed, parked under the trees and further down the road, police vans and army vehicles. The buses let out their passengers at the main road and from there the people streamed across the veld. Lots of them carried umbrellas and were dressed smartly, as if they were on their way to a wedding. Many in the crowd wore the white T-shirts showing the Third Chimurenga slogan, their ribs showed through the cheap cotton like the staves of a barrel. The drought of 2002 threatened to be every bit as bad as the dry times had that hit the country in the Nineties. An excited, happy, hungry throng; soon there were hundreds climbing off the buses and walking up the hill, marshalled by the police.

I waited for the CIO to decide what to do with me. Clearly something was up, because they really didn't care about me, they didn't want to detain me, but equally I could see they couldn't let me go. The reason for this was suddenly clear. I heard it high overhead, everyone heard it, people began pointing, and there it was, a white helicopter in the blue sky. It was the Big Man himself. I had walked straight into a Mugabe rally.

TWO

BOB'S MY UNCLE

They made me leave the car and walk across the fields. Hundreds were pouring off the buses now – those lumbering beasts you see careering along Zimbabwean roads, coughing noxious black smoke from the blend of petrol and diesel that fuels them. The crowds at the great official presidential rallies of 2002, like all the trappings of that great electoral road-show, were part of the scenery: people from miles around were bused in, after someone had frightened them with vivid depictions of what happened to those who did not back the Party, or sweetened their threats with blandishments – a party T-shirt, a pamphlet, even the journey itself – no small thing when you do not have the means to go anywhere. These were excited people. There was also the perverse pleasure of being shoved around by someone really important – a sort of masochistic snobbery we seemed prone to when the bully was impressive enough. I remember talking to people who had been pushed and punched by Al Gore's bodyguard when the Vice President came to South Africa to receive some accolade for his liberal disposition. I think it may have been the freedom of the city of Soweto, or something equally incongruous. Without meaning to do so, some of the bystanders got in the way of the Vice-Presidential progress. They didn't know who they were looking at. They simply stopped to gape at the limousine, at the big men with mikes stuck in their ears who flanked the Personage. They intended no harm, but the Vice President's secret-service minders knocked them away from the sacred being, scattered them like chaff – and the procession moved on. Those assailed felt mildly angry, then surprised, then cheered, and even rather excited, when they discovered who it was who had beaten them up. After all, they thought, as they rubbed their bumps and bruises, it was not every day you got assaulted by the foot-soldiers of the Vice President of the United States.

After walking for about five or ten minutes we came to a large amphitheatre, a clearing in the bush, big enough to accommodate the thousands of spectators. At the far end was a podium draped with flags, a rail behind which the microphones waited, and showing everywhere, the banners and slogans of the ruling party, ZANU-PF. The rally resembled the faith-healing meetings that were taking place around the country in the run-up to the elections. These revivalist sects punted a simple message: Mugabe was the way, the truth and the light; a vote for the Leader was a prayer to God, and a vote for the opposition was a sop to the devil. The dusty place, my police escort told me, was called the Lupane Business Centre. More hot air. There was no centre, there was no business, it was nothing more than a parade ground where the obedient populous might be conveniently marshalled, policed and disciplined.

There was though the strong tradition of hopeful magic and of trying your luck. The Lord showed himself to his subjects, who assembled to pay him homage. His eye might fall on the poorest, the unhappiest, the hungriest (hundreds at the Lupane Business Centre qualified on all counts) and the wretch would be showered with treasure. Amongst the crowd, perhaps, was my passenger of the day before, Sam, who had left his village to walk to Bulawayo to see the president. He would arise and seek out the Lord and beg him to work a miracle – and feed his village.

Such pseudo-religiosity arises out of the hotchpotch of ingredients that make up Mugabe's political creed, and which might be described as pan-African nationalism, founded upon a base of agrarian Maoism. It remains the core belief amongst pan-African Nationalists: a philosophy in which the 'peasant' is exalted, 'the land' worshipped, much in the way the Nazis revered 'the soil'. Often, what it comes down to is empty words, gestures and slogans. When your followers tire of promises and demand bread you give them bullets. The founding father of this fusion of blood, soil and African soul was Kwame Nkrumah, the former president of Ghana, known as 'the Redeemer'. In a little-known series of lectures, Nkrumah once defined the central commandment of his faith: 'Seek ye first the political kingdom.'

Thus the air of anticipation; this was an afternoon with the Redeemer, the Messiah's matinée.

It was very hot. Suddenly people were pointing upward again and, shading our eyes, we saw the white helicopter hanging above us. It hovered and some murmured, others clapped; it was a revelation, a god descending. Uniformed policemen took up positions around the edges of the crowd and a file of soldiers moved into place between the podium and the people. The crowd was boxed in by the police at their backs and by soldiers who faced inwards, their guns at the ready.

Thanks to the slim young men from the CIO, I had been given a free seat at one of those rare performances in which the President showed himself to the people. It was odd that this was Lupane. There was something else that weighed on the people whom I saw at the Lupane rally, something no one talked about, but it had never been forgotten. Or forgiven. Lupane, and the places around it, were killing grounds in the 1980s. It was here that Robert Mugabe's ethnic exterminators, the red bereted Fifth Brigade, raped, burnt and assassinated thousands. No word of Five Brigade was spoken, no graves of the victims marked their resting place, no reparation was ever made by the killers or their masters, but the ghosts of the murdered walked this land. At the shoulders of those excited people getting down from the buses, you could almost feel the phantoms throng. The ghosts were a warning; they reminded people in Matabeleland that it might happen again. Should the Leader decree, another brigade of killers could sweep through the lands and kill them, all over again. There was nothing they could do about it.

Everyone knew where they were. In this place, back in 1983, Five Brigade made its first appearance. The Brigade had only been in the Lupane area for a few weeks when their North Korean 'instruction' became horribly apparent. In a month and a half, the men in the red berets murdered more than two thousand people, often in public executions. The largest massacre, where sixty-two men and women were shot, took place on the banks of the Cewale River, not far from the meeting I was attending. Not long after that, fifty-two men and women were shot in the village of Silwane. As with other killings of that time, these murders have never been acknowledged.

All around me sat people from whose families and villages the victims of the Fifth Brigade had come. Here, too, were the agents of the State from whose ranks the killers had been drawn. All the principals in the Zimbabwean tragedy were assembled: the 'voters' – nothing but election fodder for the great machine of the state; the gruff and rather pompous uniformed police; the watchful troops under the trees, pointing their rifles towards the crowd; the CIO agents who had abducted countless men and women during the years of the terror, and 'disappeared' them; and the muscular young men of the Party Youth Brigades.

And here, descending from the heavens, was the President. The chopper put down about a quarter of a mile away and a dust cloud sprang up. I heard a low murmuring like distant thunder, or like a river in flood. It was the crowd gnawing at itself in hungry expectation. Then, suddenly, he was amongst us, hemmed in by watchers and guards and welcoming officials, making his careful way through the crowd towards the podium. It was less a walk than a pro-gress; he took five minutes to reach me and then he was almost invisible behind his platoon of minders. They wore sober suits and ZANU-PF scarves and looked rather like mourners at a funeral. Bright colour was the prerogative of the President, and the First Lady. He wore a golden shirt with an oval portrait of himself over the right breast pocket, and a white baseball cap, and he waved his fist as he walked. The people cheered and waved their pamphlets, their flags, their fists, their umbrellas. There was something immensely rigged about the cheers, the flags, the crowd – even the Leader seemed to be hamming it up, as if this had been done too often. And of course it had. The tales of Robert Mugabe's triumphant processional arrivals at Harare airport are legendary for their unchanging hoo-ha: the armed out-riders, the ululating women, the slow and heavily defended motorcade that moved from the airport to State House. If you cross Julius Caesar with Hendrik Verwoerd, and add a dash of his old friends and mentors, the North Korean Kims, father and son – Chong Il and Il Sung – you get something of the look and flavour of the man. The derisive appellation for Robert Mugabe in later years has been, 'Kim Il Bob', the very model of the modern tyrant.

Robert Mugabe, on the public platform, had the role taped; he embodied its absurdity, its menace, its suffocating fragrance, its location midway between Hollywood and Hell, its supernatural pretensions, its angry self-importance. He fulfilled that strange requirement of a tyrant, expansion. Each time you looked there seemed to be more of him. More of *them*. Despots flowed, one into another, consort-ing, and merging like mercury. Like called to like, cousins in corruption. Mugabe scooped cash from the Democratic Republic of the Congo, where the young dictator, Joseph Kabila – heir to the former dictator, his father, Laurent Kabila – payed for thousands of Zimbabwean troops, keep-ing himself in power by granting Zimbabwe lucrative concessions in diamonds and timber. Colonel Gadaffi of Libya kept him in houses and oil.

The President walked now amongst his people; he mounted the platform. His generals took up positions behind him, looking very much like a plump chorus line. Stuffed into their uniforms, in their bemedalled self-importance, they seemed to reveal more naked flesh than night-club strippers. Next to the President walked the First Lady, wearing a turban and flowing robes emblazoned with the medallion portraits of her husband. She waved a clenched fist, less practised, less convincing than the club her husband showed so deftly at his right ear. The crowd received the First Couple as a crowd might receive the stars at the Hollywood Oscars, though with more reverence, as if they were witnessing, here and now, the saviours of the world. The difference I suppose is that the Hollywood stars are made of celluloid; they may be beautiful, enviable, rich – but they do not breathe the perfume of power, they do not possess, in their trim or surgically improved persons, the power needed for changing the world, healing the suffering, feeding the hungry, bringing grace to the soul of the people. They are not lords of life and death. They do not embody the possibility of miracles, or draw to them the sorts of desperate supplicants like the woman who believed in Christ so deeply that, 'If I could touch but the hem of his garment I would be cured.' Movie stars are adroit charismatics, well-paid ghosts, luscious shadows projected on to a screen. They are pictures, and pretty pictures cannot have their enemies beaten, locked up, or liquidated. For that you need a particular kind of star, a death star, someone whose power is intermingled in his ordinariness. That is what makes him seem so approachable, the sense we have that he, the leader, the tyrant, is just like us, a real human being, made of flesh and blood; he is the monster next door. The true tyrant is palpable, like bread, like terror; he has blood in abundance; he promises to shed his own for his people, his nation, his dreams. He ends by shedding the blood of his people with the stern resolve of a moralist who knows he is doing it for their own good.

How substantial, how fed, Robert Mugabe looked. All

those on the platform simply bulged: his wife, Grace, in her flowing robes and her turban; the army officers, positively rubicund in the forty-degree heat, sweat running out of their caps and coursing down their faces.

The crowd were reaching out to touch Robert Mugabe; they pressed forward for contact with the demi-god; the soldiers pushed them back or hit them with rifle butts, but they didn't feel it, they were entranced, almost ecstatic. There is something in a crowd – in all of us – that is drawn to the dictator; he has what the crowd desires – again the word – blood. Blood is what the tyrant has in plenty. The trouble is that however much we may need him, he does not need us.

Then, too, there is the peculiar seduction that takes place. Sex is intertwined in the gear of rampant authority. In the swank and swagger and strut of it one sees the manners of the catwalk. In modern fascism, in the tyrannies of the twentieth century, whether left or right, there was a degree of high fashion. Narcissism. This was the unexpected side of men who could hang a village without compunction, then worry about how they looked in this tunic, or those boots, or that hat. There was something paradoxical – strangely, amazingly, almost girlish – about booted, holstered author-ity. Certainly, as I watched Robert Mugabe mount the platform, there was a mincing elegance; it was more than feminine, it was distinctly dainty. When he was seated he joined his knees together and seemed to reach for an invisible skirt to cover them.

The President began to speak. He did me the good turn of breaking into English at key moments when there were messages he wished to convey to the wider world. The cameras of the Zimbabwe Broadcasting Corporation tracked him – the state broadcasters, who put out constant propaganda for the Leader, were the only journalists allowed near the presidential rallies. The President had banned all foreign reporters and refused entry even to such anodyne news gatherers as the South African Broadcasting Corporation which might have been expected to be sympathetic.

Mugabe began by attacking the head of the Roman Catholic Church in Matabeleland, Archbishop Pious Ncube. The prelate's crime had been to criticize the regime for its callous and cruel treatment of Zimbabweans and its particular crusade against the people of Matabeleland, long detested for embracing the 'wrong' sort of politics. The President began with a disclaimer: he did not wish to create what he called 'bad blood' with 'Men of God', but – and upon that 'but' the crowd leant silently forward. Such disclaimers are part of the President's arsenal; he is a sly and devious man who has never, in his two decades as leader of his country, ever admitted to anything. He has always had a very great fear of being caught in the act. Of exposure. His way has been to tell his critics what they wish to hear, and then to go out and do whatever he chooses, leaving action to his ministers. But 'bad blood' was what he was there for and we all knew it, bad blood was in his veins, bad blood was exactly what he wished to see flowing, if faithful followers would step forward and rid him of such meddlesome priests, with their tiresome addiction to God who had, treacherously, won over the loyalty of priests like Pious Ncube. The President had found this God wanting, and abolished him. Another, more appropriate deity has been appointed in his place. Had the Archbishop not heard the news? Why did he not lift up his eyes and see who stood before him, in a green and gold shirt, a baseball cap and spectacles?

'Archbishop Ncube' – the President sighed, he looked to heaven where he foresaw a happier life for the bishop if only he would hear the message of the President – had gone too far. 'We will respect him if he remains within the confines of the church but, once he shows off his political tentacles, and if those tentacles are harmful, we will cut them off . . .' The President wished his audience to share his honest mystification with the graceless and unreasonable behaviour of the troublesome Archbishop who protested about the poor and hungry. 'I don't understand how his mind works. Today we won't say down with him – but after hearing what he has to say we will certainly know what to say about him. He is a man who has been giving us trouble, but I don't know why. I don't understand it.'

It was chilling stuff: the crowd were silent: who would be foolish enough to risk being misunderstood by the President?

Next he turned to the white farmers. They should get off their land; he had taken farms away from many of them, but many still remained. 'The job is not finished. Others have not yet got the farms. The country is ours.' Then he saw off the foreign foe. Let the enemy outside Zimbabwe rant and rave; let Britain impose sanctions. Sanctions would only serve to harden his resolve, and confirm what everyone had always suspected, 'The white man is evil.'

He worked the crowd. His rhetorical gifts were considerable: he played to his listeners, he soaked them in his venom, blowing on the hate, keeping it warm. It was rather like Mark Antony's speech after the assassination of Julius

Caesar. It was a cunning, calculated, feline incitement to violence, a silky appeal to morality and reasonableness – interwoven with a certain reproach at the foolishness of men who were misled by black bishops, by evil white men, by the plots of foreign enemies, by the opposition of cowards like Morgan Tsvangirai, Gibson Sibanda and Welshman Ncube. Those who opposed him, and the Party, were the enemies of the Revolution and the white man's pawns who had taken no part in the struggle against the armies of Ian Smith: 'They didn't want a fight – so they fled the war . . .'

As memories of the war of liberation fought by the black Zimbabwean guerrillas against the old white Rhodesian regime have faded, so Robert Mugabe has amplified his role in that war, until he has grown so large in the propaganda that passes for Zimbabwean history that it looks sometimes as if it was a battle waged single-handedly by Robert Mugabe and his ZANU guerrillas. Everyone else, and particularly Joshua Nkomo, who led the other war party, and the other guerrilla army, ZIPRA, have been airbrushed out of the picture.

The people stretched out in their thousands around the platform on which the man in the baseball cap waved his fist in the air. They have been assaulted, lied to, starved and murdered by this man. He has stolen their country – and, if that were not bad enough, he is robbing them of their own liberation.

There remained the question of hunger. It was there, it could not be got away from, it stared out of the thin faces of his listeners, it was almost like walking through a forest of very dry twigs, things kept snapping underfoot. Into the Leader's voice crept that note of righteous exasperation. He had been working day and night fighting off the church and its evil tentacles; he had confiscated farms from white people and given them to landless peasants; he was fighting sanctions imposed by Britain and the 'white' world, and what thanks did he get from the people of Zimbabwe? They continually told him they were starving. Well, he had a message for them: they were not starving; he had given orders, trucks would be arriving regularly with maize: 'Everyone will get food. No one will starve. We have a task force on food . . .'

I wondered where in this crowd Sam was sitting and whether he would have a chance to tell the President how hungry the people in his village were. Somehow, I hoped not, because it might well be that bringing such complaints to a President who is already doing so much for you might seem ungrateful, might be met with pained misunderstanding and who knew what might happen to you then?

One of the most extraordinary things about attending this meeting and hearing the messages from the man who descended from the sky, was that he knew, everybody knew, that of the thousands gathered there to listen to him, very few would vote for him. There had been too much blood spilled in Matabeland. No one spoke of it, neither the victims nor the perpetrators, but the ghosts pressed closely. Since the terror of the early Eighties, an almost unbridgeable gulf had opened between the Shona-speaking rulers of Zimbabwe and their Ndebele compatriots. At every poll since 1985 the people of Matabeleland had consistently voted against the ruling party, ZANU-PF; it was a way of keeping faith with their dead.

The President now moved on to deal with the dead. It was nothing less, he said, than the duty of people in Tshlotsho and Lupane to vote for him. He said it with a dangerously plaintive look. The people of this area, he said, should not 'let us down', and to stiffen their resolve he invoked their lost leader, a man he had demeaned and destroyed. Voting for Mugabe was what Joshua Nkomo would have wished. His voice deepened, he all but brushed a tear from his eye. It was a towering display of hypocrisy. When Joshua Nkomo was alive, Robert Mugabe waged an incessant campaign against his old political rival. When the dissidents made trouble in Matabeleland in the early Eighties and certain of Joshua Nkomo's ZIPRA guerrillas were said to be involved, Mugabe saw his chance. He cried treason and unleashed the army, and then Five Brigade, to eradicate the 'dissidents'. The real aim was to break the will of the Ndebele people to resist – and it worked. His soldiers killed, and went on killing, until Joshua Nkomo capitulated. In 1986, Nkomo signed something called a Unity Pact, he was appointed Vice President, and thereafter ceased to matter in Zimbabwean politics. His physical death was a formality.

Poor Nkomo, suborned in death, even as he was out-manoeuvred, and outgunned in life. In a final indignity he was renamed 'Father Zimbabwe', whose dearest dying wish, confided to the President, was that land should be taken from the evil whites and returned to landless blacks. 'He left us a legacy of land reform. Let's uphold his wishes by uniting in our fight to regain our land.'

Then it was all over. There was a little singing, a little dancing, the First Lady, Comrade Grace, made what is a regular donation at these rallies. She gave $250,000 to the local school, and six sewing-machines to local seamstresses. Then the President moved slowly and solemnly out of our sight and we were made to wait until, with the beating of mighty wings, and a great wind that disturbed the butcher birds in the long grass, the helicopter lifted into the heavens.

THREE

PERFUME OF A TYRANT

I was about five when I met my first tyrant. His name was Hendrik Verwoerd. He was my neighbour and we lived close to each other in one of those green Johannesburg suburbs that named its streets after Irish counties: Kerry, Wexford, Donegal. So much in South Africa conspired to remind one of somewhere else. I sometimes think it helped people to forget that, for half a century, we had been locked up in an institution for the mentally disabled. My Irish grandfather used to say to me: 'Christopher, shall we be taking a walk and stare at the Doctor?' I didn't know Verwoerd was a tyrant then, and I'm sure he didn't know either; it's a role you have to grow into. My mother said, 'That man spent the war knitting socks for Mr Hitler.' The year I'm talking of was 1948: that was my year for staring hard.

Dr Verwoerd, genial and pink, with a lick of thick pale hair and flinty eyes. It was his skin I noticed first: it was stretched tightly over his bones like a drum skin. Each afternoon we went walking past the Doctor's house and my grandfather would lift his stick, wave it at the sky and curse softly to himself. The black man assigned to act as my Nanny also behaved oddly when we were about to pass the place. He hurried me to the other side of the road, as if the house hid some terrible contagion. I just stared. I tried to work out what sort of socks the Doctor would have been knitting for Mr Hitler.

At that time, Dr Verwoerd edited the propaganda paper of his party, a kind of Afrikaner *Pravda*. He didn't stay in our street for long. When his party of racial puritans came to power in 1948, he left my suburb and went off to join the new regime. None of us knew what was coming. None of us ever do. The man who brought Dr Verwoerd into his government headed a new 'purified' Afrikaner Nationalist Party, a revolutionary movement that stood for the triumph of sacred tribe and holy blood over all infidels. His name was Dr Malan. Like many of his sort, he had a warm admiration for the Nazis, hence my mother's appraisal of people like him as knitters of socks for Mr Hitler. Though, to be fair, Hitler-worship amongst 'purified' Afrikaner Nationalists had less to do with race-theory and more with a desire for revenge, over Britain in particular. Afrikaans Nationalists were not really any more fervent Hitlerphiles than were Irish Nationalists, but they would have gone to bed with the devil if it had meant scoring a victory over the old British enemy. They had lost the Anglo–Boer war at the turn of the century, but they had never given up the dream of independence. When General Jan Smuts, the visionary intellectual, misread the mood of the country and calamitously lost the election in 1948, together with his seat in parliament, the Boer party understood politics was war by other means and votes were better than guns: and this time they were making no mistake.

Dr Malan launched his country and his tribe upon the road to independence, solitude and disaster, but it was a mish-mash, this new tribalism. His people knew, more or less, what they were in favour of – they were for racial 'purity'. They knew better still what they were against – just about everything: racial mixing, raffles, horse racing, Asians, liberals, communists, priests, missionaries, Jews, foreigners of all sorts, with the one exception of a handful of Protestant Nordic peoples, and even then in very small numbers, since Scandinavians and even the protestant Dutch sometimes showed themselves to be distressingly louche in sexual matters, and lamentably blind when it came to telling with that obsessed inner eye who was, or was not, certifiably 'white'.

Dr Malan was succeeded by J. D. Strydom, sometimes called 'The Lion of the North'. These names loomed in the sky of my childhood like baleful suns. However, people learnt to live with them, even, dare it be whispered, to relax in their heavy presence. People said of Dr Malan: 'Well, he's not that bad. Better the devil you know . . .' Then, when Dr Malan was succeeded by The Lion of the North, they said: 'There you are, at least Dr Malan was a reasonable man, you knew where you were with him, but Strydom is a fanatic.' Soon they were saying of Strydom, 'Well, he's not that bad. Better the devil you know.'

And they were right. None of these leaders was particularly dangerous – in the tyrannical sense of the word, because they were, in essence, reactionary men. They traded on the Afrikaner's bitterness, his bellicosity, his need for vengeance against 'the old enemy', his burning feeling of inferiority in the face of his white compatriots, and Jews, the English, Asians and internationalists – together with his fear of his black African compatriots, who might one day overwhelm the children of Calvin, the white tribe of Africa, and drive them into the sea. What Malan and Strydom did was to introduce special measures that favoured their own people, the only 'true' pure Africans, the anointed natives. Henceforth, they were to have their own schools, their own banks, their own morality and their own world. Those who did not like it could go back to where they 'belonged'.

So began a trend which continues in Africa today, and very fatally so in Zimbabwe, a form of favouritism some-times called 'indigenization', or 'Africanization': ugly words that mean something simple. They mean – unless you are amongst the chosen, the elect, the party, the tribe, the ethnic laager – you are superfluous to requirements.

In their instincts, Dr Malan and The Lion of the North were tribalists, but they were not visionaries. These first leaders of the purified Afrikaner 'nation' were in the pro-tection racket, they were feudal chiefs, tribal godfathers. They had no answer to the question: 'If you exclude many of your compatriots because they are of the wrong tribe, what will you do with them when they keep hanging about? In short, how do you propose to get rid of them? What is your final solution?'

The responses of most whites had been intellectually shoddy: you locked them up, you shot them, you starved them, you kicked them around, you pretended they did not exist and you hoped the question would go away.

One man knew that the question wouldn't go away any more than would nine-tenths of the population. He was my old neighbour, dreamer and visionary, the true apostle of apartheid, Dr Verwoerd. He grew into political life at about the same time as I grew into boyhood, and we kept pace together for the next fifty years. The party he dominated – and the creed he made the vehicle of his divine mission, the worship of white skin – was to endure from 1948, the year

I first saw him, until 1994 when, for the first time, South Africa held an open election. During that eternity we lived in a revolutionary state, and every notion of power I have mulled over since then first presented itself in some form under the white Afrikaner nationalist regime that fell like a great shadow across my country and plunged it into semi-darkness for half a century. It is often said that apartheid South Africa was an anachronistic world: I once thought so too. I'm increasingly inclined to ask whether it wasn't perhaps ahead of its time.

What made Hendrik Verwoerd a revolutionary was his appetite for theory and his will to power. He was prepared to face the question others had shirked. He had found the solution, and in this man who had once planned to become a religious minister, the missionary urge was strong; he was prepared to do what it took, he was going to improve the destiny of black people, whether they liked it or not. He had the answer that would be intellectually respectable, that would stand up to scrutiny, that was modern and, even, compassionate. He saw the winds of change were blowing in Africa in the direction of sovereignty, freedom and independence and he came up with a solution that embodied all these goals. He would set the Afrikaner free by setting everyone free. He would keep the Afrikaner separate and pure by keeping everyone separate and pure, within their 'homelands'.

What was to be done with 'others', your neighbours, excluded from this idea of South Africa – those who watched you strengthening your stockade, your laager, and growing rich and fat? His answer was – you declare them 'independent'. Everyone would be independent, in their own countries, under their own flags, and their own presidents. Parallel freedoms for all. Every 'race' under the sun would be penned in ethnic stockades and kept apart by law, barbed wire and bullets.

It was a doctrine built on complex ideas, and white South Africans were traditionally uneasy with ideas. They wanted superiority, they did not like theory. Yet they obeyed. They were in thrall to this blue-eyed mystic. Dr Verwoerd's theories may have seemed bizarre or bold or bunkum, but they fired in his followers passionate, violent loyalty. Distended, rampant power does not bring on mental collapse, rather it regularizes abnormality. Amongst those who bought into the dream, and most whites did so, it seemed perfectly normal.

Dr Verwoerd transformed the crude notion that whites were better than blacks into the mystical belief that the separation of races into parallel prisons was divinely sanctioned and intellectually respectable. In order to enforce his dream of 'homelands' for everyone, he was obliged to multiply the number of amenities that were to be equally available to each group: schools, sex, buses, toilets, governments, flags, churches, graveyards. You might then separate children from mothers, wives from husbands, brothers from sisters, and remove whole towns and villages from their ancestral lands. It seemed astonishingly cruel, but really it was truly kind. Thousands of people administered the system and they believed it was the best solution in the best of worlds. No one understood its Byzantine complexities. It required an army of people who went around pushing pencils into children's hair to see if it was curly enough to hold the pencil for as long as it took for the child to be 'classified' as 'coloured' or 'Asian' or 'white' or 'black'. Teams of surveyors drew up maps of new, separate, race-based states, to be created in a separate but equal, Balkanized South Africa which was to be carved up into eight or ten or twelve or fourteen new 'homelands'. Model townships arose in the veld, vast projects which often advanced no further than a forest of concrete outhouses. Squads of police broke into the bedrooms of people suspected of having sex 'across the colour bar', and tested the bedclothes for signs of tell-tale warmth. Opponents went to jail, into exile, to the gallows.

Verwoerd believed in it and soon his people believed in it, and then even his English-speaking opponents amongst the white people believed in it, and voted for Verwoerd in increasing numbers throughout his reign. They feared him, they respected him, they were appalled by him – but they breathed in the perfume and in their heart of hearts they gave thanks because they needed a strong man, and here was a strong man. They needed answers and he had the answers. They needed to deal with their enemies, and he dealt with enemies without hesitation or remorse, not because he was bad, but because he knew he was right. Nothing more distinguished the tyranny of Hendrik Frensch Verwoerd than his unshakable ascetic mien, his sincere conviction that apartheid was not merely desirable it was morally right and divinely ordained. He brooked no argument. The crazier the ideas became, the more white people adopted them. The country was in the hands of a tribe that had literally lost its head.

Some people watch birds, some walk with lions, I find the scent and the gestures of arrogance irresistible. Power is terrifying yet absurd, incredibly hard to believe when you see it close-up, yet achingly familiar. It is at the heart of being human, pushing others around. I do not believe in the 'wise application of power'. All power is the abuse of other people. Everyone is susceptible to the perfume, and any notion that tyranny only happens to other people is an affectation – as any grave crisis in Western affairs will show. When they feel their existence threatened by enemies, the most enlightened societies not only tear up their own freedoms, they pillory those who try to stop them.

I watched the way people in South Africa mimicked, in their behaviour, in the clothes they wore, in the inflexions of their voices, the image of the Leader, drugged by the man and whipped into line by the blood-blinded fanaticism of his party, which was the good of the state incarnated. What was it, this scent, this olfactory signature that all who smell it know? Fear was at the heart of it, and brooding malice. Power gone sour, too long shut up. Imagine if you will the smell of unwashed steel, or slightly putrid tungsten. It contained, too, the tincture of excitement, sexual and social. People fell for it. Prayed to it. It promised to make happiness happen forever.

Verwoerd was always at war; so is Robert Mugabe: he has only been able to define himself on fighting terms. War is a time when defeatists are punished and deserters are shot. The tyrant is at war against his own people and his message, endlessly repeated, is that the enemy within will be rooted out. Repeated performances add another ingredient to the mix: the over-heated plastic smell of the cracked loud-speaker, or the electronic heat of the agitated pixels on the TV screen. When the tyrant makes an appearance even the cameras seem to lick his boots. But the binding agent of the perfume is fear. Fear paralyses individuals facing their superhuman eagle-eyed Leader. Fear works on the crowd like a drug. Fear is what I saw at Lupane on the faces of the crowd come to hear the Leader, it moves people to baffled adoration – baffled because everyone knows, when they see the posturing creature on the podium, that they are being duped but they can't fight it. Instead they move forward, agog, dizzied.

Finally, indispensably, the ingredient that gives the perfume its base and colour, which thickens and strengthens it, is the smell of blood. When the tyrant spills blood it is a cleansing act, it is done with conviction. It is all for the best. Blood becomes a sacrament by which the political kingdom is purified. Murder is the morality the tyrant lives by. He is the world. He takes command of the horizon, the atmosphere, the daily routine, and sooner or later, no one thinks of anything else. He narrows the world down to a choked unhappiness, a provinciality that squeezes life and air out of the world but – and this is the important thing – people give way to it. They tell you quite seriously that this is perfectly natural, sure there are problems, but life was never perfect. They tell you things may change, perhaps, but 'not in our lifetime'; so it is better not to rock the boat, that one should be reasonable, sensible, less critical, that the ruler's heart is in the right place. He's not such a bad chap. And, anyway, isn't this or that place far worse? A police state, an iron regime, is a place where everyone has opinions but no one knows anything. As the grip of the tyrant on the windpipe of the nation grows tighter, they stop talking, it is too dangerous, too tiring, and they concentrate on living as best they might, keeping out of trouble, or out of jail, or out of range of the tyrant's police.

We are all susceptible to the fragrance and we behave in similar lamentable ways. Those who imagine they would never succumb to the paralysis, the cowardice, that tyranny induces, have never been exposed to it. Those in thrall are not deranged, they are super-normal because that is the way someone wishes it. Any abnormal behaviour is dangerous, wrong, punishable. The essential commandment of such a state is this: 'I will do as I choose and you will do as I say.' The essence of power is thus a firestorm of lies. You can't hold a conversation with it. Better to look at it steadily enough, for long enough, to get a reading on it.

In South Africa we were especially well-placed to study the climate of power. When I was four years old, a new government came into being. It was much the same as many other governments that came into power in Africa from the middle of the twentieth century onwards. It believed in 'the people', in 'blood', in castigating its enemies, in blaming the former colonial power for all that had gone wrong in the country. It shared in that baleful doctrine which has been the calamity of emerging Africa – blood-nationalism. A political creed that declared not just that all countries were tribes at heart, sons and daughters of the soil, but that some tribes were more valuable because more 'indigenous', and thus purer by blood and breeding than those others who fell outside the sacred pale of consanguinity.

We had the misfortune in South Africa to come under the rule of chieftains who had no sooner taken power in the name of freedom, than they began to inflict upon other people – black and brown, Asian and white – the same kind of treatment they had so hated when they were ruled by the British.

It is a contradiction I find insupportable, but it is a phenomenon that others find entirely natural. It is, they say, 'normal' or 'understandable', and if I can't see that, then I must have a blind spot, and so like an idiot I keep coming back to similar situations and staring at them. I sometimes think that if I stare long enough the penny will drop and I'll understand that what I'm seeing is not lunatic, cruel, crass; it is simply something that happens in the normal course of events, that things are like this, and that the only surprising thing about them is my own surprise. But there it is, and since no one seems able to explain to me why this is the way things have to be, I have to try to explain it to myself.

What Verwoerd pioneered was the way of making tribalism respectable across Africa, and once he'd found a method, the contagion raced across the continent together with its covey of modish words – 'self-determination', 'autonomy' – that made it so popular, and still does. Perhaps no other leader in Africa today more closely resembles Dr Verwoerd than Robert Mugabe. It is an odd twinning you would think, but then tyrants make strange kinships; they don't plan the family resemblance, it just grows on them.

I've been close to a few other tyrants and there is always the familiar scent. I think of Emperor Bokassa deeply, dangerously funny, founder of the Central African Empire who, back in the Eighties, moved into my hotel on the shores of Lake Annecy. When I say he moved in, I mean he took over the place. This admirer of Napoleon had been fashioned by the French army and then undone by the

French army when it backed a coup by a political rival. Bokassa had fled to France, but he was refused entry. After languishing in exile on the Ivory Coast for some years, he was at last allowed into the land he loved. Security guards were all over the place because there were many who sincerely wished to kill him.

My hotel was ideally situated for protecting a monster in flight from his own people: once a monastery, it made a well-defended redoubt. The lake lay ahead, the ground behind the hotel rose steeply, there was only one, easily guarded, entrance and so it was decided that in this once sacred place an ex-emperor might pass the time until his new home west of Paris was secure enough to receive him. The guests were asked to leave. Despots on the run are rather like banks that go bankrupt. When they are in their glory they punish you if you fall behind on your overdraft: however, when they collapse, as long as they are big enough, they can disclaim responsibility, and the police who were sent to feel your collar when you failed to pay the electricity bill now guard the bank against its cheated customers.

The Emperor was installed with his entourage. It all came very naturally. Taking over, filling the space is what modern tyrants do, for the best of reasons, and that is what makes them insufferable. Old-fashioned despots wished to do harm, it was in the job description, but the modern variety is far worse – they wish to do good, and they will brook no argument. And afterwards they are . . . well, just patriots at heart, misunderstood and mild. What is the link between the quiet man in his good suit and the mass murderer?

I would watch the despot in the garden. The shape-shifting abilities of such men were evident. There were several people inside the trim person of Jean-Bedel Bokassa. He had been an army sergeant, this small man in the grey suit, and then he'd been the Emperor who, a few years earlier, had lifted the crown and set it solemnly on his own head and stood swathed in coronation robes modelled on those of Napoleon: red velvet tricked out with ermine, tiny silvery slippers, his robes embroidered with exquisite bees made of silver and gold thread and huge imperial eagles with diamond claws. He had built his gigantic palace some miles from the capital Bangui, where a giant statue of the god-king still stood, in a crumbling garden.

Papa Bok, as friends and victims (often the same people) used to call him, went in for quiet suits and heavy crowns. He dealt with opposition figures by having them killed and keeping bits of them in the fridge. Faced with opposition Papa Bok did something superbly simple. He ate it. He once mentioned casually to the American Ambassador, William Dale, when he went to the palace in 1972 to present his credentials, that his grandfather had been a keen cannibal. It was not long after this that Bokassa announced the Imperial decree on the colour blue. All schoolchildren were to wear blue uniforms, as they did in France. Those who did not comply, or whose parents couldn't afford the new uniforms, which were to be made in a factory owned by the Emperor, began to disappear. The Swiss pastor at the Lutheran Mission in Bangui, got quite a shock one day when he was out walking near one of the Imperial farms, and came across several naked schoolgirls roped to a tree. How close it was to the Emperor's mealtime he was too flustered to say.

Papa Bok strolled and paused and strolled again. I watched him with a young girl with blonde hair and a short skirt. She must have been about seventeen, and he must have been about a thousand and one, a quiet unobtrusive figure in a grey well-tailored suit with an unassuming air for a tyrant and a cannibal. This was the man who had always shown a tendency towards excessive neatness when dealing with problems. Soon after he took over in a coup, in 1972, he disposed of the plague of beggars in Bangui by having them flown in helicopters over the Ubangui River, and pushed out. Bokassa always denied that he murdered schoolgirls – he loved children. After all he had had at least fifty-two of his own. In that peaceful setting between mountains and water, Jean-Bedel Bokassa was a quiet and restrained French gentleman. In the Imperial Palace he was a cannibal. In religion he was Catholic, though he spent a brief spell as a Moslem, after visiting Colonel Gaddafi.

Here he was, having a chat with a pretty girl in a French garden, to be followed no doubt by lunch: half a dozen oysters perhaps, and some good champagne. They walked and talked together for a while, beauty and the beast. The girls roped to the tree in the grounds of the Imperial farm would have been about her age. One of Bokassa's pleasantries, when he invited diplomats and VIPs to yet another Imperial banquet, was to lean across the table and wonder aloud if his guests really knew what they were eating. I wondered if the blonde walking beside the smiling careful emperor had the slightest idea of the man she walked and talked with. Bokassa turned to her his strangely blurred face, as if life had spent time trying to draw it and had to keep rubbing it out and trying again.

Papa Bok suffered terribly from home-sickness and, though he was safe and secure in France, one day he ran away. He left his guarded house and gave his French secret service minders the slip by doing something very unFrench.

He knew they were watching the motorway near his house but they were assuming he would drive along it, if ever he took flight, on the right-hand side. Bokassa drove at high speed and for a long way, down the wrong side of the motorway, and escaped home to his Empire. He was put on trial for murder and spent seven years in jail. When he died he was on his way back, at least in the eyes of some supporters – he was given a state funeral and praised by some forgetful compatriots as an 'illustrious' Leader.

FOUR

THE CURIOUS CAREER OF
HAROLD FERWOOD

There were three Verwoerds for me: neighbour, prime minister and the man who ran our universe. Even his own followers afterwards admitted that he had all the makings of a dictator. There is something rather touching about this admission. It came when he was dead – so late in the day! Verwoerd was no ordinary leader: he was a contagion, he dominated political life and subjugated all who worked for him, he was the atmosphere we lived in. He tyrannized his followers and the country. He had the face of a cream-puff with eyes of ice – The Divine Hendrik.

He was a much more serious man than Jean-Bedel Bokassa. Bokassa wanted to improve himself. Verwoerd wished to save the white 'race' and by doing so to preserve 'Western Christian Civilization'. Bokassa designed his country as a theatre set, and walked on stage dressed as Napoleon – the soldier turned Emperor. There is about his efforts something of the excitement of a boy building boxcars. He designed his own throne: a mighty eagle of bronze and gold, its wings outstretched, in whose lap or womb there was constructed a cunning little seat upon which he perched like a punter in a fairground, in crimson robes edged with ermine, wearing his medals, many of which carried his own face, including the Order of Agricultural and Scientific Endeavour, ready to take the ride of his life. There is something refreshingly open about Bokassa, as tyrants go. Hendrik Verwoerd ate nobody, as far as I know, but he was for more dangerous than Bokassa. He wasn't play acting, he looked to the future. Bokassa, when he got out of jail, forswore sex, booze and sin, and ended his life communing with the spirit world. Verwoerd ended like Caesar, in a pool of blood on the floor of the senate.

Verwoerd came to be seen as embodying what Afrikaners call *kragdadigheid*, a word which might best be translated as 'fighting spirit'. He dreamt of an unsullied Afrikaner purity, and his vision galvanized his people. His power was based on delusion and lies, and the wish of his followers to be deceived. His fanaticism, which came to stand for Afrikaner intransigence, was not Afrikaans at all: it was too pure, too dogmatic. It was the fire of the convert, the terrifying certainty of the newly won over, the interloper, the messianic outsider. Like St Paul, that other furious apostle of absolute belief, he was a convert to the faith he made his own. His deadly enthusiasm for purity of 'the blood' and '*die volk*' was at odds with the fact that he wasn't an indigenous Afrikaner at all.

No one said so, of course, that would have been heresy. In many ways, Verwoerd was precisely the sort of person Afrikaners instinctively disliked: a foreigner. His parents had been Dutch immigrants and young Hendrik had not been born in South Africa. He was an intellectual in a society which equated intellectuality with sedition. He was a theorist in a land where theory was scorned. He was a fastidious and strangely mild man in a society where the quintessence of masculinity was someone who kicked around a ball, the servants, his wife, or the children, often at the same time, and such energy was regarded as healthily South African.

The Verwoerd family had emigrated to South Africa from Holland, a fact they never liked to dwell upon. They came to stand for sacred racial purity, but when Mrs Verwoerd and her children climbed aboard the old tram that trundled past the Zoo Lake in Park View, the suburb of Johannesburg where I lived, my aunt would dig me in the ribs and we'd stare, even though we knew staring was bad manners, because, so the rumour ran, Dr Verwoerd's wife, Betsy, sombre and austere, was not entirely one hundred per cent classifiably and certifiably 'white'.

Hendrik Verwoerd, great champion of Afrikaner integrity – no one, went the Verwoerdian myth, was freer of British 'contamination'; and no one, until Robert Mugabe, so detested the accursed 'English'. Even 'the English' in South Africa were to be tolerated only for as long as this hateful but necessary contact advanced the racial future of the Afrikaner people. In fact, however, Hendrik Verwoerd was a lot more English than most of the native Anglo-Saxons. The man was a living lie. Paradox is the basis of power, and power is a form of fiction – it is the story of a life told from an unassailable viewpoint, and it allows the teller of the tale to induce in his followers the wish to believe everything they are told and to destroy those who don't.

When the Verwoerd family made their way from Holland to South Africa, it seems that South Africa was not their first choice. In any event, they sent their young Hendrik away to Milton School in Rhodesia, a very traditional educational establishment in Bulawayo which, with its blazers and ties and straw boaters, mimicked the spirit of the English public schools. They also gave him a new name: they enrolled him as 'Harold Ferwood', which is a nice Anglicization of his rather difficult Dutch name.

In the early years of the twentieth century, when Harold Ferwood was an industrious pupil at Milton, the school was filled with the sort of English boys who displayed that natural, terrifying equanimity that has marked the attitudes of whites in Africa. Innocence and insolence. They were little godlings, they never really thought of themselves as living in Africa at all, they never really noticed there were Africans about – except insofar as they formed part of the decoration, coming and going like useful and sometimes endearing ghosts. Africans didn't have names, they were simply 'Munts' or 'Kaffirs'. Harold Ferwood, then, was sent to school amongst boys who in their iron-clad English provincialism thought all the world was like themselves, and thought of nothing else except ball games and shooting. What an agony it must have been for young Harold, a bookish, intellectual foreigner, lost amongst the rough and ready colonials who seldom read a book and put foreigners on a par with 'Munts'. We know how he responded to his predicament; he kept his head down and pretended to be one of 'them'. He was very successful. Years later, former pupils at Milton were astonished to learn that they had been at school with the architect of apartheid, and that the quiet little Harold Ferwood was now the mightiest man in Southern Africa, Hendrik Frensch Verwoerd.

Verwoerd never got over his scorn for Rhodesia – so parochial, so small – or for white Rhodesians, and their absurd pretensions about independence. His successors inherited his contempt. Years later, after propping up white

Rhodesia in its war against the guerrilla armies of Robert Mugabe, the Afrikaner Nationalists would tire of it and pull the plug and Rhodesia would die. The white nationalist regime of South Africa at first supported Ian Smith for much the same reason the present black South African government backs Robert Mugabe – vague feelings of racial solidarity, and fears of waves of refugees washing over the border if the country collapses. When Verwoerd was assassinated in 1966, John Vorster took over and continued the policies of his predecessor, though he trimmed and fudged where he felt it was necessary. He was not a visionary, he was a political operator. While it suited South Africa's interests to prop up Ian Smith, South Africa propped him up. When the price became too high, John Vorster kicked away the prop. This was later to be called cynical, but I think that is to mistake the purpose of the Afrikaner's vision. The apartheid regime was never in the business of preserving the white man in Africa; it was dedicated to salvation of the Afrikaner in South Africa, and that was another matter.

In many ways, Dr Verwoerd has much more in common with, and would today be far more sympathetic towards, Robert Gabriel Mugabe. They hate so many of the same things, and they see as their destiny the duty to save their people and their country from gangs of marauding enemies, gays, Jews, British liberals and traitorous sell-outs amongst their own tribe. They seem linked across time in an uncanny way.

It is difficult to explain these things to those who live in safer places; who have never seen a man killed in a demonstration by police; who have never had a friend taken to jail, have never known a book banned, or met a censor, and are blissfully unaware of the icily amusing wit that hangs around police states, where jokes are edged in mourning ribbon and are one of the most delicious things about totalitarian societies; who have never remarked upon the extraordinary peacefulness at the scene of a shooting, on the silence of the dead, their utter lack of melodrama, the very prosaic nature of violent death; who have never experienced the ability of tyrants, living or dead, to transfer ideas between them.

I retain a special regard for Dr Verwoerd – after all, he was my first tyrant and he taught me a lot. I had not come across another quite like him until Robert Mugabe began to mimic the old Doctor. The resemblance was so uncanny I sometimes wondered if they were not perhaps related. Hendrik Verwoerd was an elected tyrant who crossed the line between government and religion: like modern tyrants, he reversed Charles Péguy's dictum – that what begins in mysticism ends in politics. What began for Hendrik Verwoerd in crude racial politics ended in mystical ethnic subdivisions. Verwoerd believed that South Africa was a victim of a worldwide conspiracy, directed by Britain, which wanted to destroy the Afrikaner revolution. Britain was the old enemy, the colonizer, the destroyer; Britain had tried in successive wars against the Boers, to liquidate the Afrikaner people, on the battlefield, and in the concentration camps established by Lord Kitchener, and then by economic might. This is Mugabe's belief too.

In order to safeguard the Afrikaner liberation struggle, Verwoerd ran a programme of racial cleansing unlike anything seen before. He did it with the support of his party, which had a huge majority in Parliament. The force used to separate out the black population and drive them into distant homelands was never done by decree – it was done by parliamentary procedure – votes. The modern world, said Dr Verwoerd, was keen on democracy, and so he would achieve his vision with the help of democracy. He would not hammer apartheid into place, he would vote it into being. He did so with parliamentary lawyers who drafted bills making all forms of dissent illegal, immoral and, even, sacrilegious. He did it with the enthusiastic help of his party press who throughout his rule were so servile that Afrikaans newspapers made the old Soviet papers seem positively bolshy.

Verwoerd ignored the legal opposition and he beat, imprisoned and allowed his police to murder his more rebellious opponents. He did it with the help of the courts who applied those laws unquestioningly – in fifty years of apartheid, no judge ever resigned rather than continue to work in a system which victimized most of the population. He destroyed the parliamentary system which he so scrupulously exploited, by packing the Senate with his place-men. He instituted a system of censorship so severe it resembled the Vatican Index. He accused his local critics and the press of being in the pay of communist powers, he expelled foreign journalists, he controlled the state media. He maintained that the Afrikaner was the 'true' African who had been robbed of his land by the British during the Boer War and he was going to redress that long and old injustice. He said that blacks occupied land that rightfully belonged to whites and they were to be driven off that land and stripped of their farms. They were illegal squatters, 'temporary sojourners' in white South Africa. When the

Commonwealth asked him to think again he replied that his was a sovereign state and would brook no outside interference. When at last the Commonwealth lost patience and it seemed South Africa was about to be expelled, Dr Verwoerd got in first and fired the Commonwealth. Like Robert Mugabe is cheered in many African councils, the Doctor was supported in his delusions, in his icy dedication, in his dreamy tyranny, in his absurd ideas of ethnic purity and the sacredness of Afrikaner blood, by most of his white compatriots. It was a career of almost unrelieved destruction, and it left his country so badly wounded it has still not recovered. It is forty years since Dr Verwoerd went, struck down by an assassin in Parliament, at the very seat of his power, but the scars are still fresh.

And at almost every step, Mugabe has followed suit.

Tyrants are pneumatic, they puff up like beach balls, like giant dirigibles, they inflate and grow bigger until they loom over the land like horrible Hindenburgs. I learnt this by watching Verwoerd and others of the tyrannical kidney – but none so closely resembled my old neighbour than Robert Mugabe. They are peas in a pod, brothers under the skin. Perhaps that's why Dr Verwoerd, when I saw him first all those years ago, seemed to be so tightly enclosed in his skin. A terrible emptiness under high pressure. Baleful balloonmen. Eventually they pop, but it is always too late, and the mess is terrible.

FIVE

FRIENDS AND NEIGHBOURS

It was 1960 when the structure of Dr Verwoerd's theories of race ghettos for all, sometimes called apartheid, or separate development, was established, and the success or otherwise of his policies was measured by the amount of blood shed for and against. The crux of his method may be stated like this: if we are able to silence, imprison and, when necessary, kill more of 'them' than they can of 'us', then we are winning the war.

In 1960, nine policemen were murdered by an African crowd at Cato Manor near Durban. In those same riots, Africans killed Indians whom they saw as mercantile oppressors and white stooges. In the way it seems to happen, with a kind of Shakespearean inevitability, when politics goes very badly, nature conspired to deepen the tragedy. At a place called Coalbrook in the Free State, four hundred and thirty miners, most of them black, died in an accident deep underground. Then in March, at Sharpeville Township, outside Vereeniging, police opened fire on black demonstrators, killing sixty and wounding scores of others. Shortly afterwards, in one of the most impressive marches ever to take place in South Africa, thirty thousand Africans from the black townships of Langa and Nyanga, outside Cape Town, marched on Parliament and might have taken it by simple moral suasion had they not been tricked by fanciful promises made by the authorities who coaxed them first to pause, and then to disperse.

On 9 April 1960 a man named David Pratt approached the Prime Minister as he made a speech at the Rand Easter Show, and fired several shots into Verwoerd's head. Those shots should have killed him. Instead, Verwoerd's body-guard fainted, the Prime Minister was taken into intensive care, the bullets were removed and he hung between life and death for several days. He pulled through. In the climate of nationalist hysteria – where politics was equated with religion, the policies of the government with the will of God, and Hendrik Frensch Verwoerd with the saviour sent by the Lord to lead his people out of the land of oppression – his escape was seen as a miracle. From that point on, those who opposed the racial religion of the Doctor were not merely political ingrates and enemies; they were heretics to be cast into the outer darkness.

In quick succession Dr Verwoerd took South Africa out of the Commonwealth and then out of the real world. The Sixties were the start of a surreal era that saw the country slipping into a nether-world where unbalanced and brutal things became the norm, because someone 'said so'. It was a traumatic development which left South Africa lonely, reckless, prey to delusions of grandeur, some very violent, and in the charge of a man who no longer discussed or debated. He simply went ahead, guided by his own inner lights, and neither official opposition, now thoroughly impotent, nor even the Doctor's own lieutenants, had the measure of a man who had become a demi-god. He was the serene and self-anointed prince of the new religion of skin colour; he was the bulwark of Western civilization, of

European culture, of civilized values, of democratic principles, of the rule of law. He was repository of fairness, justice,
honour and peace. He said so, and if you demurred you
went to jail. Harold Ferwood had come a long way.

By 1960 Dr Verwoerd was a very modern autocrat. He
exemplified the modern dictatorial state, which attaches a
very high priority to 'the law', yet it is run by outlaws,
backed by a majority in Parliament. Judges chosen for their
political reliability interpret the laws in a way that the
regime requires, and the police and other law enforcement
agencies, public and secret, work to ensure that people obey
these laws. One of the old clichés of complaint in South
Africa, was that the government 'rode roughshod over the
courts'. In fact, however, it was far worse than that. The
government had no need for those tactics, it had only to get
itself elected with a large majority, pass the bills it wished to
pass, and rely on the judiciary to do its duty. It was the
regime that made the laws that appointed the judges and
then expected them to ride roughshod over the people. And
so they did, with remarkable equanimity. It was a sign of the
extent to which the perfume of tyranny drugged and
befuddled anyone who came into contact with it.

South Africa in the early years of the Sixties had begun to
descend into a darkened arena where only the police held
sway. Terror in a dictatorship is an extreme and perverted
form of moral therapy. It is intended to incapacitate its
victims while at the same time being good for their souls.

In 1965, I was sitting in a small café across the road from the
University of the Witwatersrand. There had been protests
that morning against detention and banishment, there had

been marches, and the police had arrived and arrested students. I was drinking coffee when I heard a broadcast by the Rhodesian Prime Minister, Ian Smith, telling the world that he was unilaterally declaring independence from Britain. The date was 11 November. The voice on the radio was high, reedy, quite unlike the gravelly English we spoke in South Africa. Words were clipped, bitten off, flat. It sounded rather like a mechanical announcement from another planet, and in many ways it was. I'd been to Rhodesia a couple of times and found it really rather pleasant. They were not mad, as we knew madness. There were no politics as we knew them, only groups of farmers with strange semi-English voices. Salisbury, the capital, seemed to me no more than a suburb in the bush. I possessed all the usual arrogance of a South African who knew in his bones that no other country south of Cairo was worth a moment's interest.

The flat tones of Ian Smith on the radio in the University café, the words he used, were strange, cracked – 'We have struck a blow for the preservation of justice, civilization and Christianity, and in the spirit of this belief we have this day assumed our sovereign independence. God bless you all.' 'Justice', 'civilization' and 'Christianity' – dangerous words that we lived by, though we knew they had no meaning. We built law courts and they had never made for justice. We washed, those of us with access to running water, but it never civilized us. We went to church in our droves, but we were never Christian. We were a society so thickly hedged with lies that only the very young or the very stupid were able to avoid contamination. Lies sat at the heart of our language, they were sewn into our syntax. No one would have uttered the words Ian Smith used without taking precautions. Dr Verwoerd had annexed them all – culture, western civilization, justice, honour, fairness – and devalued them. They all meant the same thing. They meant, when used in public places, or over the radio, nothing more than that we were the occupying power and we would fight anyone who crossed us, and kill those who injured us. Used without permission, those words were dangerous – in South Africa you could get locked up for using the words Ian Smith used.

Through the window I saw the policemen mopping up outside the University. The clock on the South African Breweries building across the road showed a few minutes to one o'clock. As always there was this piercing sense of unreality in the bright highveld light, but I think I was vaguely aware, as an astronomer is aware when he finds evidence of the birth of a new star, that I had been present at the arrival in the South African firmament of a brand new tyrant – Ian Douglas Smith.

I have often thought that what Ian Smith should have said when he ended his declaration of rebellion was not, 'God bless you all' – but, 'God help us all.' What began with the UDI speech was despotism of a peculiar sort. It did all the usual things; it destroyed its enemies, it gagged the press, it rode people down, and it carried large guns. It was oafish, bloody, humourless – elements common to rabid authority and to most autocratic states – but what distinguished Rhodesian despotism was an ineffable smugness, a kind of shopping basket savagery of small men who had never before been expected to think of anything but cold beer and Sunday bowls, a spot of golf, a bit of shooting, a walk in the fields of their gigantic farms, supper in the suburban ease of their households where white people, if they were decent and successful, always observed one rule: they never did anything. Doing was poor, it was vulgar, it was what you had servants for. The point of servants was to serve white people, to be patronized, despised and, when rebellion showed, to be locked away, or worse.

Perhaps one should not be too harsh. After all, the thinking that came out of the Rhodesian rebellion was at least a discernible cerebral movement. It was an attempt, the first known attempt, by whites settled in Africa to ask themselves who they were and what they were doing there. The answer that even fewer would have wished to contemplate was that the job of white men in Africa had been petty tyranny. Ian Smith confronted the question and answered it in a way that Cecil John Rhodes would have understood and approved. The white man in Africa was a genial despot and he should fight for his right to remain so.

However, what his speech that day in 1965 really showed was that Ian Smith had got a whiff of the perfume. He wasn't alone. Black leaders were just as prone to the falling sickness, and by the mid-Sixties there was not a single freely elected leader in any African state from the Cape to Cairo. Tyranny came to Rhodesia in 1965, just as it had come to South Africa in the person of Dr Verwoerd, and, once lodged it would not be got rid of for decades.

Fate had not finished making playful yet merciless connections between my first tyrant and me. I moved to Cape Town after I finished University and I went to work as an editor in an Afrikaans publishing house. Dr Verwoerd was in Cape Town then, too. He was there as Prime Minister. On a September afternoon in 1967 he was in Parliament; he slipped into the front bench ready for the afternoon session. While he was sitting there he was approached by a parliamentary messenger named Dimitri Tsafendas who pulled two knives from his tunic and stabbed him through the heart.

When Dr Verwoerd was assassinated, the notion so carefully preserved in Afrikaans circles that he was a politician, a leader, a human being, a thinker, and not a demi-god, was exposed for the protective manoeuvre it was. People had simply been in awe of Verwoerd. In my Afrikaans publishing house people could not bring themselves to speak to me on that afternoon when Verwoerd was struck down by Dimitri Tsafendas. They stared at me as if I ought to know something, to say something, perhaps confess to my involvement in the murder. For after all, I was an English-speaker, and all English South Africans were by nature liberals, and liberals were known to harbour murderous thoughts towards the Doctor. Hadn't David Pratt been a leading member of the liberal community? And he had tried to murder the Doctor. This view was even more dramatically acted out by one nationalist MP, P. W. Botha, who was destined to succeed Dr Verwoerd in some years' time. Botha marched over to the sole genuine liberal in the House, the Progressive Party member for Houghton, Mrs Helen Suzman, and with trembling finger pointed her out as the real force behind the assassin.

It took the killing of the Leader by an alien (Dimitri Tsafendas was an immigrant, a Greek sailor of mixed-race parentage) to allow this charge of murder by association to be so publicly stated. It allowed my colleagues in the publishing house, and indeed Afrikaners generally, to say out loud what they feared to say before then, to express what all blood-nationalism has at its heart – the need to defeat the enemies who are out to destroy you; the belief that you must act first, and incapacitate, knock out all opposition. This philosophy when extended becomes a means of denying to others any real human feelings and of removing them from the world.

Dr Verwoerd was gone but he continued to fill the world. It is as if at some point in the steady accumulation of power, the body of the despot begins to swell, the skin stretches to accommodate the internal expansion and signs of it appear in the face, which grows smoother, shinier, brighter. If you look at portraits of Stalin you see the phenomenon: it is as if someone not content with the face of the man as it was in life has painted it up, made it rosier and more artificial, rather like a face painted on a balloon. The pictures of Hitler show a similar maquillage. Sometimes the portrait of the leader has literally been touched up to make it nobler, to burnish the skin, polish the moustache, to add brilliance to the keen eye of the Father of the Nation, and the Beloved Leader. The aim of this cosmetic work is to ensure that the sacred image assumes a consistency that can be recognized, reproduced and respected – for its magical ability, in a world where everything changes, is that it is able to remain its unchanging self. The aim is also to increase what marketing people would think of as brand recognition, and it is useful when the image is to be reproduced thousands of times, as in the case of Stalin, or Lenin, or Mao, or Hitler, on book jackets, badges, coins, flags and shirts. It is, finally, a very good working tool when in the end the sacred object of the people's esteem may be laid in a glass coffin and preserved for eternity, to be visited and adored by millions of his subjects.

No one put Dr Verwoerd in a glass cabinet, but in a sense they didn't need to. Not one of the leaders, all of them authoritarian, many of them bullies, who governed South Africa in the long period from 1948, when the Nationalist Government first took power, until 1994, when it finally collapsed, had Dr Verwoerd's uncanny capacity for inserting himself into the landscape, into the very marrow of his country. When he was struck down it was the Party that dictated, in the manner of the Soviet system, and its leaders were not redeemers but a series of brutal managers.

The assassination of Dr Verwoerd is in many ways emblematic of the country, and to a great extent he summed up in his death what he had made of the country. The murder could not have taken place where it did, or as it did, without the measures that Hendrik Verwoerd had put into place. The Houses of Assembly, the South African Parliament in Cape Town, like all government institutions took great pride in observing the separation of races laid down by law, statutes that Hendrik Verwoerd had first envisaged as Minister of Native Affairs. No Asian or mixed-race or black person was permitted in the House except through a separate entrance provided for the purpose. Once inside the building a 'non-white person' would use the toilets, corridor and drinking taps set aside for persons of 'other races'. These were Verwoerdian laws. This was the Verwoerdian vision. The only time 'non-white' staff entered the House was silently and secretly under cover of darkness to do what such staff always did: to dust and clean and repair and then depart. As a result, it became very difficult to find whites willing to work in menial positions. Dimitri

Tsafendas was 'coloured' but he needed the job, and he looked the part – in the parlance of the time he 'passed for white' – and so he was employed as a parliamentary messenger. Dr Verwoerd had been struck down by a man who was in a sense his own creation.

Tsafendas claimed to have been acting on the orders of a giant tape-worm coiled in his belly. It spoke to him, it told him to kill Verwoerd. He was judged to be insane and spent the next thirty years in mental institutions. It is a moot point as to who was the loopier. Insanity has never been a drawback in South African politics; often it has been rewarded with high office. Like the rest of us, Dimitri Tsafendas was an inmate in an institution. One day, our director was murdered by one of his patients. It was very bloody: it was also, in our terms, all perfectly normal.

SIX

THEM AND US

I used to travel in Rhodesia in the mid-Sixties and Seventies, the years of UDI, and a very strange time it was. I liked it because it threw some light on South Africa which was a country almost impossible to fathom. Living there never helped you to understand the place, it only enriched your sense of confusion. Although South Africa and Rhodesia were neighbours, the history and nature of the two peoples were every bit as different as those of Canada and the United States. Only geography and the most superficial similarities linked them, and then only in the eyes of those who were not familiar with Southern Africa. Even the fact that both countries were ruled by white minorities, did not give them a common bond. Yet somehow the mirror that was Rhodesia reflected something of the strange realities of South Africa.

The whites of South Africa were two sharply divided groups, uneasily bound together by an accident of skin colour. English-speakers were the confused fragments – neither British nor African – left behind after Britain withdrew from the country at Unification in 1910. The other group, the Afrikaners, did not see themselves as fragmentary; they did not regard themselves as 'settlers' and they did not acknowledge the British conquest of their country. They believed with great passion, and good reason, that they had belonged to their own Republics, the Transvaal and the Free State, and to Africa, long before Britain interested herself in the region. They did not regard the Boer War as being anything other than armed robbery, a brutal take-over by a hated enemy.

South African whites had been in the country a long time compared with those recent settlers in Rhodesia who were relative newcomers to Africa. The first white settlers arrived in the Cape of Good Hope in the middle of the seventeenth century. But further north, across the Limpopo river in Matabeleland and Mashonaland, those black tribal domains that were to become Southern Rhodesia, very few whites had been seen before 1890 – just the occasional hunters, missionaries, explorers, and a few adventurous parties of Trek-Boers.

There was another difference. It had to do with respectability. South African whites, Afrikaners as well as English, were adventurers, chancers and buccaneers. It is true there has always been an attempt to dignify the first white settlers in South Africa – Dutch, French Huguenot, Germans or British – as refugees in search of peace and freedom. The Huguenots, fleeing religious persecution in Europe, which followed the Revocation of the Edict of Nantes, had the best claim to be true refugees. The others made up their stories as they went along. The Dutch were fierce lovers of freedom. The English settlers were yeoman farmers, the best of British stock, striving to civilize a savage place.

These portraits are nonsense. The 'Dutch' who landed at the Cape of Good Hope in the mid-seventeenth century were only very patchily Dutch. A lot of them were mercenaries hired by the Dutch East India Company, and the Dutch East India Company was not choosy about who it signed up for its voyages of exploration, embracing rogues, thieves and freebooters and, in many cases, the dregs of the Berlin gutters. The Dutch 'settlers' in the Cape in the mid-seventeenth century had a lamentable record; they built no roads, opened no schools. They installed themselves on large farms serviced by slaves, and when they sometimes planted vines it was easier to have a slave walk through the vineyards cracking a whip when the locusts descended than to change their methods of farming or their lifestyle, which consisted of sitting comfortably and having somebody else do the work. There were soon so many slaves in the Cape of Good Hope, something like three for every one white settler, that it became known as the Cape of Slaves.

The British who first colonized the Cape, and more particularly those who rushed to the Highveld when diamonds and gold were discovered in the 1880s, were as mercenary and as ruthless as the men who manned the ships of the Dutch East India Company. These incomers were known as 'Uitlanders'. They would never have claimed to have had a vision or a philosophy of life. They wanted to get very rich, very quickly, and go home. The mining camps were rough places, and the miners had little time for the British class system, though they invested heavily in the notion of effortless white superiority: so they jettisoned the first but took the second for granted. They looked no further than their digging claims. They were venal, narrow, energetic and resourceful. In the Kimberley diamond diggings or the Jo'burg goldfields, no patriotism was evident, nor any Imperial idea of the amplitude that Rhodes expressed. In the gold and diamond fields people were too busy grubbing for riches.

What the Uitlanders felt for South Africa was little more than an appreciation of servants, sunshine and space, accompanied by spates of furious moneymaking. If they felt anything more, it manifested itself in a sentimental attachment to its wildlife. Love of animals in Africa has always had a sinister undertone because it went hand in hand with a signal disregard for the people of Africa. The Uitlanders did not have an unshakable belief in their British destiny that made them lift up their eyes to the hills – they only wanted to annex them.

That was a destiny best expressed by Cecil John Rhodes who believed that: 'The British are the first race in the world, and the more of the world we inhabit, the better it is for the human race.' It was an attitude of those who followed Rhodes into the new lands beyond the Limpopo. He was interested not in money for its own sake, but in the power it brought him. Those other races – like the Boers and the Blacks, savage and lost to the modern world – would have to be swept away if Africa was to be turned into the sort of profitable company that Rhodes regarded as being the entity closest to perfection. The key word in Rhodes's remarks about Englishmen in Africa is 'inhabit'. Rhodes didn't mean 'live in', what he meant was 'conquer', then extract from the captive country as much of the treasure as you can carry, then go 'home' to Chiswick or Tunbridge Wells.

Rhodes and his invaders had as their target the usual lure – gold. Their ambition of taking over the gold and diamond fields of the Transvaal and the Free State had been achieved with the ending of the Boer War. Now he turned his attention to the virgin lands further north. Together with his acolyte, Leander Starr Jameson, Rhodes saw the land beyond the Limpopo as a huge and tantalizing commercial space. It was very bad news for the people unlucky enough to be living there. As Paul Kruger remarked from his Swiss exile, after Transvaal Republic had been extinguished, the goldfields were in British hands and the independence of the Boers was dead, and he too was dying: 'Rhodes was one of the most unscrupulous characters that ever existed.'

Rhodes's vision may be briefly summarized: he took the view that everyone else would be happier when he and his fellow millionaire mine-owners took charge. Healthier, and morally improved. What made Rhodes happier made subject people happier. Indeed, it is probably wrong to make a distinction between their commercial activities and their Christian faith since they hardly ever did so.

It was a pattern repeated again and again from the Belgian Congo to the Cape of Good Hope, and it was an idea striking in its brutal vulgarity. The thesis was this: by wrecking your land, and ruining your people, I will become richer and you will become better and more civilized human beings. The destruction of your country will considerably improve your moral fibre. What is good for my shareholders, in short, is good for your soul.

The last was the real killer. This idea remained popular long after Rhodes's dreams had been semi-forgotten. It lingered on in places like Southern Rhodesia, Northern Rhodesia and Nyasaland, well into the second half of the twentieth century, when Ian Douglas Smith and his Rhodesia Front party argued that since they were rich, powerful and white and, above all, truly British, they represented the last true hope for Western values and

Christian ideals. Echoes of this delusion were in the speech
I heard on the radio in the University café on 11 November
1965. Ian Smith explained his act of rebellion with all the
perverse logic that Rhodes had invented. His declaration of
UDI, Smith said, was not treason. Treason lay in the 'un-
British' behaviour of the British government and the refusal
to do the decent British thing and recognize that white rule,
and only white rule, would save the black people of
Rhodesia. The ghost of Rhodes was there in Ian Smith's
extraordinary words: 'We have struck a blow for the preservation of justice, civilization and Christianity . . .'

It seems to me that the root of the problem in Africa was that
forever, in the eyes of their European overlords, stretches of
Africa were not countries at all; they were merely companies:
the Dutch East India Company; Belgium Incorporated; The
Rhodesian Mine Owners' and Farmers' Association. It was a
terrible fate, a truly modern horror. Bad enough in South
America where countries were taken over by conquistadors,
who extinguished the local populations in the name of God
– in a way, this was worse. Places like Rhodesia were taken
over by stock-jobbers who found themselves free to do in
Africa what they were unwilling or unable to do at home.
They might increase their self-esteem and improve their
social standing all at once, by ripping off the natives and
gouging out the wealth in the dream of one day going
'home' rich and respected. Did it make them monsters? No
– it seems to me much worse than that. These countries were
taken over by suburban moralists, men who imposed on local
populations a set of insufferable Anglo-Saxon pieties that
they had no intention of abiding by themselves. Places

like Rhodesia and South Africa were not invaded by buccaneering colonial pirates, nor by sober Puritans hoping to build heaven on earth; they were invaded by men with the souls of company secretaries. Those who battened on Africa didn't have murder in mind; they had murder on the balance sheet. 'I dream of Africa and golden joys . . .' Shakespeare remarked, but that is to put too good a face on it; it is to suggest some magnificent venality about the clerks who raided Southern Africa. They were just petty invaders with cornershop minds, accounting clerks with guns. They were after gold all right, and diamonds, and anything, or anyone, they could sell or trade, but there was this difference: these functionaries, these wide-boys, these smash and grab settlers were after something more in Africa, something they thought was cheap and endless and which in the end rotted their souls. They wanted to rip off the entire world from horizon to horizon. They wanted blacks to do the work for them, and they also wished – in the arrogance that is always astonishing – to extract from this light-headed life a sense of moral self-satisfaction. As a result I think there are no more morally prescriptive people on earth than the white minorities of Southern Africa. There was never any dignity to it; the god they worshipped, these travelling bookkeepers, these murderous share-jobbers, was the god of the bottom line, the profit margin. Their small universe was bounded on the one side by ball games and on the other by balance sheets.

Nowhere was this truth better exemplified than in Rhodesia, a huge stretch of southern Africa that took its name from a spectacular robber baron whose rampant urge to own as much of the continent as he could take in a lifetime was equalled only by his conviction that armed robbery was a holy vocation urged on the English 'race' by God himself. Rhodes turned Africa into a cash crop, grabbed its best land, stripped its minerals, moulded vast tracts in his own image. He bought, sold and robbed it blind. He romanticized it and, it must be said, he loved it. Africa was a dream, and a business. In a long-forgotten speech made over thirty years ago, Robert Mugabe offered a definition of Rhodes's followers: 'Avid fortune seekers who brought to the fore a bigoted Briton, one Cecil John Rhodes who, by outbidding, outclassing, throttling, cheating and deceiving his fellow partners and speculative opponents alike, had emerged as a millionaire committed to the territorial expansion of British colonialism'. Under the circumstances, Mugabe's definition erred on the side of charity.

The cost of these investments by invasion was large. It ruined Africa but it also wrecked the invaders, it turned them soft and stupid, and then it drove them mad. Theirs was a dispiriting desire for large amounts of loot and low workloads. It made them detested by their black serfs. It is one thing to be oppressed by barbarians, it is quite another to be murdered by men in shorts who have grown so fat and lazy and greedy that they crush you simply by existing, by their presence in the adjacent space of what used to be your country.

What was called the British Pioneer Column crossed the Limpopo and reached what came to be called Cecil Square, in Bulawayo, on 12 November 1890. The Column was after gold. This was later to be sublimated and its rather unpleasant and steely outlines softened into something more palatable, it was a quest for 'honour' and 'peace' and 'civilization'. This became a vision so unexceptional in so many white communities in Africa that many otherwise sensible people sincerely believed that their form of armed robbery was a sacred vocation.

Joseph Conrad's brief damnation of white traders in the Congo in *Heart of Darkness* has two advantages over Mugabe's analysis of Rhodes: it is more shapely, and more devastating. A group of whites arrive on yet another treasure hunt in the Congo, members of what Conrad calls the Eldorado Expedition – the name would serve for much of the European colonial enterprise in Africa: 'Their talk was the talk of sordid buccaneers: it was reckless without hardihood, greedy without audacity, and cruel without courage; there was not an atom of foresight or serious intention in the whole batch of them, and they did not seem aware that these things are wanted for the work of the world. To tear treasure out of the bowels of the land was their desire; with no more moral purpose at the back of it than there is in burglars breaking into a safe.'

That was the air that hung over Rhodesia in the years after UDI. The country seemed a vast and stultified suburb, filled with insufferably self-satisfied people who were sure they were doing the right thing. It is one of the great mysteries, I think, to any South African visiting this hospital ward for the incurably complacent, back in the years that followed UDI. How could this small remnant (there were never more than 220,000 white Rhodesians, and we could have lost them all in the Transvaal) believe they were winning? We were not like Rhodesians, our position was so much stronger and yet we knew, many of us, that it was hopeless.

If Rhodesia in the Sixties and Seventies had little to teach South Africa, we had lots we could show them. Rhodesia continued under Ian Smith in its rather prim and steadfast rebellion, with constant borrowings from the rich store of repressive devices pioneered by South Africa. There were laws against publishing certain writings, and laws against releasing certain detainees; there were detentions and arrests all the time. There were security laws like the Law and Order (Maintenance) Act. They sounded very fine. They gave Ian Smith power to lock up people more or less as he chose. However, Rhodesians were as wary of being mistaken for South African barbarians, as South Africans were of being mistaken for Rhodesian wimps, and these measures were presented in Rhodesia as somehow more legal, more respectable, than the racist laws down south – the sort of measures the House of Commons would have taken, had it wished to lock up the opposition. The South African government looked with benign condescension upon Rhodesian efforts to shut down the black majority; at least they were trying to be at least half as awful as we were.

By 1972, black leaders like Robert Mugabe and Joshua Nkomo were in detention and so, very soon afterwards, were white critics of the Smith regime like Judith Todd. The pattern established in South Africa set in hard. People were to be abused, assaulted and, from time to time, if not done to death, then left to die in their cells. Judith Todd, who had opposed UDI from the start and had also stood out against successive attempts by the British government to cobble together a deal that would let Smith off the hook, was locked up. When she went on hunger strike she was force fed by the medical staff, one of whom was a boozy doctor named Baker Jones, on whose watch the dissident Leopold Takawira died of diabetes which had gone undiagnosed. Her account is modest and unforgettable: the tubes, the injections to relax her muscles, the involuntary vomiting, the drunken doctor overseeing the treatment, the heavy-handed nursing sister, punishment for recalcitrance. The details gave way to bleak comedy when Ian Smith declared he was 'unaware' of her hunger strike, and told an interviewer: 'If Miss Todd does not wish to eat the food given to her, that doesn't worry me a good deal . . .'

By this stage, the Smith regime was afloat upon a sea of lies and self-deceit. It was always a little view, a mean and vindictive vision. To read the spokesman of the Smith regime is to find yourself not among thieves, but among canting moralists, smug sphincter-tight minds, drowning in their own complacent clichés. Desmond Lardner-Burke speaks for the times. He was – and it was very difficult to read with a straight face his ancient title – Minister of Justice in Ian Smith's rebel regime. Lardner-Burke went to the banal heart of the matter when he saw the collapse of the Belgian Congo in the early Sixties as the beginning of the end of the white man in Africa. He remembered that when the Congo crisis took place, 'We looked out at thousands of Belgians who fled in panic from the Congo, and this caused our first riot, as the African in Rhodesia considered that the European was on the run; he had come out of the Congo, he was fleeing from the African, and therefore the African Nationalists tried their riots in Rhodesia to see whether the European would start running from Rhodesia as well. They found that this was not the attitude of the Rhodesian European; he was here to stay.'

This comment is remarkable, not only for its stealthy refusal to ask why the Congo was in chaos, and whites were fleeing; or its refusal to admit that Africa was awake and moving; but also for its indifference to something now very advanced in Africa. The day of the demagogue had come.

Through the Seventies, the contagion that had been peculiar to South Africa was spreading – not only to Rhodesia, but also to other black African states where, increasingly, power was the consideration of rulers, indifference was the lot of those unlucky enough to starve. Jail awaited those who disagreed. The rule of brutality was growing and Ian Smith's coup or putsch was really no different from a dozen other armed insurrections which would bring a plague of dictators to Africa, each rather worse than the last.

Yet you were struck not by violence, or anguish, or even mild concern. It seemed that whites had never been better off. However, the jails were filling up with prisoners, the bush was crackling with guerrilla activity, the isolation of their country was increasing all the time, and their distance from Africa was almost complete. But when you spoke to Rhodesians or watched them at play, they gave no sign of being even slightly worried or, stranger still, even remotely aware of it.

I used to watch groups of Rhodesians leaving for home from Johannesburg Station and one day I wrote about it:

> They look up.
> The rains have been heavy and beside the tracks
> water has gathered in temporary pools
> the wind drives coldly across
> panicking the small grasses
> so that they fling themselves face down
> in its path. The travellers' eyes are aimed
> at the higher, benevolent grasslands
> softer, more shapely than the sour veld,
> and as blonde as a sunburnt woman.

With the precise shifts of rifle-sights
their eyelids adjust their gaze
as they pass on and upwards.

Rhodesia is a location in the sky
somewhere above Africa where the sun is kind
to English skins and no winds blow.
A country of tourists who stayed
and were conscripted. Africa spreads below,
a game park to be preserved by selective culling.
If necessary the Zambezi will be stopped
that mother is assuring her son, firmly,
lest the waters of Kariba redden with Chinese.
Will she live to see his safari suit
swell with beer at Meikles,
sweat darken his hat and stain its leopard skin?
The station falls behind until it is as small
as England, and drops away.

'Rhodesian Leaving For Home from
Johannesburg Station' (1974)

As one tyrant gave way to the next in Africa, they seemed
mirror images of the despots who governed in Southern
Africa, in Rhodesia, and in Mozambique – with this difference: the men who took over in the Congo, in Ethiopia,
or in Guinea, marched their people into prison, and
plundered and ruined, yet they were more interested in
rhetoric and self-preservation than moral homilies. Watching the depredations of black leaders, you were free to feel
horror, but at least you were not overcome with the nausea
that ruled in much of white Southern Africa, induced by the
self-approving pieties expressed by our leaders and their

followers – a nausea that grew more marked if you travelled amongst those white minorities.

The closest that Rhodesians under Ian Smith ever convincingly came to a definition of what they stood for, was a celebrated remark made by him in 1976: 'I don't believe in black majority rule in Rhodesia – not in a thousand years.'

Terrible words. Slowly at first, and then in spates, Rhodesia was bleeding to death. Although the guerrilla war, led by Joshua Nkomo and Robert Mugabe, had begun back in the early years of the 1960s, it was only in the latter part of the Seventies that the killing began in earnest and finally put an end to indifference and to the Smith regime, but not before something like forty thousand people had died, most, but not all of them, black.

The warring parties signed peace accords at Lancaster House in London in 1979. Elections were held and the party of Robert Mugabe, ZANU-PF, swept to power. In a football stadium in Harare, in 1980, the British flag was lowered and the new Zimbabwe was born. Its new leader made a most extraordinary appeal to his defeated white compatriots: 'If yesterday, I fought you as an enemy, today you have become a friend . . . If yesterday you hated me, you cannot avoid the love that binds you to me and me to you.'

What counts in a tyrant, as Ilya Ehrenburg pointed out when reflecting upon Stalin, is not what he says or even how he comes across, it is rather to distinguish, if one is lucky, his essence. The essence of Mugabe was dissimulation, and surreptitious, unforgiving, malevolence. On 4 March 1980, when it became clear that he'd won a large majority in Parliament, and that his total of fifty-four seats was more than all the other parties put together, Mugabe exuded generosity. He talked about the time having come 'to beat our swords into plough-shares'. He urged people, black and white, to 'forgive and forget'. He appointed two white officials to serve in his government and he even kept on, briefly, the old Rhodesian joint Commander in the war against the Zimbabwean guerrillas. He retained the services of the Head of the secret police, the Central Intelligence Organization. Mugabe also retained, and this was not very much remarked upon at the time, many of the most draconian security laws, which had been invented by Ian Smith and his government. He told the *Herald* newspaper in 1980, on the eve of his victory, that he was determined to bring about 'true democracy based on equality where there won't be any discrimination on the grounds of race or colour. It would be a failure of policy on our part, a failure of our struggles.' These were words that would come back to haunt, not Mugabe, but the country.

He was welcomed by the West, by many die-hard Rhodesians, and in particular by churchmen who saw in Mugabe's religious zeal, a mixture of Marxist homily and the Christian zealousness he had learnt at school. His beguiling ways so hypnotized whites that they moved, in many instances, from outright hostility to a kind of defensive fawning on a man they soon came to call 'good old Bob'. Indeed to read through the newspapers and magazines of the early Eighties is to be struck by the surreal air of calm and contentment that settled over the new Zimbabwe soon after Independence. The danger seemed to have passed, and whites went back to doing what they always did: looking out across their immense farms, playing rugby, and drinking lots of cold beer. What could be better? They felt that radical change in the country was painless and that 'racism' in Africa was over. They were home and they were free. Whites would never be hounded and harried in quite the way they harried and hounded Africans. When Mugabe came to power they thought it was kiss-and-make-up time. Here was proof at last, in Africa, that the two forms of belief, communism and Christianity, were as one, reconciled in the bespectacled, schoolmasterly person of Robert Gabriel Mugabe. He had achieved this synthesis by dissolving the best of both creeds in the molten passion of his pan-African nationalism.

The appointment of the Reverend Canaan Banana, a Methodist minister, as Zimbabwe's first President, was seen as another example of the recasting of traditional Christian and liberal values in a revolutionary new African form. There was a grain of perverted truth in this; Mugabe had a semi-religious temperament. At one time he considered becoming a priest. However, his true religion was actually the violent vision of Marx and Lenin that found its most terrible disciple in Joseph Stalin; and his theology, like Stalin's, was couched in that extraordinary language that Soviet leaders invented, a grammar that, rather like Soviet architecture, was loud, ugly, menacing, and from which all human particulars were excluded, a language that substituted for people, for living flesh and blood, neutral abstract nouns like class, structure, cadre. In the windy talk of convinced Marxist revolutionaries like Robert Mugabe, these words swing like hanged men.

For Canaan Banana the Christian lineaments and moral blandishments of Robert Mugabe were, years later, to turn into a terrible trap. Affected as so many were by the euphoria of the Mugabe accession, the new President went so far as to compare the sacrifices of the guerrilla fighters with Christ's passion and death. This adulation of revolutionary Christianity, embodied in the person and party of the Leader, was to land Canaan in court years later, charged with buggery, his wife in exile in England, all the brave talk of that brave new world in tatters.

Why the Church, so undeceived by Ian Smith, was so taken with Mugabe is hard to fathom. Anyone reading his speeches made before he came to power, sees that he made no secret of his contempt for Christian belief. They were written on the battlefield, and sometimes broadcast from exile, when the ZANU-PF guerrillas were fighting the forces of Ian Smith. They carry the title: 'Our War of Liberation' and they reveal a man in the grip of rage and malice, and steeped in a mystical attachment to his Marxist convictions. They are political sermons peppered with jargon, eerily light-headed, laced with those terrible abstractions that have brought death to so many – 'elements' and 'class enemies', 'liquidation' and the victory of the 'toiling masses'. They also reveal an adulation bordering on idolatry for Mao and Fidel Castro, for Kim Chong Il and Samora Machel. They display an intense dislike, bordering on hatred, for the 'white man' and all his works. They embrace a kind of pan-African Marxism, founded on the Soviet, that is to say the Stalinist, model with bracing additions of Mao Tse Tung to whom he owes his overheated emphasis on the peasantry. It is similar to the agrarianism, the soil worship, with the peasant as God on earth, that Pol Pot and the Khmer Rouge were about to put into deadly practice in Cambodia. They say one thing plainly and they say it again and again – nothing and no one will stand in the way of the Leader and his party once he has taken absolute power.

Still, it is hard not to sympathize with those who were taken in. They wanted to believe, they needed to believe, and Robert Mugabe gave sweet and moving promises, all of which have turned out to be without any tincture of substance. If you look at any of his speeches of the triumphal period of his accession in 1980, the same note is hit again and again. Here is a quotation at random: 'If ever we look to the past, let us do so for the lesson the past has taught us, namely that oppression and racism are inequalities that must never find scope in our political and social system. It could never be a correct justification that because the white suppressed us yesterday when they had the power, the blacks must oppress them today because they have the power. An evil remains an evil whether practised by white against black or by black against white. Our majority rule could easily turn into inhuman rule if we oppressed, persecuted or harassed those who do not look or think like the majority of us. Majority is never mob-rule.'

It sounded good. Robert Mugabe usually reserved his expressions of affection for words and phrases drawn from banal party discourse but filled with passion. Love letters from the rostrum; a grammar edged with emotion; a warmed airstream wafted towards friends and detractors which, like some disabling gas, knocked them sideways, something semi-erotic, a deadly affection, the capacity to inspire and receive violently excited devotion: Mugabe hit every note his listeners wished to hear, protestations of love that astounded his enemies. Then he began systematically to destroy every one of them.

This ability to say one thing and to do another has baffled his opponents ever since. For some insight into his mind, Adolf Hitler's summation of the ingredients of power is useful: 'Politics,' Hitler told his dinner guests one evening in 1942, was 'the attainment of a goal by all conceivable means: persuasion, cunning, astuteness, persistence, kindness, slyness but also brutality.'

SEVEN

DOUBLE VISION

I began travelling in Eastern Europe not to get away from home but because I could not get away from home. After the mid-Seventies, South Africa was closed to me, my work banned. As a result I found I was spending more and more time in places where it was possible to study the world which I had left, a world which also lived in parallel lines. I went to West Berlin and I did what few West Berliners were able to do, I went to East Berlin, and what was once called the German Democratic Republic (how quaint that name sounds now). The GDR was barely German, never Democratic and, far from being a Republic, it was an obedient outpost of the Soviet empire. An absurd, touching, fiction rather than a country, it was haunted by ghosts of the old Germany and the Nazi disaster that few talked of, and ruled, ultimately, by Russia, a former enemy, now the fraternal partner. 'We are the *real* Berlin,' people told you, and that was odd. Odder still – they meant it.

Berlin, West and East, was an island deep inside East Germany. Twin cities with almost the same name, divided by a wall, and there were times when each denied point-blank it knew anything at all about the other. It was foreign but it was home; I knew where I was. When a place has been pummelled and stamped on, glorified and destroyed by one sole proprietor, the city, the stones, make a record, a sort of speaking likeness. West Berlin was filled with a kind of bright hysteria. The city was like an old veteran that has been badly wounded in the war: half its head had been shot away, but the heart was still beating, and still in the right place.

Flying into West Berlin, the plane dipped to a level where it could be tracked by Soviet radar, and one's head dipped with it, as if you were passing under barbed wire, into no-man's-land, or at least a political wonderland cut in half by a barrier the locals pretended not to see, a concrete wall that was hardly ever discussed but if you walked in any direction you'd sooner or later run up against it. A curving, smooth-lipped wall (two walls – with a minefield between, and barbed wire, dogs and border guards, search-lights, viewing platforms and warning signs). The whole extraordinary erection was brutally bare and grey on the Eastern side. Its Western face was painted, pocked, coloured, angry, pissed upon, thick with jokes, threats, funny faces and funeral markers, a theatre of irony and anger set in concrete.

Berlin was a rump city, a severed city, its western section divided into zones of occupation: American, French, British. The eastern portion was divided between Russian and German overlords. The West Berlin underground trains rattled beneath East Berlin and never stopped at the deserted stations. The roads of West Berlin ran forward until, suddenly, they were halted by the Wall. Berlin had become a distant theatre of the Cold War: secret agents, daring escapes, cunningly concealed compartments slung below trucks, flights by hot air balloon across the Wall, midnight dashes through the sewers, gunfire and bleeding bodies.

Along the length of the Wall small tabernacles remembered with a name or a photograph those who didn't make it.

Above and below all, there was the ghost of Hitler. No other despot except Stalin achieved so completely the terrible and murderous mediocrity that is the hallmark of modern tyranny – nor its range, its reach. The modern tyrant as Vladimir Nabokov observed so superbly, deliberately conflating Stalin, Lenin and Hitler – moves into the available space in the world, he takes over the available people, he becomes the majority. In time, he becomes everywhere. More correctly, time is his. The present moment exists as the opportunity to settle scores, to correct things. The future exists as a form of revenge yet to come. The past, all that strange time gone by, however you wish to describe the period anterior to the arrival of the dictator is not the measure of former events that had a life of their own, since nothing and no one, not even the dead, has a life unrelated to that of the despot. That is why this past time, or dead time (we might call it history), belongs to the State and is the property of the tyrant to be manipulated as he wishes. History becomes a matter for the police, and the censors.

Tyrants take over time and space, but they go further: they colour the world a uniform grey, they infect life with a lethal dullness, they provoke in their victims not only terror, but also a kind of fatal lassitude. This inertia is the same in all places ruled from the centre upon the basis of some prevailing idea, irrespective of political direction, left or right, which is really no more than decorative colour, the gift-wrapping around murder.

In the area around the Wall was war-torn desolation. A great tousled patch of nothing, once the site of the

Potsdammer Platz which had been, before the War, among the busiest intersections in all of Europe. The old prints show it to have looked rather like an immensely hectic Piccadilly Circus, at the heart of the old metropolis of Berlin. Now it was simply a muddy disconsolate vacancy. It was also the suburb of pre-war embassies, which had once been so smart and so rich, and now looked like victims of some below-stairs revolt by the proletarian vegetable orders – with creepers spreading across their rich frontages and reaching through open windows into empty rooms. The Potsdammer Platz, as Berlin taxi drivers liked to say, was not a development zone. Reminders of a cataclysm were every-where: the Hitler bunker; the site of the Gestapo torture chambers in Wilhelm Strasse; the fragmentary remains of the old Anhalter Station: just a crumbling façade and a few headless statues on what had been the roof. Before the war, the Anhalter Station despatched sixty trains a day all over Europe, to Dresden, Rome, Vienna.

Berlin was not just history for me, it was pattern, connection. Without Hitler and the Nazis, the racial vision of Hendrik Verwoerd and his men was not feasible. With-out the ground work done by the British in the early forms of concentration camps where so many Boers perished, the new improved model used by the Nazis was not explicable. Without Hitler's pioneering destruction of whole peoples, not for 'evil' reasons, but in order to 'improve' them out of all recognition, it was not possible to understand similar murderous corrections used in several societies; used, it should be said, with a degree of equanimity that is very peculiar when seen close up.

Friedrichstrasse was a grey shadow of its pre-war tinselly self. It was now a spatter of pizzerias, and a rash of small and rather bad bars, and it ended abruptly as it hit the Wall at Checkpoint Charlie. The graffiti I most cherished summed up all of the West Berliners' sharp irony, and their exasperation at the foreigner's obsession with their madly familiar, imprisoning fence: 'What are you staring at? Have you never seen a wall before?'

West Berliners detested the Wall. There was something ugly and shaming about it, but they learnt to live with it, they jogged along its grey length, daubed it with graffiti from one end to the other. Except on rare occasions when it thrust itself into view with some spectacular escape or shooting, or some important politician came to call and made a speech about the Wall, West Berliners simply tuned it out. They did much the same with the War: though signs of the cataclysm remained – ruined churches, bullet holes and shrapnel marks spattering the sides of the chic boutiques, in places like Fasanenstrasse in central Berlin – it was really not done to point them out.

There was always something inconsolable in the air of West Berlin.

East Berlin, by contrast, always pretended to be somewhere else. People in East Berlin talked about their city as 'Berlin', the capital of the only legitimate 'Germany'. For a start East Germany was a police state. Though most of the countries of Eastern Europe were police states, none provided a homesick South African with quite such familiar terrain: a divided country with a divided capital, an artificial state that had been constructed for political reasons soon after the end of the Second World War and whose divisions, marked in stone by the Berlin Wall, had endured almost exactly as long as the Colour Bar, erected by my old neighbour Dr Verwoerd, had endured in South Africa.

There was no talk in East Berlin of the camps, or the Nazis. They had been led to believe, they did believe, that they were the good Germans, the socially responsible Germans. As for West Berlin, well, they preferred to ignore the existence of this impostor, stuck away in the middle of one hundred and ten miles of East German territory, an island of lies and deceit. You watched the TV but you ignored the 'unreal' city from which it came. In the 'real' Berlin, east of the Wall, real soldiers would be seen changing the guard in the Unter den Linden, still doing the goosestep, wearing steel helmets shaped like soup plates. I would cross over into the East at Checkpoint Charlie for the pleasure of not believing what I saw. The bus would clatter into no-man's-land, and the East German border police clambered aboard and began checking passports, luggage, faces, atmosphere. The banging under the chassis of the bus told you that they were doing their mirror check. A long rod with a mirror on the end, rather like a massive dental mirror, was used for checking the underparts of the bus for any contraband like Bibles or meat or films or people who might have been wired to the exhaust pipe in an attempt to smuggle them into the land beyond the Wall, the workers' paradise.

To pass from West to East, through Checkpoint Charlie was to take a trip that made you experience again the strange realization that the dictators of our time were oddly alike. From the Hitler bunker, the ruined redoubt of the tyrant who lost, to the flourishing tyranny of the victor, was a few minutes' ride: as if the spirit had not been stilled but transmuted; as if there existed between them distinct familial ties; as if one dictator might hide another, a linkage perfectly expressed in the satirical Matrioschka dolls on sale in the Soviet Union in which Gorbachev opened up to reveal

Brezhnev who revealed Khrushchev who hid inside him Stalin who produced – the demon who began it all – the little bald effigy of Lenin. Indeed, it might be argued that Hitler was the soulmate, the twin, the promulgator of Stalin – that without the Nazi invasion of the Soviet Union, Stalin would never have become the military commander of unexpected gifts, nor the undisputed tyrant of all the Russias, nor perhaps the most murderous leader of our age. Hitler was, to some degree, the making of Stalin. One of them lost, and killed himself. The other died in his bed, raving mad, cursing all around him, imagining that Jewish doctors were killing him. And when, suddenly, he was gone, the story used to go in Russia, a story tinged with that glacial wit so heroic in the old USSR, the doctors about his bed puzzled over the recumbent corpse of the man everyone called simply 'the Boss'. They checked and rechecked for hints that he might still be alive – it would have been fatal to be wrong – but there were no vital signs and so they turned to each other and solemnly agreed that, yes, Joseph Stalin was dead, but this was by no means the end of the matter. There was the tricky question: 'Who is going to tell him?'

In West Berlin to talk of Nazi tyranny was natural. Across the Wall, to talk of Soviet tyranny was treason. Everything was different there, new world, new species, *Homo Soveticus*. It was another place. The little Trabants rode hither and thither. Bottles of pickles in the shop windows wore a dusty face – shop windows I soon discovered were places where they exhibited what they didn't sell, goods that were not available. It was not strange, there were powerful reasons for the paucity of means, it was all perfectly normal.

The trumpet blast of housing units, flats, apartment

blocks, slabs of concrete on Karl Marx Allee, that great boulevard that swept through the heart of East Berlin – time itself seemed to have set hard in those block-houses where thousands lived. They loomed like bouncers, or soldiers, or giants; they were not like anything I'd seen before. They dwarfed the world. They were ugly beyond imagining and they were threatening.

I began to understand architecture as a form of speech. It told you what a country was thinking and, in particular, since buildings were an expression of power, because they require money and muscle to erect, they told you more clearly than newspapers or political talk about the way things were. They were signs I could read. This was particularly useful in totalitarian countries where newspapers were organs of party propaganda and you could go to jail for holding the wrong kind of political conversation, and where conversation anyway had been reduced to a kind of code which was really only understandable if you had been trained to use it.

In places like East Berlin, people lost the ability to communicate directly and reduced their language to the oblique, to the wry, resorting more and more to gesture, to the pause, to the lifting of the eyebrows to communicate what was forbidden – sometimes even fatal – to say. Buildings, however, couldn't do that, they couldn't shut up. Like music, buildings went straight to the point. The buildings of East Berlin, the apartment blocks that stood shoulder to shoulder along Karl Marx Allee, were not first and foremost places in which people were housed. They were expression of power. So were the ridiculously polished and pampered museums and galleries, restored to their old magnificence at enormous cost. They were there, and had been triumphantly recreated from the rubble of war-torn Berlin, not because anyone cared about the pictures or the art they contained, but because they advertised the superiority of the System. They insisted with their heavy, peculiar, polished menace, the great museum, the immense gallery, that this was what socialism could do for the masses. In East Berlin they had the finest museums, the fastest swimmers, a superior political philosophy, and the purest form of democracy. They had the City Hall, the German State Opera, the Old Library – all of them grand and substantial ghosts. It didn't matter whether they were used or not. Restoration of these old buildings was a mixture of ideology and conceit, a protest whereby progressive forces, 'the future', kept up, in a disdainful way, a few of the more redoubtable and interesting landmarks of what was regarded as a sad, brutal, wasteful, foolish and hateful epoch. The young revolutionary state of the GDR preserved a few of its aged, mummified relatives on permanent display, relegating living beings to great rabbit hutches built of concrete. A small and rather sad painted fountain in the middle of Alexanderplatz was surrounded by the deeply depressing architecture of the 1950s. The fountain had been switched off and the open space of the square was cold and empty. Over there was the Brandenburg Gate, standing like a stage prop, or a huge papier mâché construction of a Hollywood film set. It didn't look real. Nothing looked real. Nobody passed through that gate any longer. Through its arch you got a very clear view of the Wall running behind it.

To preserve in costly mausoleums, the cherished arte-facts, paintings and jewellery of the largely bourgeois past, while turning your city into a massive jail filled with prisoners and apologists – a place where no one mentioned

the War, or the Jews, or the Wall, where the need to mollify
their Russian conquerors who had taken and then raped
Berlin had induced in the people a kind of somnolence, as if
the centres of their brains that controlled memory and anger
and hurt and grief had been closed down, and they had been
reduced to sleepy, strolling automatons – this regression
into adolescence, this playground behaviour, was something notable in oppressed societies. Grown people began
to reproduce the comportment of schoolchildren. They
ganged up on each other, they spied on each other, they
sought to curry favour with the Head – or at least they tried
to avoid being noticed at all by the authorities because to be
seen was to be vulnerable, and they reported on each other
all the time. When, some years later, the DDR collapsed,
and the files of the secret police were opened, the great
surprise in the West was the revelation that half of East
Germany spent its time spying on the other half. Just about
everybody seemed to have worked for the Stasi. Even
apparently 'dissident' intellectuals had been compromised. A
society ostensibly developed for the common good was
shown to have been based on lies, malice and treachery, not
as a by-product of its ideology, but as its very essence.

I used to wonder why I felt so at home in East Berlin.
After all, I understood and spoke the language very inade-
quately. I had little in common with the people or the
system – this was a European communist republic run along
Soviet lines, and I came from a nationalist, African ex-
British colony – but it didn't matter. I knew instantly where
I was – in a word, I was *home*. You had only to look at the
people in the street to spot the kinship. They were walking
wounded, small and careful and without apparent resting
places between the great slabs of stone that loomed above

them. They had that look I knew from the white people in South Africa; they looked like pasty-faced inmates from some house of correction. The German Democratic Republic, the GDR, was not a country, it was an institution, a confined space, a cross between a mental home and a boarding school where everyone, except the teachers, were designed to be ever juvenile, on trial, on show, on parole, on notice. East Germany, and in particular East Berlin, bore that other distinguishing mark of a tyrannical society: the eternal immaturity of its citizens who have never, will never, be trusted by their minders to lead their own lives or to make up their own minds or to go their own way. Such juvenile delinquents were told in long preachy harangues, for our masters were infused with a desire to be ethically as well as ethnically superior, that we were champions of white western Christian civilization. The sermon preached to the citizens of East Berlin, those mute and yawning congregations, told them that they were bright new standard-bearers of a socialist paradise towards which history, destiny and scientific materialism were carrying – rather slowly it was true, but too bad for slow coaches – the rest of humanity. In East Germany I found myself in an institution which claimed for itself a mystical superiority which was nowhere to be seen, though where to question the vision of perfection trumpeted at you by the party organs was worse than treachery, it was heresy.

East Berlin was a nest of lies, welded together by the party and the secret police, a society that claimed to be modern and progressive but which you saw, at every turn, was slow, shallow, shadowy, stupid and corrupt: the sentry in his tower; the citizen on his knees; the tall, demented psychiatric nurses hovering over the small scurrying infantile classes whom they oversaw, instructed, sometimes reformed, and, where it was necessary, sometimes shot. The juvenile citizenry watched what they said or read or thought, never stopped or talked in public, went home to their kitchens and revealed in the early hours of the morning over a glass of vodka at the kitchen table that not only did they not believe, but they were not idiots, they were not taken in, and they loathed their guardians with a bleak and bitter contempt that far exceeded anything conventional foreign enemies would have dreamt of saying about them. They knew that they were, after all, people, just like people everywhere, and they bitterly resented their confinement and, even more, they resented the way in which they were expected to lead the lives of childish fools. It was very liberating to find people who thought as you did. It was comforting to know that you were not alone, even though in our case, white people in South Africa had had another destiny thrust upon them. They were said to be superior, gods in white skins, but the truth, everyone knew, was quite the opposite. Authoritarian societies do not make exceptions to the rule. They are small closed places run by very few people in whose hands all power is held. And the people in charge are determined to make fools of the ruled. That is common to most despotic regimes. It is only the nature of the foolishness that changes.

The Wall, said the party functionaries, had been built to increase the happiness of all Germans, and to promote peace and friendship. Dr Verwoerd said the same about his racial barriers thrown up between black, white and brown people. In South Africa we built walls of skin, made homelands for our serfs, and deposited them there. And even that was a lie. We could not do without those from whom we wished to distance ourselves. We thus devoted our lives to maintaining a system which was not merely cruel and silly, it was a myth. We gave up everything – an identity, responsibility, imagination, freedom – in order to do nothing but keep an eye on our servants, when we weren't keeping an eye on each other. It was the primary responsibility of the State to interfere with its citizens, and it was the duty of citizens to interfere with each other. Someone's job was incidental to their true existence. You proved the reality of your existence by the degree to which you obeyed the Regime. It alone conferred authenticity. The things people claimed to be in 'real' life, their professional occupations, hung loosely and unconvincingly on them, like borrowed clothes. No one was really a plumber, a midwife, a butcher. Everyone was, firstly, a particle of dust owned by the state, and only later were they engineers or train drivers.

Much the same thing happened in Eastern Germany. Before you were a doctor, or a poet, or a train driver, you were a member of a new species. It was an historical responsibility and the State accorded special privileges, separate schools, exclusive shops and favourable status to a small number of the politically élite who recognized their destiny. I fell in love with Eastern Europe because in many ways it was a cure for my homesickness. The country was run by the police on behalf of the Party, and run very badly.

Those who have never lived in police states imagine they must be very efficient. Exactly the opposite is true: there is intimidation, imprisonment, censorship and murder, but these things don't make for efficiency. Despite Mussolini's reputation for getting the Italian trains to run on time, totalitarian systems are inefficient. It is an inefficiency bred, I think, out of the need for control and out of the fundamental belief that, since every aspect of human life is political, it requires the right political direction, from the right authorities at the time. Which is why the useful fiction, so comforting in freer societies, that politics can be kept apart from daily life, is viewed with incredulity by those who have been locked into an autocratic country where everything, from the production of poetry, to the refinement of petrol, is a political matter, because politics is another word for control and control is an absolute obsession, a suffocating, boring and dreary chimera that drives the rulers mad and alienates the ruled who can do nothing about it except to fall back into the bleak and bitter and increasingly wordless wit that is one of the great achievements of those who lived under the old Stalinist regimes.

East Germany presented the form of communist tyranny in a peculiarly faithful manner, perhaps because it wasn't the originator but the disciple. It showed that East European 'socialism' produced cruelty and absurdity, much as did life under apartheid, with its rabid right-wing mumbo jumbo. And people got to like it, they defended it, they compromised with it. Its victims were not consulted as to their feelings. The greatest treachery, the greatest corruption of tyranny was perhaps not simply that the ruler set out to betray his people but that they were increasingly willing to betray each other, and themselves. It is also a question of atmosphere, of air, or the lack of it. Societies where control is paramount and all-pervasive, inspire very naturally this feeling that everyone is watching everybody else, that everyone somehow 'knows' everyone else. This is not paranoia as some might think – it is simply good sense. It is always strange to live in a country where constantly you have the feeling that everyone is in some way 'related'. This comes about perhaps because of the peculiar bonding that goes on when people are forced together, to watch and think and act together. Totalitarian societies are immensely, even lethally, boring, drawn, cramped, pressed. There are only a handful of ideas and the rate of repetition is high, and because people go round doing and saying more or less the same things all the time, they build up this feeling of almost claustrophobic intimacy. You watch, and you know you are being watched. Your ability to communicate is halved. For one thing it is dangerous to say what you think and feel and, for another, the ability to express yourself is impaired, a lot of the time people just say the same things. There is, however, more wit in a shrug, more originality in a sniff. Your gestural language, your monosyllabic and ironic language, is considerably enriched. Trapped in the jungle of ideology where words are the province of the rulers and change comes according to the whim of the tyrant, and lethal, lacerating, hideous boredom interrupted by spasms of fear is your lot, you fall back on jungle language: a wink, a sigh, a glance that is quite enough to stop someone in his tracks.

It is also assumed you can measure the magnitude of the tyranny by the bodies it leaves. This is not the case; you measure it better by the amnesia it creates. On some sort of Dictators' Top Ten, Hitler and Stalin and Pol Pot may seem to lead the field, measured by the millions they murdered, but that is false. Dead bodies are inevitable but incidental to modern tyranny which relies for its force on persuading people to kill others and to sacrifice themselves for the common good. Those who rebel or demur are to be exiled, imprisoned or destroyed – not as some special measure, something out of the ordinary, but as something natural, wholesome, healthy. In this respect, despots like Robert Mugabe or Erich Honneker, are very modern. Where they fall behind is in their inability to command the blind devotion, and thus the lives, of millions of believers.

However, the model still works, even if you lack the great operatic congregations of hysterical followers known by Hitler, Stalin, Mao. So long as you can use terror, and you command an inner core of enthusiasts, then yours is the power and the unchallenged capacity to destroy enough of those who dissent. And how many is enough? One may do. A hundred may be better. Enough is simply a question of whatever it takes to solve the problem.

The word whispered today in Zimbabwe, amongst those who fear the Regime, is that famine threatens to kill half the population, say six million. To some of Mugabe's men, this might not be such a calamity because by controlling food supplies, they can see to it that the 'right' people perish and since the people of Matabeleland are among the fiercest of unbelievers what could be better than that nature should conspire to punish them? It is something that frightens hungry people in parts of the country that voted against the Party and the President. No one forgets Robert Mugabe's first campaign to stamp out 'dissidence' in the new Zimbabwe – the Matabeleland Massacres.

EIGHT

MURDER IN MATABELELAND

The election of Robert Mugabe in 1980 pleased so many that no one mentioned how very odd it was. Here was a man who hated open scrutiny. No one expected him to win. The smart money was on Joshua Nkomo, the senior partner in the guerrilla alliance fighting the Rhodesian army, but, although the guerrilla armies, ZANLA and ZIPRA, led by Robert Mugabe and Joshua Nkomo, had joined together to form the patriotic front to fight the war against Ian Smith, this merger was dissolved before the elections. It's also worthwhile recalling that Joshua Nkomo's party, ZAPU, or the Zimbabwe African People's Union, was the original liberation grouping formed by Nkomo back in 1961, and it was Mugabe and others, dissatisfied with Nkomo's leadership, who split off to form a second major liberation movement, the Zimbabwe African National Union or ZANU, a few years later, in 1963. In other words, Mugabe was the political offspring of Joshua Nkomo and, in the grave and inexorable rhythm of some Shakespearean tragedy, the son rose up and struck the father dead.

The new Zimbabwe was to be dominated by a single party, ZANU-PF, directed by a politburo that would rubber-stamp the orders of the Leader for life who answered, when he answered at all, not to his people but to his Central Committee. That was decided. What was not clear at the time of accession in 1980 was exactly how to bring this desired ambition to pass. Mugabe's belief had always been that bullets would decide the fate of white Rhodesia, that war was the way to power, and that the means of destroying the white regime of Ian Smith lay in his own guerrilla army, the Zimbabwean African National Liberation Army, or ZANLA. His fighters, he declared in a war-time speech, were 'revered and adored by the people as the vanguard of their liberation struggle'. He foresaw a long bush war, ending when the victorious guerrillas swept into Salisbury, grubbed up the bourgeoisie, the capitalists and the settler vermin, destroyed their black stooges and the other running dogs of capitalism and imperialism, and founded a one-party state along North Korean lines. Other models were Fidel Castro and the Cuban Revolution, and East Germany, which had been instrumental in providing funds, military assistance and training to Mugabe's liberation army. The German Democratic Republic was also the model of the sort of steely Marxist correctness, rigour and discipline that Robert Mugabe always found to be politically indispensable virtues. The only passion he showed was when speaking – preaching might be a better word – about the virtues of 'scientific socialism'. Here was a man who focused his passion on 'the toiling masses' who were to be 'guided', and upon whom one day the burden of destiny would be 'discharged'. When he dedicated himself to the toiling masses, he rose towards the loved object, he achieved rhetorical tumescence.

At the Lancaster House peace talks, in London in 1979, Mugabe reluctantly allowed himself to be coaxed into standing in an election he was sure would be loaded against him. To everyone's amazement, including perhaps his own, he won a huge victory. This result had the unintended novelty of bringing to power, through universal suffrage, a convinced revolutionary who detested bourgeois democracy. The outlaw who had expected to have to shoot his way to the bank, had been presented with the keys to the strong-room by a delighted manager and his grateful staff, and invited to help himself. It was rum stuff.

Quite how it was done is still not clear – although Mugabe's party made sure of the votes in the areas where it was already strong by threatening voters who cast their ballots for the wrong party, a method he was to use ever afterwards – but the results were there, his party, ZANU, had the support of the country. Joshua Nkomo was trounced. The father of Zimbabwean nationhood cast at the backs of the departing British rulers this memorable *cri de coeur*: 'You gave them one man, one vote, and look what they have done with it!'

Robert Mugabe was not a man to be taken in by conventional success. He had not spent years in exile, and in jail, and fighting a bush war, in order to preside over what was in effect an effete consultative Western democracy. He had promised to expel, or extirpate, the white 'settlers', redistribute their farms to poor peasants, and liquidate all black opposition who were far more pressing a danger than the exhausted and by now thoroughly baffled whites of the old Rhodesia. He had been elected to office; but now the time had come to take power. Sentiment was given some place in the proceedings, the new Leader made several extraordinary speeches pledging love and forgiveness, and then he went back to war.

★

The country of Matabeleland, in southern Zimbabwe, is populated in large part by Ndebele people, while in the north, the majority belong to the Shona grouping. Although, in Robert Mugabe's words, all indigenous people are Zimbabwean, and the Ndebele are indigenous to the region, it is also true in this mad land that some Zimbabweans are more indigenous than others. Robert Mugabe was a Shona and the Shona were the ruling clan. This did not matter so much when the country rose against the white regime of Ian Smith, but, when the war of independence had been won, and Robert Mugabe installed as prime minister, the alliance between Shona and Ndebele fractured. Fighting broke out between the guerrilla armies of Robert Mugabe and Joshua Nkomo soon after independence in 1980. The State of Emergency, which had been introduced by Ian Smith, was reinstated and remained in place for the next decade.

In November 1980, clashes in Bulawayo left fifty-five people dead and wounded ten times that number. There was talk at the time that the cause of the fighting had been an angry speech by the ZANU-PF minister Enos Nkala, in which he promised to 'crush' Joshua Nkomo. The belief in ruling ZANU-PF party circles was that Joshua Nkomo and his ZAPU party, embittered by their defeat in the general election, were planning a coup against Robert Mugabe. There may well have been some truth in it. The bitterness was very real.

In 1981, more fighting between the former guerrilla partners left one hundred and sixty-seven dead. Senior leaders of Nkomo's guerrilla fighters were put on trial in 1982, charged with treason. That year Robert Mugabe formally fired Joshua Nkomo, calling him a 'cobra' in the house and accusing him of attempting to organize a military

take-over by hiding caches of weapons. In response, Joshua
Nkomo said something that was to go on resounding down
the years: 'I've never done anything wrong and Robert
knows it. I tell you, this is for personal power.'

The six defendants in the first treason trial were acquitted
but immediately arrested under the Emergency Powers
Regulations, another familiar instrument Robert Mugabe
inherited from Ian Smith and used with even sharper effect
than his predecessor. In July 1982, six British and American
tourists were kidnapped on the road between Bulawayo and
Victoria Falls by unknown 'dissidents'. The kidnappers
demanded the release of their leaders who had been detained
on charges of plotting a coup against Robert Mugabe. When
the government refused, the tourists were murdered. Two
men were later found guilty of their murders and were
hanged. Doubt still persists as to who the real culprits were,
but it hardly matters – for the kidnap of the tourists became
the pretext for launching in Matabeleland one of the most
sustained programmes of torture, terror, kidnapping and
murder that the country had ever seen.

The instrument of this action was to be Enos Nkala, an
Ndebele himself, an old and loyal ally of Robert Mugabe, a
cell-mate from the year of struggle and now his Minister of
Home Affairs. Nkala was perfectly plain about his intentions
to reduce all opposition to the Mugabe government within
Matabeleland to a trickle of blood. The Ndebele who were
calling for a war of liberation would be 'shot down' he said.
Enos Nkala occupied a special place in the massacres of
Matabeleland. He was Robert Mugabe's chosen executioner and he showed himself well up to the job. He became
known to some as – and I recall the vehemence with which
his name was spoken – the Butcher of Bulawayo. His role

may be juxtaposed with that of his Leader: Enos Nkala's job was to liquidate the enemies of the regime by all available means; Robert Mugabe's role was to express wounded innocence when asked about the terror launched in his name by his government and directed by his ministers.

Robert Mugabe also turned to North Korea for help in suppressing 'dissidence' in Matabeleland. The North Koreans had long been Mugabe's models and mentors. He admired North Korean politics, a mixture of Stalinism with additions of agrarian communism that derived from the most radical of Mao's lethal drives to exalt the peasantry into the deity. The bond between Mugabe and that god-king Kim Chong Il, 'Beloved Leader' of North Korea, was strong.

By 1982, the special military force trained by the North Koreans, known as the Fifth Brigade – or, sometimes, 'Five Brigade' – was unleashed: red berets, AK47s, trucks that kept breaking down, and death everywhere they went. 'Plough and reconstruct,' said their commander, Colonel Perence Shiri. 'Reconstruct' is a word that, in Africa, has people running a mile; it often means murder.

Claiming that Matabeleland in general, and Joshua Nkomo's former guerrilla army in particular, was fomenting violence and 'banditry', Mugabe launched the Fifth Brigade upon 'dissidents' among the Matabele people. The men of the Brigade were mainly Shona-speaking soldiers trained to detect, and extinguish, those who opposed Mugabe's rule and his party. They did so with a ferocity that even today stops people speaking freely of the events that took place between 1981 and 1986 across Matabeleland and, most lethally, in Lupane and Tsholotsho. Places where I sat in my car, waiting for the CIO operatives to make up their minds what to do with me, had been the Zimbabwean killing fields in what became known in Shona as 'Gukurahundi', 'the rain that washes away the chaff from the last harvest, before the spring rains'. It is still spoken of with a shiver.

Five Brigade were destined to be remembered. Their mission was set out by Robert Mugabe in a speech in Matabeleland in 1983: 'We have to deal with the problem quite ruthlessly . . . Don't cry if your relatives get killed in the process.' Five Brigade were a force apart and nothing stood in their way. How extraordinarily superior they must have seemed to the people in the villages they torched and destroyed, how very modern. They came from the evolved 'scientific' world, a world which believed in 'hygiene', in order, a world which, when it was ordered to exterminate the local population, obeyed immediately, not with noise and sensationalism, but with quiet efficiency. Five Brigade burned victims alive, tortured them with electrodes, drowned them, locked them in camps where they succumbed to starvation and disease, and then threw their bodies into mass graves or dumped them down old deserted mine-shafts. There were times when Five Brigade exceeded its own records of cruelty. In order that the families of their victims should suffer as extensively as possible – for the Ndebele find it intolerable that the dead should not be properly buried and decently mourned – Five Brigade insisted that the bodies of the executed be abandoned in the bush to be disposed of by vultures and jackals and other scavengers.

Some time after 1985, when the killings were in full spate, Enos Nkala was appointed as Mugabe's Minister of Police. He was characteristically plain-spoken: 'My instinct tells me that when you deal with ruthless gangsters, you have to be ruthless. I have locked up a few honourable members [of Parliament] and I think they will have their rest for a long time to come before they reappear to continue with their dissident activities.'

During the liberation war against the guerrilla forces of Robert Mugabe and Joshua Nkomo, the government of Ian Smith locked civilians in closed villages and supplied them with just enough food to prevent starvation; the aim was to stop them feeding the guerrillas. Mugabe took things a step further; he did to his own people what the white government of Ian Smith had never dared to do. He declared open war upon them. By the time he had finished, those who were not obedient were dead; and those who were not dead were either starving or terrified.

The continuities between the Smith regime and the Mugabe government, in method and in murder, have been uncanny. Robert Mugabe retained many of Smith's police, and his army commanders. He retained most of his security legislation: the State of Emergency was formalized; the right to detain people without trial, as well as the right to detain people after their trial, even if they were found innocent, were also retained, strengthened and used.

What could be said to flavour the brand of savagery that Robert Mugabe inflicted on his people and what distinguished it from the cruelty of the previous tyrant, Ian Smith, and his collection of bone-headed, whip-wielding ministers, was the spurious religiosity which accompanied the bloodletting. Five Brigade were very fond of Biblical allusions, and several of its commanders appropriated the name of Jesus. These 'black Jesuses' had power over life and death, and they liked their terrified victims to be aware of their supernatural status. Soon after the terror was launched in

Matabeleland, the Minister of State Security, a title even then to strike fear into the hearts of one and all, Emmerson Mnangagwa, who ran the CIO, told a meeting in Victoria Falls, in 1983, that the government had been fairly patient with the 'dissidents' thus far, but there was an option that might have to be tried, the soldiers might well begin burning down all villages where their enemies could be hiding because, said the minister, they were like so many cockroaches. He went on to liken Five Brigade to DDT, the insecticide that would destroy them.

Later that year, Minister Mnangagwa fell naturally into quasi-Biblical terminology when he warned the people of Matabeleland that they had a choice: they could either co-operate or die. The minister handed down this message in the form a parody of Christ's Sermon on the Mount: 'Blessed are they who hunger and thirst after justice, for they shall find peace.' Mnangagwa chose rather to speak in the voice of the god who lived not in heaven, but in State House in Harare, and his sermon was short and sharp: 'Blessed are they who follow the path of government, for their days on earth shall be increased. But woe to those who choose the path of collaboration with dissidents for we will certainly shorten their stay on earth.'

The methods used by the Fifth Brigade were explained to me by a man I shall call Henry who lives in Tsholotsho, an area infested by Fifth Brigade soldiers for much of the early Eighties: he remembered a raid on his village when he had lost three brothers, his small son and his sister:

'The soldiers came before dawn and they carried bazookas and grenades and they made us get up and they said we had dissidents and we said, "No", so they shoot my brother there in front of us and we are crying and they say,

"Show us the dissidents," and we don't know what to say and they shoot again, just like that and my son who is only small and my sister fall down and they say, "Leave them – if you touch them we will kill you." Then they say, "Take them into the hut," and we take them in and they say, "Here is petrol," and we pour petrol on the hut and they light it and the hut burns and they say, "Now you dig a pit here," and my brother and me dig the pit and they make us stand in the pit and they shoot and my neighbours fall on me and I wait to die and I don't, and the hut is still burning. And then they go away. I don't know why. And I am alone there.'

It took a number of killings before the churches, which had been far quicker to protest when Ian Smith was in charge, managed to arrange an audience with Robert Mugabe, in late March 1983. By this time things were so bad they could no longer be hidden; bodies were piled or buried or burned in very great numbers right across the province. The Prime Minister listened with sympathy, the clerics reported; he seemed to be 'genuinely shocked and saddened'; and he turned to Emmerson Mnangagwa and asked: 'Why didn't you tell me that?'

It was an extraordinary performance. There is about Mugabe a terrifying meekness, which those who know him have remarked upon: a dissembling modesty mixed with cunning. Why the churchmen should have taken this seriously might be explained by an almost Chamberlain-like desire to receive from the Leader some form of reassurance with which they might assuage their own unease. The need, indeed the wish, to be deceived has marked the dealings of friends and enemies over the years. The delegation was barely out of the door, when the Prime Minister attacked them as meddlesome priests. They were, said Mugabe, 'a band of Jeremiahs . . . and sanctimonious prelates . . .'

The concerted murder of Matabele people went on until late July 1983, when Five Brigade was withdrawn for what was called 'retraining'. Now food supplies which were controlled by the Government, were sharply reduced. The drought was bad in Matabeleland and the regime in Harare saw food, or rather the withdrawal of food, as a way of further intimidating an already terrified population.

The nature of the retraining the Fifth Brigade had received became clear when they returned to Matabeleland the following year. The terror campaign went well beyond the hunt for 'dissidents'. Men, women, mothers and babies, old and young, were shot, burnt, bayoneted, tortured. Families who made the mistake of mourning their dead were shot by Five Brigade as a warning to others that tears would not be tolerated. One of the more favoured methods of execution was to herd women and children into huts and set the thatch alight. Many thousands of people were done to death by government forces in the early 1980s in a fairly small area of Zimbabwe. Many more were injured, tortured, raped, or they simply disappeared. Others were burnt out of their homes or chased off their land.

The numbers who died have never been confirmed. Estimates start at 'over a thousand', by the International Commission of Jurists: this refers to the number who died in the month between January and February in 1983. The Lawyers' Committee for Human Rights adjusted this figure upwards to one thousand five hundred people killed during late 1982 and March 1983. The most extensive report is by the Catholic Commission for Justice and Peace, based on interviews with over a thousand respondents carried out between 1995 and 1996. The Commission published in 1997 a patient, sober, meticulously documented report of murder, rape, robbery and torture – though 'published' is perhaps too confident a word: the Commission's report has never appeared in full, or in public, just as the massacres were never acknowledged by Robert Mugabe. The Commission put the figure of confirmed dead somewhere between three and five thousand, but concluded that the number was almost certainly much higher – at least twice that figure. This tally does not include the missing. Sometimes entire families were murdered, leaving no witnesses. Joshua Nkomo reckoned the total number of dead to be closer to twenty thousand, though the more cautious agencies have always regarded this figure as inflated. No one really knows.

The Matabeland murders proved to be as modern as any massacres by Stalin or Pol Pot. Mugabe's security apparatus established camps where enemies of the state were conveyed, and there beaten, tortured and murdered in their thousands. Zimbabwe was a small country, with a population below ten million in the Eighties, when Five Brigade, stalked Matabeleland. There was barely a family in the region that was not touched. It may have been, as some accounts suggest, that seven or ten or twenty thousand perished – but totals do not make a tyranny, method makes a tyranny: the way it induces the most well-meaning to live a lie. Tyranny is a matter of texture, a question of feel, and there is an unmistakable characteristic: it will murder while it moralizes, and it will build camps while it talks of freedom.

There is an edging of self-righteousness, as well as a tendency to sentimentality, in those despots of our time, the

Uncles, and Beloved Leaders and Number One Brothers and Leading Peasants, the Saviours, Redeemers, Daddas, Papas and Uncles: a desire for recognition, for some sympathetic understanding of just how hard these conscientious clerks of death must work, what little thanks they get, how ungrateful the victims seem. And, how perfectly 'normal' the killers of our time will show themselves to be at the end of a long day in the killing fields. In a phrase, how like ourselves they are.

The use of terror against defenceless populations has its own remorseless logic. In the elections of 1985, Robert Mugabe won seventy-one per cent of the seats on the Common Roll and the ruling party increased its majority to seventy-five per cent. However, in Matabeleland almost everyone voted for ZAPU, the opposition party of Joshua Nkomo. It was another slight Robert Mugabe was not prepared to tolerate. Enos Nkala, who was running the war in Matabeleland with relish, had this to say:

'Let me assure you that the policy of reconciliation towards ZAPU has been withdrawn . . . We want to wipe out the ZAPU leadership. You've only seen the warning lights. We haven't yet reached full blast.'

Nkala promised to lock up everyone in ZAPU if he needed to, including its leader, Joshua Nkomo. He wasn't joking. He had already locked up a couple of hundred ZAPU officials, and five ZAPU MPs: he had also jailed the mayor of Bulawayo and his entire council.

In 1986, Gukurahundi was declared a success and the peace of the graveyard descended on Matabeleland. Joshua Nkomo was on the ropes. There was in his increasingly perilous statements of that time no sign that he saw the disaster about to engulf him. His great antagonist and the architect of Ndebele humiliation – by terror, starvation, and murder was Enos Nkala, but the man pulling the strings was Robert Mugabe and Nkomo never seems to have grasped that he was in a war to the death with a man who defined himself by crushing his enemies, real or false, at home or abroad.

Poor Nkomo. He could only protest: 'We do not want war and we have no means to fight a war. If Minister Nkala wants, he can come and kill us. If I knew what to do to satisfy Nkala I would do it – but I do not know what to do to satisfy him.'

Robert Mugabe knew what to do, and a year later, in December 1987, he led Nkomo, now completely groggy, to the conference table, and they signed a peace deal known as the Unity Pact. It was all over. So was the notion of opposition. Nkomo became, once again, a 'president' of sorts – and vanished as a significant force in Zimbabwean political life, though his substantial ghost hung about for some years longer, rather like a large and reproachful wraith, telling everyone he knew how badly treated he'd been. No one was listening because they knew Nkomo was no longer alive, he was merely pretending. A story tells of Nkomo reproaching his neighbours for rustling cattle from his Vice-Presidential ranch, which was in the countryside where the Fifth Brigade had been active. 'You should treat my property with respect,' said Nkomo. Those who had suffered through the years of the Gukurahundi killings were not impressed: 'When you give us back our sons, we'll stop taking your cows.' In the same month as he signed the Unity Pact, Robert Mugabe pushed through Parliament a consti-

tutional amendment that made him President of Zimbabwe
– a position, it was clear, no one else would hold while he
remained on earth.

Looking back, it would seem that Robert Mugabe was
on the road to tyranny soon after coming to power. Within
seven years, in the name of freedom, the Leader reigned
supreme. There had been the killings in Matabeleland, the
corruption and criminality of his regime – all this was
awesome enough, but it took something more to propel
Mugabe into the front ranks of tyranny: it took plunder on
a very grand scale, a theft so large, so brazen, it defied belief,
and in fact there are those who still don't believe it. Justice,
freedom, the economy, the press, the government, the past,
the future, the hopes of millions were swallowed up by a
ravening ambition to own the lot. Here was the sign of
Mugabe's real seriousness. Here was a man who stole his
own country.

It seems to be a rule in the revolutions of the twentieth
century that those prepared to die for freedom cannot be
trusted with its achievement. And those like Mugabe, who
suffered under European despotisms, have an uncanny way
of mimicking their former oppressors as soon as they come
to power. Robert Mugabe exhibited this unconscious
mimicry to the point of parody; he did not just behave like
other models of darkness, he looked and sounded like them.
It is as if absolute power turns those who possess it into
brothers under the skin. They begin to impersonate each
other, no matter how far apart they may be in time or
culture or politics. In an age which deserved to be called the
time of tyrants, Mugabe was absolutely quintessential: in the

facial furniture, the tiny moustache that visited his upper lip like a fleeting salute to other brothers; in the sneaking love for tunics, gear, podiums, fists; in his attitude of brooding solemnity; in his record for murder, and his elusive malice; in the madness that swirled around him and to which otherwise apparently sensible people were horribly susceptible. Despotic consanguinity, a gift for mime – dictators did not die but merely passed on their tunics, and their torture chambers, to the next generation. The incoming candidate might change small aspects of himself – his hatreds, his hats, his moustache – but, for the rest, he wears the family face.

NINE

GREAT ABOLITIONISTS

Zimbabwe, under the rule of Robert Mugabe, has often declared itself to be 'Stalinist'. Mugabe's men embraced the brand-name without embarrassment – but I suppose an embarrassed Stalinist is a contradiction in terms. 'Stalinist' was a badge of pride worn by party functionaries and party hacks who found it frightened effete Westerners. However, it was never very accurate. Zimbabwe was a very imperfect copy of the master model, except in two important aspects: the cult of the Leader who could do no wrong, and who was portrayed as the redeemer of his country rather than its ruination; and a collection of very nasty camps in which many people died. Stalin brought to tyranny a malicious desire, not only to destroy all who opposed him but to know and judge every aspect of the life and death of his victims who are crushed not by anything as crude as bullets or boots or bayonets – certainly not; they are judged and over-whelmed by the revolutionary purity of the Leader. In that respect Mugabe has proved very close to the master.

When the terror squads, the secret police, the army, and Five Brigade were sent to Matabeleland in the Eighties to put down 'dissidence', it was a murky and murderous business, but it had a design: it was to be violent but invisible. It was to leave no trace. It was to be everywhere and nowhere.

Mugabe made that clear in 1982 when he told the passing-out parade of the soldiers the North Koreans had readied for this operation: "The knowledge you have acquired will make you work with the people, plough and reconstruct. These are the aims you should keep in yourself." There was to be blood and terror but no one was to say so. Terror was to be followed by oblivion. The Leader was to rise above it all, untainted by the savagery of his police, his security agencies, his ministers. He was to remain the smiling and avuncular freedom-loving father of his people.

Even today you will find it hard to get anyone to talk openly about what happened. Terror is an effective silencer and instils a wish to forget. Amnesia is the refuge of the executioner but also of the victim. Killing on that scale is an onerous business, it requires time, facilities, and privacy, and the logistics of accommodation and disposal are formidable. Also, it must be carried out in such a way that not only those who gave the orders but those who willingly participated may be able to deny later that any such thing happened. Half a century passed after Stalin's Great Terror of the Thirties before Russians were able to talk and to remember.

I went to Moscow in 1988, and it was a time when the evidence of Stalin's camps was coming to light. If I had felt strangely at home in the divided city of Berlin, Moscow seemed even more familiar, with its special schools, shops, limousines and clinics for the favoured few of the ruling clique, with the 'propriska', the paper 'pass' Muscovites carried to prove they were legally living in the city. Moscow, for a South African, was full of intensely haunting normal things – omnipresent police, insolent officials, the overweening, ridiculous Party, strutting power, fierce yet absurd – and at the back of it all, just beginning to push their way into the public consciousness, the prison camps from which so few returned.

Moscow was a Stalinist city, he was in its bloodstream and in its skyline. He had been dead for thirty-five years but he was everywhere, the semi-divine being whose people rioted upon news of his death on 5 March 1953 and who was compared by his praise singers to spring sunshine. My friend Viktoria remembered Stalin's death. She'd been about five at the time and she could recall a frenzied ugly grief that broke out in the centre of the city. The sky she said was lit up with an enormous picture of the dead dictator, 'A portrait of Stalin flying in the air'. People were trampled by the hysterical crowds, a young boy she knew was crushed in the tumult. She fell ill, she ran a temperature and her grandmother sat by her bedside and said to her, 'People shouldn't be glad when a person dies, but it's very good that he died. Maybe, maybe there won't be so many tragedies.' After Khrushchev's denunciatory speech against Stalin in 1956, her grandmother allowed herself another crumb of comfort, 'Now we have some chance.' Her grandfather, an architect who enjoyed Stalin's esteem, took no chances even so, and in the corner of his study he always kept a small trunk. Viktoria remembered how she used to play on this suitcase. It was only much later that she realized that it held her grandfather's clothes, ready for a late night knock on the door.

In 1988 Stalin, like the power he wielded, was gone and yet he remained apparent as a kind of background radiation penetrating every aspect of Russian life. His presence could be detected still, in many ways, and in particular in the suffering of his victims, and in the machinery needed to exile them, or murder them – he can be traced in the memory of victims who survived and in the names of the camps. Many of these camps had been anonymous, but now they were being named and visited and explored: Solovki, Minsk, Magadan, Potsma, Karaganda.

It was permissible at long last to begin to number the victims, but it was an impossible task and one that the historian Roy Medvedev did with great caution. Arriving at a figure solely for the terrible years of 1937 and 1938, when Stalin's persecution of his own people was at its height, presented most difficulty. After pointing out that the destruction had been perhaps even more bloody during and after the war against Nazi Germany, and in the years that followed, Medvedev suggests that in 1937/38 between five and seven million were 'repressed' (imprisoned, banished, murdered). He continues: 'Most of those arrested in 1937–1938 were put in "corrective labour" camps that peppered the country. Considerable numbers of those who came from the top party and government echelons were shot soon after arrest, or after investigation, on trumped up charges. Death sentences were recorded at one time. I used to think seven hundred thousand to eight hundred thousand were shot. But many, it appears, were shot on secret orders, in the camps. So a more realistic number would be one million.'

Khrushchev's denunciation of Stalin at the Twentieth Party Congress of the Soviet Communist Party in 1956 had still not been published when I got to Moscow in 1988. The enormity of Stalin's crimes was deeply felt by those Russians who believed that their revolution, and their country, had been hijacked by a murderous crook. On 26 November 1988, Mikhail Gorbachev, General Secretary of the Communist Party of the Soviet Union, and President of the USSR, made a speech to the Supreme Soviet of the USSR setting out his principles for restructuring the country. Gorbachev's solution to the first stirrings of the spirit of independence was something he called 'Glasnost' – openness – but of course not too much. There should also be something called 'Perestroika' or 'restructuring' – but not too much of that, either. The rule from the top was to be relaxed but it was to remain the rule. It was not a position he could sustain. People were talking, mouths, memories, suitcases, cupboards were opening, and out tumbled the skeletons.

There is something recalcitrant about human beings. You may break them down, burn them, send them up a chimney, bury them in pits in the forest and pour lime over their bodies, and somehow they persist, endure. The victims of Stalin's camps were making themselves known; their relics kept turning up like revenge notes to the living world. In 1988, for the first time in the Soviet Union, Moscow newspapers were publishing reports of the discoveries of killing fields dating back to 1937 and 1938. Five were discovered and examined in the Minsk region. Here were burial pits and enough evidence to reconstruct how people were executed and even, sometimes, at what time of day it was done, as well as the kind of social classes they came from.

In a place called Kurapaty, near Minsk, for example, people were shot after dinner, and on into the night, until the small hours. The killers were the NKVD, the secret police, and the victims of these executions were laid out in pits, covered lightly with sand and the next load laid on top of them until the pit was full. What shocked the researchers was the large number of women who'd been shot, as well as the wide spread of social classes, ranging from peasants from nearby villages to middle-class victims who left behind them glasses, medicine bottles, women's high-heeled boots. The researchers then calculated the numbers who had died in these killing fields and concluded that with the average number of corpses to a grave being in the region of two hundred, if you multiplied that by the number of graves found – five hundred – this gave a figure of more than one hundred thousand victims. However, since the researchers knew of many more graves (at least one hundred had been covered over and lost when roads or gas mains were laid), then it was clear that the total number of victims had been much higher. The researchers wrote eloquently of the burial pits, the smashed plates and cups, the way the long strands of women's hair clung to the bullet-riddled skulls. They reported from a pretty forest filled with birdsong and they evoked again in their grizzly discoveries the extraordinarily mute tenacity of victims who would not be done away with.

I went to one of the first meetings of a group called Memorial. These were elderly people who had survived the camps: engineers, poets, politicians, Party veterans, dispossessed kulaks, peasants – those who had been classed as 'enemies of the people'. Of course, their wives and children had also been tainted by association and became in their turn 'class enemies'. Back in 1917 Memorial had a predecessor, called The Society of Former Political Convicts and Exiles, formed by members of early politically subversive and revolutionary groups that had challenged the old Tsarist State: groups like the Committed Terrorists of People's Will as well as various anarchists, Bolsheviks, Mensheviks and social democrats from places as far apart as Poland and

Lithuania. It was estimated that these people had spent a total of 10,086 years in prison, 1,041 years in exile and 3,086 years in leg irons. None of it helped. Once the revolution they had helped to usher into place had been taken over by 'the Boss', as Joseph Stalin was known, some of these early victims of the earliest camps were persecuted once again, or made to agree with the relentless persecution of more millions of victims, whom Stalin called 'Enemies of the Proletarian Revolution, Agents of Capital and Saboteurs of Soviet Construction'.

I used to go and look at pictures painted by Stalin's court painters. The artists were warned to favour his right profile and men like Shurpin and Gerasimov, in their devotional portraits of the Leader, show him contemplating the great sweep of the Russian steppe, adopting a prayerful contemplative pose. He was the mountain range that loomed high in everyone's life. He was the aged eagle. The songs he encouraged were dreadful – with lines like 'Hello country of heroes, country of dreams, country of scientists . . .' but everyone sang them all the same.

Stalin killed millions, yes, but it is his method, his familiarity, seen through the prism of his subsequent incarnations, that fascinates me. The pervasive belief in the goodness of the Leader, who has been misled by his minions, is so widespread that it must also be one of the essential components of the syntax of terror. Consider again Robert Mugabe's wide-eyed questioning of his minister when stories of the killings, rapes and the deadly camps of the Matabeleland campaign had become impossible to ignore: 'Why didn't you tell me that?'

★

Though they are the signal examples of the form, it was not Nazi Germany nor the Soviet Union that supplied the model, or template, of what we think of as that place of imprisonment where non-combatants were 'concentrated', in order that they should be more easily controlled. The concentration camp was invented by the British in their war against the Boers, at the start of the twentieth century. There had been earlier attempts at concentrated settlements of women and children, in Cuba in 1898, but the system as we know it was brought to its deadly perfection in South Africa by Lord Kitchener and a British administration.

The Nazis then introduced the idea that prisoners might be concentrated in camps for work, moral improvement or murder, sometimes for all three. They also introduced the idea that what they did there was so horrible, it could not possibly happen, and accounts of death camps could be denied, or blamed upon the exaggerations of 'enemies'. This sleight of hand was adopted by others, most notably Joseph Stalin and, more recently, Robert Mugabe.

The most extraordinary past example of this form of illusion is Treblinka, a place that vanished sixty years ago, but you can still go there and see it, even if it isn't there. It is not to be confused with its namesake, a village a few miles away, a tiny place with a rail-siding, which is the still extant Treblinka. The site of the death camp is not to be confused with anywhere else. The 'real' Treblinka is a black hole in the forests north-east of Warsaw, into which nearly a million Jews vanished in a little over a year, between July 1942 and August 1943. Once, there was a fake railway station in the forest, a mock timetable in the waiting room, a clock on the wall whose hands always pointed, it was said, to six o'clock, and a door marked 'Exit'.

Treblinka ceased to exist, except in memory, shortly after the armed rising that took place on 2 August 1943. The rebellious prisoners killed a number of guards and escaped into the forests that stretch as far as the Russian border. They were hunted down and killed. Then the camp was dynamited. It is Treblinka's 'not being there' that so fascinates me because the camp, though vanished, is so palpable. In the summer, when it is green, the forest mounts a kind of dark surveillance. There is a line of concrete sleepers recalling the railway line of death, and waves of standing stones, like a stunted Stonehenge. Some of the stones have names cut into them, remembering the victims. Otherwise there is nothing, only a dove calling in the dark forest, the fluting repetition of the insistent notes.

In winter, Treblinka freezes and the road into the forest cracks up. The railway sleepers are buried under the snow which is two feet high around the standing stones which now make the place look like a graveyard on tiptoe. Polar winds knifing across the River Bug kill all sensation. The empty space is emptier than ever. The reception building is open to the wind and snow and its walls are split by the frosts. The faces in the elderly photographs on the wall are filmed in ice. Henryk Goldsmiz peers dimly into the world, the stippled pores of the blown-up newsprint of his old photograph only just managing to hold his face together – Henryk Goldsmiz, dead these sixty years. Treblinka isn't there, but the empty space has a terrible gravity, it hangs on the heart.

Killing in the modern camps is invariably accompanied by that twentieth-century affectation, high-sounding moral claptrap. The victims are told they have to blame not their killers but themselves for the political failings that have landed them in hell. In Cambodia, for Saloth Sar, otherwise known as Pol Pot, otherwise known as Brother Number One, and his army of peasant teenagers who marched into Phnom Penh on 17 April 1975, the centre for re-education was a prosaic school on the edge of Phnom Penh called Tuol Sleng. It is an unremarkable and functional building in which the classrooms were turned into cells, prisoners were chained to the beds, many of which still remain, and thousands of people were tortured and executed. It is thought that perhaps as many as twenty thousand people may have died in these corridors and these classrooms. Some were clubbed to death in the quiet school grounds, some were tortured in an atmosphere of scholarly cruelty; and all, in the eyes of their executioners, died, as it were, to improve their moral standing. Among the orders scribbled by the demented jailers on the cell block walls, I found this item: 'Don't be a fool. For you are a chap who dared to thwart the revolution. While getting lashed you must not cry out at all.'

These camps, however, are no more than variants on the original, invented by the British administration of Lord Kitchener, and used to imprison Boers during the guerrilla struggle between a band of farmers and the troops of the Empire, with which the twentieth century began. The British concentration camps anticipated what was to come. They pioneered the methods: brutality beneath the cloak of earnest, steely good intentions, silence, denial, willing accomplices, trained staff – things later to be so well known in Germany and Russia and Asia, and which enabled various tyrants to murder large numbers of people while maintaining a steadfast moral tone and an air of injured innocence.

The camps multiplied around South Africa, and were to be found in the Transvaal, Natal, and the Orange Free State. Into these rural pens were driven women and children, relatives of the Boers fighting in the field, and the dispossessed owners of the farms and lands that the British forces had torched and destroyed. The enormous speed with which the camps developed is remarkable. The concentration of prisoners began in 1900 in a modest sort of way, a few families here and there. By October of that year, the camps contained one hundred and eighteen thousand Boer dependants – women, children and elderly men – and forty-three thousand mixed race or 'coloured' prisoners. The camps were justified by Lord Kitchener, and others, as enlightened solutions to very messy problems, places where prisoners would be given shelter, health care, lessons in hygiene and decent honest work. If you had burnt the farms, killed the men and destroyed the crops of your enemy, then surely it was more humane to lock up his family in a safe place where they could be fed and receive medical treatment as well as correctional training, rather than to abandon them to starve in the veld? What made the argument all the more convincing was that the Boers were seen as Neanderthal brutes, dirty, ignorant and barely human. Faced by evidence of these camps, the British public refused to believe what they heard. This was not surprising since the view taken by most enlightened British statesmen, from Kitchener to Kipling, was that the Boers would have to be re-educated to fit in with the 'new' world, even if it meant – and this seemed likely, even desirable – that they were extinguished in the process. That was sad but inevitable: not only were they wicked, dirty, unkempt religious fanatics, they were not suited to the twentieth century.

Over twenty thousand people died from all manner of diseases, from measles to heartbreak. The death rate vexed and disconcerted the authorities who considered it a form of Boer backwardness, and even ingratitude. People who had been evacuated from their ruined homesteads repaid their jailers by dying in large numbers. In their willingness to blame the deaths on the victims' own lamentable lack of hygiene, modernity, or up-to-date political thinking, the British with their rudimentary but effective death camps showed themselves to be as modern as anyone else.

The camps of Zimbabwe also showed the hallmarks of the real thing. They are said never to have existed, or, when their existence is admitted, they are said to have been errors made by too-zealous officials; they are said to have been set up without knowledge of the Leader; they are said to be nothing but lies spread by the enemies of the country. But they did exist, and I have been to see the remains.

The Matabeleland camps grew out of the need of the death squads of Five Brigade, the CIO and the other police agencies, during the Gukurahundi campaign, to find a way of housing their victims and then disposing of them. To begin with, in the early Eighties, when troops swept though the countryside killing and beating as they went, it did not much matter about fixed camps because much of Matabeleland, as well as parts of the Midlands, were one giant prison camp. Random killings, hut burnings and assaults took place openly. Public terror was the aim. In Matabeleland North the method of exposure was used: the bodies of the victims were left to predators and the families forbidden to bury the remains. Bodies were also buried under huts, or in mass graves beneath torched villages. The savagery of the early attacks on civilians is caught particularly well in the measured tones of the report of the Catholic Commission for Justice and Peace: this is the only account ever rendered of the killings, a remarkably cool and sober record of great suffering:

> Five Brigade passed first through Tsholotsho, spreading out rapidly through Lupane and Nkayi and their impact on all these communal areas was shocking. Within the space of six weeks, more than 2000 civilians had died, hundreds of homesteads had been burnt and thousands of civilians had been beaten. Most of the dead were killed in public executions involving between one and twelve people at a time.

It was just the beginning; after naked terror came adaptation. Public murder and overt torture, of many people in a confined region over a short period, has a shock value to begin with but it becomes less productive. More secretive methods of terrorizing people must be found. Soon there were camps across Matabeleland of which, perhaps, the most notorious was Bhalagwe Camp, in Matabeleland South. According to eye-witnesses, anything from eight to sixteen thousand prisoners passed through Bhalagwe. To be locked up there meant beatings and physical torture.

> There was a change of strategy on the part of 5 Brigade in 1984. They had apparently realized in 1983 that is was not possible to kill hundreds of well-known people in front of hundreds of witnesses in their home villages and expect the fact to remain hidden. In 1984, the new strategy of translocating many thousands of civilians and grouping them in Bhalagwe, where

everyone effectively became strangers, has made it much harder now to identify either exact numbers or names of the dead. Most detainees did not know the names of those they were detained with. People also cannot remember exact dates on which they witnessed a certain number of people beaten to death or shot, so it is not possible to sort out eye witness accounts in a way that prevents double counting of deaths.

Conservative estimates put the death toll in Bhalagwe at around one thousand. The bodies were buried in makeshift graves within the camp, and shipped out by night. Local villagers near old mine-workings, such as those at Antelope Mine, remembered the trucks arriving every night. Once the bodies had been dumped down the mine-shaft, grenades were tossed in to destroy the evidence. This had also been a method used by the troops of Ian Smith in his war against the guerrillas of Robert Mugabe. As the CIO was the agency responsible for the logistics of the Gukurahundi repression, it is very likely that some of the officers who tipped the bodies of their compatriots into mine-shafts, when the Smith regime was in power, were the same men who repeated the exercise under Robert Mugabe.

In the Nineties I went along to Antelope Mine. A few days before, searchers had pulled out a grizzly haul: eight skulls and a variety of other human bones. On a bright morning I stood by the mine-shaft and waited as the miners clambered down into the darkness. Certainly they had been finding clothes and bones. Everybody was jumpy; the police kept confiscating whatever the miners found. The police were often followed by CIO operatives, themselves no strangers to skeletons – several had just turned up in the cellars of the CIO headquarters back in Harare. When the miners were winched to the surface they said water was rising in the shaft and they had found nothing more. They shook their heads like disappointed fishermen. Perhaps tomorrow?

Later that morning, in a village close to the old mine-workings, I listened to a man who put flesh on the bones from Antelope Mine. 'We found hip bones, trousers, shirts, ankle bones, some with their socks still on. Others were wearing cycle clips, and I remembered my brother who rode off on a bicycle when the soldiers imposed a curfew. He never came back. Finding those bones was God's will. His way of speaking to His people. Why don't the churches do something? Apart from the Catholics, the churches keep silent, but until the churches speak nothing will happen. They spoke up under the Smith government. Why don't they speak now? If they don't speak we will never know the truth.'

In Moscow, in 1988, as the victims of the purges were making themselves felt, Stalin still had plenty of supporters. There were letters to the newspapers defending the honour of the Great Leader and sharing his paranoia about enemies who plotted to destroy the revolution. If people died it was because Stalin was forced to fight against the provocations of the time; attacks by 'kulaks' and 'white guard officers'. The masses were misled by these enemies, who changed their places of residence and they had to be hunted down and exposed because they had infiltrated the communist party and sabotaged it from within.

Robert Mugabe talks in the same way of Zimbabwe's

enemies; he has his kulaks, too, the landed white farmers. When you ask the defenders of Mugabe about the camps and the killings in Matabeleland, they remain defiant. There were no camps, they sometimes say, and even if they existed then the numbers who died in them are over-blown. Robert Mugabe's Information Minister offered an explanation which uncannily echoes the apologists for Stalin. This minister did not simply defend his Leader, his words displayed the need, the urge, the requirement of tyrannical states that you sacrifice yourself or your family to enrich the destiny of the Leader: 'I also lost uncles and relatives during the Gukurahundi. Even my uncles lost their close relatives during this period, but I am not as bitter as everyone else in Matabeleland.'

There was in the speech of this flunky all the characteristics of the professional servant to the contemporary tyrant: a murderous reasonableness, a willingness to condone murder, a grasp of the crucial things that go together: business and blood. There was, too, a certain weary irascibility at naïve and old-fashioned misunderstanding of the Leader's divine motives. It was simply too bad that people should go on dragging up the bodies of those best left to oblivion; victims who, if they had been asked their opinion, would surely have agreed that the President should be left in peace, and not be subject to this malicious misunderstanding that was not merely uncalled for, but out of date.

The dead, however, keep floating to the surface. In 1999, Robert Mugabe, in one of those manoeuvres that have characterized his rule, appeared ready at last to address the ghosts of those who perished in Gukurahundi. A government committee was formed to examine the background to the killings and pay compensation to the victims for what

Mugabe called 'moments of madness' – but no funds were made available and within weeks the idea was dropped and the committee was dissolved. Again, Mugabe's spokesman found a form of words to explain why this was another good thing. There he stood, this ineffable lackey, a living bridge between the Supreme Leader and the grateful dead. The victims themselves, he implied, would have backed suspending the enquiry – had they not been detained elsewhere – but we could take his word for it: the Matabeleland Massacres had been blown up out of all proportion by those 'bent on causing trouble to the nation'. So the President (and he has done this over the years with cases of judicial or state murder) had decided to draw a veil over the events by invoking the Official Secrets Act. The enquiry, like the victims, had been formally abolished.

TEN

BROTHER'S LITTLE HELPERS

In Moscow, in the late Eighties, I was able to compare the testimonies of other ordinary men just doing their jobs. The memoirs of former Cheka operatives like Mikhail Schrieder were being printed for the first time. Schrieder was a witness to the methodical paperwork that accompanied Stalin's mass murder. He was revealing on what were its 'administrative' details: methods of dealing with people shot during the particularly bloody purges of July to August 1937, and on through to January 1938, a period of almost unimaginably rapid execution of tens of thousands.

He explained how lists were made. A simple large 'R' beside your name meant instant execution. Many of the victims were lifelong, passionate Stalinists, 'innocent communists devoted to the Party and Stalin, veteran Bolsheviks, non-Party specialists, and other personalities who somehow stood out against the mass of people'. Also shot were 'practically all leading Party functionaries and government officials, former social revolutionaries, all communists who were, even in the most indirect way, related to Trotskyites, many former Anarchists and Mensheviks, as well as the entire families who worked on the "Chinese Eastern Railroad".' It gives a measure of how mad the times had become: these unfortunates were done away with because, in Stalin's tortuous mind, they were suspected of being 'Japanese spies'. Schrieder himself was arrested in 1938, though he survived.

Lev Razgon was another witness, and what a story he told. In 1977, he had been in hospital together with a fellow named Grigory Niyazov. The two men shared their experiences of the camps: Lev Razgon had been jailed for seventeen years as 'an enemy of the people'; Niyazov knew the camps from a different perspective – he had been the man who shot people. It was rare to come across the institutional Stalinist executioner in such a good state of preservation.

Grigory Niyazov began his work as a jailer in Omsk in the Thirties and showed such promise that he was promoted to 'a special project', working close to the railway-line near Khabarovsk. The project turned out to be the execution of Stalin's political prisoners, who arrived by train. Large pits, often on a hillside, were dug by inmates of the local prison. In return for their work, these convicts had their sentences shortened and received better food. Political victims were taken to the execution pit and lined up. Niyazov remembered how the victims often cried out that they were communists and that this was wrong. They were shot as they spoke. Burial gangs from the jail then arrived to fill in the grave and dig new pits for the never-ending batches of victims. It was steady work, said Niyazov, relatively easy, too, nothing like the penal labour of felling timber.

After they had finished for the shift, the executioners would drive back to their barracks and have a couple of drinks. Asked if it weighed on his conscience, Niyazov said: 'Conscience? No, it didn't torment me. I never thought about it and if I did, it was as if nothing had happened. I'm only beginning to feel some pity now – if I see some old man suffering, I am so sorry for him I even burst out crying sometimes, but for them – I'm not sorry for them. No pity whatsoever – as if they never existed. No, I didn't feel sorry. I didn't think about it. I slept well. In the day I'd go for a stroll. There were beautiful places there. But it was very boring. No broads.'

Stalin's victims died for standing in the way of the dictator's dream of an unsullied, obedient universe. They died in many cases for what might be called 'moral' reasons, so that the health of a nation, the progress of humanity – those deadly clichés – would be advanced. Many of them were so mystified by the terror of 1937/38 that they assumed it must have been some sort of fascist conspiracy. How else could you explain that the father of his people, the Great Leader, exalted and benign, was ordering, watching, and enjoying this massacre of his faithful followers? It is one of the terrible Russian ironies that many of Stalin's victims continued to believe, right to the end, in Joseph Stalin.

It takes staff to fulfil a dictator's dream, trusted, clever, competent people, with dedication and the ability to withstand long periods of boredom. Torture is repetitive work. Power, at its outer edges, is a grind. It keeps saying and doing much the same things, and the perks are limited. There are no broads and a pretty rigid repertoire. It is not only deadly but dull. Its clerks are expected to be efficient not excitable, ruthless but restrained. There is room for sadism but it doesn't win promotion: too flash, too noisy, too messy. The job is bloody but the best demeanour is clean, quiet. Dress it in uniform and you see it straight away.

It is in the relation of the chest to the waist to the knees to the careful curl of the knuckles on the swagger stick, to the exact cock of the cap. It is in the attractive reduction of the male to a shapely machine whose look lies in the precise line, the gait, the perfectly controlled swagger. The construction gives off again that scent, that smell, when you have superior beings, special creatures, proud and booted captains, *Übermenschen*, divine favourites, tough hombres, fleshly clockwork marching to a higher rhythm. Take away the cap and badges, however, and the killers are indistinguishable – from us.

Consider Dirk Coetzee, a pleasant enough guy – liked a laugh, a beer, loved his kids, his motorbike, his country. He was a secret policeman from South Africa, whose speciality was killing people. One day, in the Dorchester Hotel in London, I sat with Coetzee, then on the run, and over tea we talked about the people he'd killed. Coetzee was lost in London, he dreamed of the Transvaal, and his laugh skipped around the big room like a flat stone on water. He added interestingly to my understanding of the perversions of power.

Coetzee came from an Afrikaner family raised in the severe apartheid mode where race was religion, white nationalism was sacred, and blacks, Jews, and other races were beyond the pale. His father was a postal official, his mother worked in the local butchery. Dirk had been an unhappy child; he stuttered badly and the only way he found he could cure his stutter was to curse. Like Caliban, he cursed everyone. He was on the road to nowhere, he dropped out of school, went to sea, and spent a few years on a frigate.

Then, in 1970, he found his métier. He joined the police

force and he became a dog handler, a scuba diver and, by 1973, was a warrant officer serving in Rhodesia. In those days, the South African government was giving tacit support to Ian Smith, rather as today it props up his successor, Robert Mugabe. Coetzee and his tracker dogs were sent on a clandestine posting to help the white forces of Ian Smith fighting the guerrillas of Mugabe and Nkomo. He worked out of Mount Darwin, north of the capital, Salisbury. Coetzee remembered the Rhodesian bush war with affection. His job was to move in after a suspected terrorist incident, bringing up the dogs to aid the trackers who followed enemy spoor, flanking the forward troops. He relished making contact with the enemy – the fire-fight, then the first lessons on how to dispose of the bodies of enemy dead. The method was this: you dug a grave, shallow but broad enough to handle around seven bodies at a time. The bottom of the grave was lined with plastic, then a thin layer of earth, then tree branches, and the fire was started: 'It was fucking horrible,' Coetzee recalled. 'It's the hands and feet and heads that go first. They go so fast. But that way, you see, there's no chance of identification. And then we buried them. Never more than three or four foot. It's enough.'

In 1997 Coetzee joined the Security Police. He worked hard, he was a quick learner. If you wanted to blow up the United Nations offices in Swaziland, Dirk would do it. If you wanted to dynamite a rail-line, Dirk was your man, and if you wanted people removed, Dirk was first choice. Coetzee brought a clear memory to his recollections, and he had kept neat notes and showed them to me. They were models of clarity. His specialities had been the uses of poison, the disposal of bodies, and covert assassination. The victim to be murdered was kidnapped, and then drugged –

this was not a matter of kindness, but because the South African Security Police never gave its operatives the thorough training Stalin would have approved of. The victim was drugged, said Coetzee, because 'Nobody involved had the courage to shoot a helpless and fully conscious man at point-blank range.'

This was the method he had used for a certain Sizwe Kondile, who was taken from his cell, drugged, driven to a remote spot in the veld and shot in the back of the head. A Makarov pistol with silencer was used for the job, and the body was burnt. In the Rhodesian war, destruction of face and finger-prints was enough, but in the South African secret war all the evidence had to be destroyed, and that meant a long wait. It took seven to ten hours before nothing but ashes remained. The executioners sometimes built a barbecue, grilled meat and 'broke out a few beers' while waiting for the flames to consume the victim. Drinking sustained killing.

One day Coetzee was asked to do something very particular. He was to arrange for the murder of a black lawyer named Griffiths Mxenge. The victim was a well-known ANC supporter in Natal, and the usual methods of making him vanish were judged unsuitable. Coetzee hired a gang of hit-men and told them he wanted it to look like robbery. Mxenge was held up on his way to work, and stabbed to death. The assassins stole his jacket, his watch and his wallet. Then they collected Mxenge's new white Audi from the parking lot and drove it to a remote spot on the Natal North Coast. It was a long drive through the night, but there was music and booze and sing-alongs to make time pass. The killers burnt Mxenge's personal effects, then they burnt the car. It was another job done.

It turned out badly, however. One of Mxenge's killers, who had been jailed on other charges, spilled the beans, Coetzee was fingered and, when his minders disowned him, he did a runner, headed for London and turned himself over to his old enemies, the ANC. The ANC were very welcoming. Coetzee was a useful source of intelligence, he was good 'staff', and his devotion to his new masters was as genuine as it had been to the apartheid regime. He wanted to go home and work for the new secret police in the new South Africa.

I had an idea the new people would look favourably on him. He was the right stuff, and he still had a lot to give: 'I'm a dedicated policeman in my heart and soul.' He talked nostalgically of the flawed but honest values of professional secret police officers: 'They're not angels. I've heard of Gabriel's angels, up above. I've heard of Hell's Angels. But police angels I've never seen in my life, and I've been around a long time.' Then, after a moment's reflection, he added with the frankness that would have fitted him for any job that dared not show its face: 'We were thugs. Mostly thugs.'

What was paradoxical about these agents, Niyazov or Coetzee, was that they were committed enough to do the job but imperturbable enough not to care who they were doing it for: it did not mean that, should the lackeys lose their king, they would weep or tear their hair or throw themselves on to his funeral pyre. Not at all. That would be to mistake their professionalism. What they would do would be to switch sides and – here was the miracle – do it without qualm. They would serve the old enemy with exactly the same dedication with which they once hunted him down. The security operatives who switched when Ian

Smith went will switch again when Mugabe goes, and keep their jobs and their pensions. They will keep their insufferable belief that they were right and righteous and respectable. Will they also keep their sanity? Will they sleep at night? I know the answer: in a word – easily.

Dirk Coetzee remembered and rejoiced in the camaraderie felt among professionals in a closed and private world: 'The security police were a law unto themselves, who in effect controlled all special police work, and whose world was impenetrable to all but those within the security family.' The members of the 'family' talk the same language, one of suggestion and understatement, a lingo at once light and frightening. Coetzee remembered the relief of not having to explain to those who took the absurd view that words meant something: 'To stand up in court and carry on about the exact words used between security people is often quite ridiculous. We do not say: "Dirk, ask so and so to take a knife and kill Mxenge with it." Rather I would use words with the drift of – "Why not make a plan with Mxenge?" And on consenting, [I would] be told not to use a rifle but to make it look like robbery. This would mean, among many other things, that Mxenge should not, like Steve Biko, disappear . . .'

On the run, in exile, far from home, he craved understanding, he missed the 'family' – outsiders never understood the assassin's need for sympathy. Only the 'family' knew. It was a kinship that cut across culture, epochs and ideology: the 'family' knew how it felt, after a hard day in the execution ditches. You had a drink, took a walk . . . after all, someone had to do the job.

★

Heinrich Himmler, perhaps the most modern and most merciless of Hitler's lieutenants, pioneered the notion that the overworked butcher requires support in times of stress. He was also particularly fond of animals. He understood Coetzee's qualms, that it is not easy to kill your fellow human beings in cold blood. There was also the laborious business of actually mechanically executing dozens within a small space. There were the sheer physical logistics: how many people were to be killed before the men deserved a meal? There were problems of shifts, transport, supplies and ammunition; there was the disposal of human remains; it was always heavy, messy thankless work. It weighed on a man to shoot children, it was only natural.

Himmler told a meeting of SS leaders, in Poznan in 1943: 'Most of you know what it means to see a hundred corpses lying together, five hundred, or a thousand. To have gone through this and yet – apart from a few exceptions, examples of human weakness – to have remained decent, this has made us hard . . .'

That was perhaps the first time cold-blooded murder was found to be character-building. Himmler spoke for the new class of killer/accountant, a class that took off after that: punctual, reliable, the man who signed off a trainload of victims to the ovens and then went home to the family, schooled to serve the leader whose orders are always reasonable. Robert Mugabe's orders to the Fifth Brigade before they fell on Matabeleland reek of this reasonableness: 'Where men and women provide food for dissidents, when we get there we eradicate them. We don't differentiate when we fight, because we can't tell who is a dissident and who is not.' What is needed is obedience, yes, but also patience, a penchant for figures; there must be thugs – but numerate thugs who will keep good books on a family shot or a village torched by reducing them to a number, tidying those figures, correcting them, justifying them, signing them off with a sense of duty done.

After the killing in Matabeleland was over, a Zimbabwean paratroop commander, Lieutenant Colonel Lionel Dyke, summed up things in this way: 'You often have to be cruel to be kind. Had an operation like [the Fifth Brigade's] not taken place, the battle would have gone on for years and years as a festering sore. And I believe the Matabele understand that sort of harsh treatment far better than the treatment I myself was giving them, when we would hunt and kill a man if he was armed. The fact is that when Five Brigade went in, they did brutally deal with the problem. If you were a dissident sympathizer, you died. And it brought peace very, very quickly.'

Himmler could not have put it better.

ELEVEN
PAST REMEMBERING

When overwhelming power fades it goes so quickly you have to struggle to remember what it smelt like. Some genuinely forget, others cannot bear to remember. Two weeks later, 'the change' seems ancient history, two months is an eternity. Amnesia sets in, and denial, with people saying, 'It was never like that', and 'I was never involved', and 'I knew nothing about it' and even, 'Things were better then . . .'

Maybe there is some truth in these lies, after all. When long-standing lunatic and corrupt tyranny is the only show in town, each citizen plays a role and it feels like it goes on forever. Then the show suddenly shuts down, and it all seems long ago and far away – unreal. It was a bit like that in Moscow, when Gorbachev turned up the house-lights and people were free to talk. Some said, 'Was Stalin that bad?' Or they didn't remember – genuinely, painfully, sincerely forgot. Those who did remember seemed boring, or stuck in the past. It was that way in South Africa when much of the white electorate so liked apartheid they voted for more of it, at every chance they got, for half a century, but when it died you couldn't find anyone with a good word for it. That's the usual miracle, post tyranny. Where did it go, that hate, that misery, that cruelty, that suffering?

Where did they go – those people who told you, loudly and often, that this was the only show in town, so knuckle down and accept it? But if cynicism and amnesia takes care of most of those who can't remember, what about those who really and truly believed. Are their hearts broken?

In October 1989 I was in East Berlin when Erich Honecker stood beside the visiting Soviet President, Mikhail Gorbachev, both muffled in coats and scarves. Their round pale frozen faces made them look like hailstones in hats. They were on the freezing rostrum watching the military hardware of the Warsaw Pact armies rumble by. Here was an alliance destined to endure for decades: they believed it – so did everyone else. Yet, within hours of that parade, the East Germany cities of Leipzig and Berlin were in uproar as massive demonstrations against the regime began rolling through the streets.

A few weeks later, I was in West Berlin to give a talk at the Hochschule, and I stayed just off the Kurfürstendamm. Tens of thousands of people were in the streets of East Berlin, while in Poland, Czechoslovakia and in the Baltic provinces of Estonia and Latvia, masses were on the move. If being a citizen of the Eastern bloc was a form of employment, then hundreds of thousands were walking off the job – but where were they headed?

On the night of Friday, 10 November, the East Germans began smashing through the Wall. You went to bed, and you could hear the demolishers working, chink – chink – chink; 'Woodpeckers' they called them. All night long the steel beaks of their chisels pecked deeper into the grey concrete. Every morning there were new gaps and tears in the fat, self-important barrier. Every morning there were those who said things would settle down (there were surprising numbers who believed in two Germanies and two systems), but the woodpeckers chewing away at the concrete didn't hear them.

People who rather preferred two Germanies also mistook the importance of symbols. Once upon a time a great wall stood between East and West Berlin. Built of stone and stained with blood. One night, without warning, it began to crumble and only the rich bird-life along its lethal, heavily mined and hateful length would mourn its passing. Anyone who imagined that things would settle down did not, as they say in Berlin, have all their cups in the cupboard.

Exhilaration was spiked with fear. What was to be made of the thousands of troops the western allies and their Russian enemies had kept amassed along this crucial border, where it had long been said that World War Three was very likely to begin? There were bad memories. Where exactly were the borders of Germany itself? And why had Chancellor Kohl, on a visit to Poland, declined to state that the post-war boundaries were movable?

The unthinkable became perfectly normal. East Berliners, the 'Ossies', were everywhere. No one knew what to make of them. Three Mayors from the East had committed suicide. It was the opinion of otherwise pacific matrons taking coffee in the Kempinski Eck, the plush, glass-fronted observation room on the Kufurstendamm, that the former leader of East Germany, Erich Honecker, should 'do the decent thing', and follow suit. But nothing 'followed', everything was new, you made life up as you went along.

The Ossies were to be seen striding through the most distant suburbs – how those people walked! – in a city where no one else walked. They'd gather in groups to stare at children playing in a park. They'd stroke the park furniture. They'd goggle at a man washing his car. They gathered in great crowds outside the BMW showrooms. It was utterly beguiling. They strolled into West Berlin looking like dazed children come to visit Xanadu. They crowded the pavements outside the non-stop strip shows on Kantstrasse, or they poured into places with names like Big Sexy Land on Martin Lutherstrasse. The strip joints reduced their entry fees and offered two free beers to what they called 'our good-humoured Eastern guests'.

The East German border guards, determined to shoot you on Monday for attempting to cross the Wall, on Tuesday became guides and helpers to elderly people who had trouble negotiating the jagged holes in the broken concrete: 'May I help you, Madam, step this way . . . watch the minefield, sir . . .'

There were those who grieved. If you genuinely love your adopted despotism, what will you do when it dies? If you are like a young man I met in Namibia some years ago, you grieve bitterly. The German Democratic Republic had been a haven, an inspiration, and a military godfather to several African regimes. Young men set off for East Germany to be trained as soldiers. In what was then South West Africa, the guerrilla organization called SWAPO (South West African People's Organization) sometimes allowed children to be transferred from its refugee camps in Tanzania, to schools in East Germany, while their parents fought a bush war against the South African army.

That's what happened to Matthias. It was 1979, and he

was four years old when one day, without warning, along with a batch of other young children, he was taken from a refugee camp in Angola and flown out of Africa. He remembered running up and down the aisle and crying hysterically as the plane gained altitude. He remembered how the crew took him into the cockpit to sit with the pilot and watch the instruments, in the hopes that it would calm the boy. When the plane touched down Matthias found himself in a faraway land covered in shining white crystals. It was winter. The snow had been heavy and he had never seen snow. He was in East Germany. He felt sure he had come to a land built of sugar.

Matthias was taken to the School of Friendship near Magdeburg and there he was to live for the next ten years. He was taught to speak German and more importantly to feel German, to read the great poets and to tell the difference between snow and sugar. He was taught to be a good German, a socialist and a republican. He was given the kind of triple-layered authenticity that the GDR alone claimed it could bestow on its citizens because, after all, they were real Germans – not like the fraudulent people on the other side of the Wall who called themselves German. Matthias was taught about Goethe, but he also learnt about guerrilla tactics. Important officers from the guerrilla force to which Matthias would one day belong, as his parents did, came to the School of Friendship and taught Matthias how to read a map and how to use a grenade and how to shoot.

Sometimes these important visitors made lengthy speeches about colonialism and liberty and revolution. Sometimes, Matthias remembered, the speeches went on for so long that some children fainted. On one occasion they were promised sweets to celebrate the birth of their new country, Namibia. The candy never reached the kids. The teachers got in first. Perhaps that's how things tend to go in revolutions – someone else eats your sweets.

Matthias was learning to defend his distant country, to march, to recite slogans: 'Down with Imperialism!' At morning roll call, their instructors chanted: 'Future loyal defenders of the Namibian Revolution, be prepared!' and the children answered stoutly: 'Ever prepared!'

Africa, however, was far away and fading. Matthias was becoming a German boy and the teachers at the School of Friendship became for him the family he'd never had. He and his friends thought of home, when they thought of it at all, as being perhaps a bit like California. Their country, they knew, was rich in diamonds and composed mostly of desert. It was also almost permanently at war. They went on, these young defenders of the Namibian Revolution, daily promising to answer the call, but the call did not come. It did not come when their country became independent in 1988. It did not come in 1989 when the Berlin Wall came down.

It was after this that something began to change. German boys began throwing stones at the hostel. Matthias was puzzled, 'After all, the boys throwing the stones, they'd been our friends . . .' One day, a year after the Wall had fallen, and eleven years after he had arrived in the land made of sugar, he was told to pack. He was going 'home'. It was every bit as much of a traumatic tearing loose from a known and loved place as his departure had been when the plane lifted off out of the bush of Africa, and Matthias ran screaming up and down the aisle. When they got the news about going home, some of the children wanted to run away, others were resigned. After all, they said, what was the good of staying in a country where people were throwing stones at you? So they packed and they were flown out, their absence unmarked by anything other than their tears because, simply by being in East Germany, these 'borrowed' children were like so much else, a State secret. It was forbidden to report their presence, or to photograph them – although Matthias had some illegal snaps that showed him as he had been in East Germany, happy and smiling.

Matthias arrived back 'home' in the new Namibia, and there was a great party thrown in the capital, Windhoek, to welcome warmly the young lions of the Liberation. There was singing and dancing – but the festivities were a mask; they disguised for a while the fact that the party was over. Matthias, the young defender of the Revolution, had come home too late.

Calls went out for the parents of these children to come forward and take them home. A lucky few recognized their own kids, but that wasn't common. After all, parents and children had been separated for over a decade. Some who put themselves forward as parents were simply after the small sum of cash each child had been given, but there were children who simply went unclaimed. That is what happened to Matthias. When his own parents failed to come forward he found foster parents.

The family Kopf were settlers of German stock who owned a game ranch in the western part of Namibia. As his foster parents they paid for Matthias's schooling. He was sent to a boarding school in Swakopmund, on the west coast of Namibia and he came 'home' at weekends. Mrs Kopf felt about Matthias the way any mother would. The Kopfs were admirable parents – they had taken Matthias in because he had nowhere else to go and they provided a warm and loving home – but they made a distinction between fostering and adoption. Mrs Kopf put it this way: 'You can't just go and adopt somebody. You have to realize that you will have them then for the next years. We never adopted Matthias.'

I met Matthias when he'd been 'home' for some years. He was then nearly eighteen, a grave, quiet, intense boy given to brooding, to dreaming. Matthias remembered who he'd been before he became a lost child; he had been a hero of the Namibian Revolution and the way in which he told me his story, of how he fell from grace, was more revealing of the structure of tyranny than anything I've ever read. He was one of the 'lost children'; in German they were known as *Niemandsmaenner* – nobody-people. He showed his snaps taken in East Germany – a boy who wasn't anybody, pictured in a country that had ceased to be. He recalled for me with a spasm of anguish, sitting on his bedroom floor, how very happy those days had been.

'They were good times. Everyone was kind, we travelled. We went on holiday. We stayed with our friends at the weekends.' Matthias laid out his relics on his table, they were his clues to his past: his flags, his pictures, his coins, his memories. He had the flag of that happy human paradise – the German Democratic Republic. These little bits of nothing, these morsels, reminded me of the bread-crumbs those other lost children, Hansel and Gretel, scattered behind them as they walked deeper into the forest so as to have something at the end of the day that would guide them home. It worked for a while, their map made of crumbs, but then one bad day the birds ate the crumbs, devoured the map and the kids were lost again.

Matthias had not acquired an African identity, he had

been deprived of his German identity, he did not have a passport. He looked like an African teenager, he sounded like a German boy but, in truth, he wasn't anything. He was a ghost. Matthias had turned from flesh and blood into thin air. The lost boy had become the invisible man. Matthias was unhappy and he was homesick. He was also living on borrowed time. His stay at the Kopfs' was almost over. He was about to write his final exams. 'He'll have to learn to stand on his own feet. Matthias has talked of future plans. He talks of going to study in Canada. But who's going to pay for that?' Mrs Kopf asked. 'That's the trouble with children now. It's natural enough, but their heads are full of dreams.'

Matthias's head was certainly filled with dreams, crazy dreams, but then he had too many heads. There was his African head, and his German head, and there was his *Niemandsmaenner* head. He dreamed about the School for Friendship in faraway Magdeburg. Matthias could not help his pain, he missed the way the world was, when he was at home, in the only home he knew, when his brothers and sisters were his friends at school, when no one threw stones and when he knew what he was, a German boy growing up in the 'real' Germany. Matthias was now one of those exiles who could never go home; the country he once lived in had vanished as surely as Atlantis.

Matthias remained a patriot, he wouldn't hear a word against the old GDR, he was a missionary for the country he had loved and lost. It represented for him all that is good and kind in the world. No wonder he clung to it with all the desperate intense warmth that only a lonely and bereaved child can know. No wonder he held to what lay behind him and refused to move on, to forget, to come to terms with things. No wonder he remarked with quiet sincerity that the system of socialism in the old East Germany was the best the world had ever known. No wonder his foster parents considered him to be very badly mistaken in this belief.

As it turned out, Matthias had moved from one authoritarian state to another. The new Namibia was, to all intents and purposes, a one-party state ruled by a President who took the view that once elected there was no need to go through the humiliating procedure a second time. The Namibia he came back to was East Germany without the cruelty, but it had all the numbing stupidity and the distrust of its own people that typified such places, all the familiar rant, and it was run by another of the brothers under the skin, Sam Njomo. That was scant consolation.

I wished for his sake he was not so afflicted because I feared there was no cure for his form of radical longing. He went on believing in the dignity, the friendliness, the honesty and moral probity of the German Democratic Republic. The more time passed the more Matthias invested his memories with warmth and love. It was hard not to see and sympathize with his arrested development.

Maybe, too, this was an explanation for the perpetually adolescent nature of police states, and the way their citizens went about impersonating 'real' people, or 'grown up' people. In a country that has shut down, gone blind and deaf, there are no 'normal' people, only servants, victims or supporters of the ruling power, all of whom play a role in someone else's dream. Countries under dictatorship invariably inflate the notions of country or patria in order to reinforce further the regime whose aims are always and only political. There is nothing but politics in a tyranny, it is the only currency available, and since it is counterfeit, made by the rulers, it drives out all good money; other currencies –

language, law, civility, religion – all are downgraded. That is why, perhaps, all of Matthias's most passionate feelings, his ideas, his longings, were for the political emblems and relics of the life he had known.

There were other, more bureaucratic, reasons why Matthias did not fit into the new Namibia. He raised far too many questions. Who was he? What was his real name? What happened to his parents? The Namibian authorities had been unable to trace them. There was no record of his birth, so they could not issue him with a birth certificate. Without a birth certificate he did not have any claim to nationality, and so, for the moment at least, he was a citizen of nowhere. Matthias seemed to prefer that; he knew all about vanishing places and people who weren't there: 'I can't say for certain that I exist.' I had the feeling he was trying to be helpful. If he'd known how to do it he'd have vanished. That would have spared his foster parents, and his 'new' country, considerable problems.

TWELVE

TITO'S DREAM

After the fall of the Wall the gate to the east was open and I travelled that way over the next few years. I got to Belgrade in the spring of 1992 just as the war in Slovenia, a short sharp war, was ending and the civil war in Croatia was getting sharper. I came by train, through Germany and Vienna, where a fellow traveller warned me about highwaymen who were, mostly, Hungarians: 'They get on with knives, and will not take no for an answer. Never sleep with your head towards the door . . .' I thought of those words as the train surged through the warm May night. They could have been carved on many a tombstone in the Balkans.

Yugoslavia was Tito's dream. To picture it think of a great new house with many rooms to accommodate the united family: Serbs, Croatians, Bosnians, Slovenes, Montenegrins, Macedonians, ethnic Albanians, Serbian Muslims, and ethnic Hungarians. Travelling across Serbia was like being in the dream just after it died. Huge unfinished houses, a dozen rooms or more, jostled for space on the bare hillsides; they sprang up unexpectedly in orchards and vineyards or between the football field and the empty factory. In one, a set of concrete stairs, climbing confidently towards an unbuilt doorway which led into an imaginary bedroom, suddenly stopped in mid-air. The windows were wide and blind. A line of washing was strung across a half-built living room. It would not be a good idea to sleep with your head towards the door.

Slobodan Milosovic had succeeded Josip Broz Tito but the old dictator still stalked the land. Tito had been a hypnotist, a communist who broke free from Soviet control, a federalist who somehow held together an improbable group of Balkan nations.

In the cloisters of the ancient monastery of Hopovo the monks had hung posters commemorating the Battle of Kosovo, which had taken place some six centuries before, a battle the Serbs had lost to the invading Turks. It had always weighed on their minds, and had appeared in their poetry, had entirely coloured their view of themselves. When the regime of Slobodan Milosovic took over the country the Battle of Kosovo became a rallying cry for every Serb, even the most liberal. 'Kosovo!' they said, again and again, as if in the word alone there was the explanation of everything. In the cloisters of Hopovo Monastery was a portrait of King Lazar who had led the doomed Serbian armies against the Turks. King Lazar raised a chalice to his chest, his crown haloed inches above his golden hair. Between the chalice and the crown floated his saintly head. It was a kind of fourteenth-century recruiting poster in a peaceful cloister. The legend below the picture read: 'From 1389–1989, we will remember Kosovo'.

I was there on St George's Day. The little church was bright with lilies of the valley placed before the blackened icons. Fading medieval frescos on the walls showed the Massacre of the Innocents. A line of baby men were having their throats slit as a prelude to decapitation. Then their heads rested beside them like hats.

A plump bearded priest sat drinking with friends in a smoky room. A bottle of plum brandy went around the table; there was jam and tea, hospitable offerings to visitors. I watched two fierce roosters chasing a frightened hen across the monastery garden. The hen hid among the kitchen herbs which shrank from her; she hid among the tulips which turned their heads aside. The pursuing roosters shook their rubbery combs; their beaks were sharp in the sun. War seemed close as the roosters eyed the hen and then each other, and the priest kept sending the slivovitz bottle around the table. I heard the clink of the teaspoon on the lip of the jam jar, then a tall elderly nun stepped between the roosters and their victim, she stepped between them and their quarrel, lifting an empty Coca-Cola bottle like a club. The roosters turned away but they did not run. The trembling hen hid behind her protector's skirts. The war was not over – this was a truce, a cease-fire, policed by a nun. In the monastery garden of Hopovo the fading daffodils had lost their heads a month before. But the tulips were keeping theirs. Bugle-lipped and soldierly, they went marching through the monastery garden.

In Novi Sad the Lecturer said: 'Men are spitting more.' She winced at the thought. 'It goes together with their macho image of themselves. It goes with the guns they wear, the way they turn their heads, the way they talk. Men and their sons – they spit everywhere these days.' Novi Sad still showed traces of its Austro-Hungarian grandeur, and its ethnic Hungarians were living in what was known as the 'autonomous' region of Voj Vodina. Here yet again was the curious way in which all words over two syllables turn into lies in sealed and breathless countries like Yugoslavia. 'Autonomous' was, quite simply, a terrible word. It was a lie given out as the truth, as something real, but also as a warning. Polysyllabic words were often threats, in a land where language was used to enforce obedience. 'Autonomy' was one of those solutions imposed by the late dictator Marshall Tito. It had been a cunning move; 'autonomy' for the Hungarians of Voj Vodina and 'autonomy' for the Albanians of Kosovo meant allowing a small measure of freedom to inconsequential groups. Milosovic stopped that. 'Autonomy' was what Milosovic now wanted for the Serbs, in a Greater Serbia.

There used to be a restaurant in Belgrade that served a good variety of dishes, though the menu explained in English that everything was served 'in the despotic fashion'. Tito's Yugoslavia, Milosovic's Serbia, Tudjman's Croatia all produced in fine detail the façade of freedom so beloved of iron-tight regimes – the pretend courts, the make-believe constitution, the fairy-tale labour laws, the electoral panto-mime, the constant appeal to civil virtues, made one wish to scream. Under Tito the fashion had been 'socialism' and 'federalism' and 'internationalism'. Under Slobodan Milosovic it was nationalism, patriotism, Serbian blood and glory. While the war in Bosnia was at its most intense, that view carried the day. Perfectly normal people repeated that they were the victims of a plot run by secret cabals in hidden rooms, directed by Americans, or androids, or Freemasons, or the Vatican. I had never been in a country, not even my own South Africa, where the police had been more visible. In the early Nineties they were the unchallenged guardians not just of law and order, but of history; they defined for a moment the Serbian character, which seemed to be caught between authoritarianism, nationalism and a profound self-pity which found fault everywhere but at home.

The border between Slovenia and Croatia was a lay-by on the motorway, manned by recently created Croatian Customs Officers who wore grey tunics over dirty trainers, and sheltered from the steady rain under red and white umbrellas supplied by Marlboro cigarettes. Each passing traveller had a price on his head, a kind of entry tax payable of course not in dinars any longer, but in that universal currency of the old Yugoslavia: deutschmarks.

The strong man in Croatia was Franjo Tudjman who was presented as an emancipator of Bolivarian proportions. He encouraged an eager celebration of his country's Nazi or Ustase past, when it collaborated with Hitler, in order to rally Croats against the Serbs, and to weld together a 'new nation'. Self-righteous, noisy, narrow, boring, bone-headed, antique, hate-driven nationalism – the sort that most Europeans swore had been dead and gone half a century past – was back with a vengeance. Every one of the old countries of Yugoslavia claimed to be pure, tribal specimens of irreproachable racial probity. Croatia was merely the most unpleasant. Work began on the new, pure, linguistically purged, Croat dictionaries. No one spoke Serbo-Croat any longer.

All Zagreb was out on the streets to salute the Leader. He kept holding elections, modern despots thrive on elections – insist on them. Nothing beats being voted into power; that way people deserve all you give them. The modern despot loads on his people his own ponderous notions of freedom.

He berates them with calls for civic decency; he bangs on endlessly about law. He organizes things in such a way that not only his rule, but also his democracy is thrust down your throat. You will have it, whether you will or no. The closed societies I have known have all possessed courts and lawyers, newspapers, dissidents, opposition movements, and these pseudo-democratic frills and flounces only made things worse; the devotion to legality has been nauseating. Hitler knew the value of elections; Verwoerd increased his vote every time he stood and so has Robert Mugabe. Slobodan Milosovic was a winner in the polls. Tudjman carried the day. Excessive devotion to the ballot box is not, as one might suspect, a rarity in police states – it is one of the symptoms. In Zimbabwean elections, amongst the most crooked in Africa, ballot boxes are treated like sacred fetishes, and rightly so, for what they represent is not freedom of expression, but a blank cheque guaranteeing unlimited power.

In Zagreb, in 1992, the cult of the newly elected 'democratic' Leader was well-advanced. Croatia was windy with war-talk and with neo-fascist rallies that seemed to have been packed away, with all their gear, since the days of Mussolini. It was extraordinary, this brassy blast of perfume from the past. All over ex-Yugoslavia little 'nationettes' declared themselves in favour of liberty and democracy, independence and self-determination, and then sent in thugs to enforce the dictates of the despot – but only Croatia wanted to reinvent the Nuremberg rally: boots, berets, badges, salutes, a rash of chequered black and white Croatian flags, a crash of martial bands, large men in ridiculous uniforms, pop-eyed with self-importance, talking about their thirst for honour, the rape of Croatia, and the pressing need to kill other people. Many of these were the same men who until about five minutes earlier had been paid up, card-carrying socialists with impeccable 'federal' credentials.

Racial background was soon a matter of life and death, and Jews, and gays and foreigners – all the usual suspects – were in trouble. Citizens of the new Croatia were being asked to prove they were of irreproachable Croatian stock. My friend Slobodan was a Serb and his daughter had just lost her job in a nursery school. A friend in government had this advice: 'Change your name Slobodan, and things will be fine.' Slobodan was worried by the number of guns worn by men drinking in the cafés. 'If you look at someone twice he picks a fight. Just let them see my papers and I wouldn't stand a chance. My phone rings all the time. "Go back to Serbia," they say. After independence they took down all the pictures of Tito, and they made us put up pictures of Tudjman instead. Is this democracy? Things are very dangerous.'

Amongst those who had not succumbed to the boots and bugles of the new nationalism there was despair. A film director deeply saddened by the collapse of the old Yugo-slavia, said: 'We see it as a lost illusion. Unfortunately, the Serbs see it as lost property.' For an historian, Yugoslavia had been a confidence trick performed by a master fraudster, Tito, who had held the constituent people of the old Federation spellbound by his magic, he had made Yugo-slavia look and feel and behave like a real country, but it was never that, the historian suggested, 'It was merely history postponed.'

Now the Serbs were at war, a war of anger, intem-perance, self-pity; a war to make those secessionists pay dearly for their ingratitude; a civil war, a war between the family. What had happened was that all the occupants of Tito's house were now trying to kill each other. It was a domestic homicidal struggle, a very Balkan war. In fact it was a series of wars that would end in the birth of a series of 'new' countries. They were wars that could not be understood in military terms, wars which the West was embarrassed by because they indulged the kind of murderous nationalism that the West had bloodied itself with for much of the past century, but which it now found unseemly, parochial, savage and lamentable. People in Western Europe were not just shocked they were offended when the Balkans dissolved into primitive tribalism. What was happening in ex-Yugoslavia was a series of wars fought to ensure the partition of very small countries – all of which spoke the same language and came from very similar stock – into tribal enclaves where only very small minorities of foreigners would be permitted, if any were allowed at all.

I went east, to the little town of Vrsac, on the Romanian border – Vrsac with its faded Austro-Hungarian flounces, its careful German cathedral, its gypsy weddings and its poets. This was Vasco Popa's home-town. He was one of Yugoslavia's marvels, and it was the poet's good fortune that he died before his country did, but then they said his timing was always good. Popa wrote the purest Serbian most agreed, and they whispered with delight, in those days of ethnic and linguistic witch hunts, that the reason he wrote such beautiful Serbian was because he was, in fact, Romanian.

It was from towns like Vrsac that the military conscripts were coming and going and sometimes never returning. Yugoslavia was one huge rumour mill. There was no news, only portents and fines, and the conscripts had taken to hiding in cellars and the military police who went to search for them had taken to wearing civilian clothes when they knocked on the doors of the small houses in Vrsac and asked the sleeping families to give up their sons. Most families gave them up – the neighbours saw to that – but where they went when they were called, no one really knew.

They told me a story in Vrsac. A boy from the town was called to the army. His family lost touch with him. The war had been bad in Croatia, and then it began in Bosnia. Still the family heard nothing of their son. Repeated enquiries led nowhere. Then came news of battles in different parts of the country. The boy's father set off for the battlefront. He wasn't sure which front, there were several, but he chose one that looked likely, down in Bosnia. He passed one police checkpoint and he was warned that if he persisted in continuing his journey then he did so at his own risk. He refused to turn back. At last he came to a field in which were lying hundreds of bodies. An officer asked him his business. 'I'm looking for my son, have you seen him?' The officer pointed to the field. 'I don't know where he is, but if you are brave enough you may look over there.'

Going south to the city of Nis, where the roadside verges sprouted poppies and policemen, I travelled the roads of Yugoslavia marvelling at the frequency of the roadblocks. The police seemed to be everywhere, hauling in motorists like demon fishermen, searching their cars for drugs, for spies, for loot, for information, for everything but an explanation of why they were doing this and why they regarded it as entirely natural. It required special training to make a real Police State. Not everyone was up to it. It also showed that the modern tyranny, at least in the matter of its

enemies, was instantly adaptable. Once upon a time the
targets of the police in Yugoslavia were enemies of the State
who were also citizens of that State, a perfectly normal thing
in abnormal societies. However, when the wars in the
Balkans broke out in the early Nineties, the police faced
new enemies, enemies within and then enemies without
and, as a result, they were busier than ever. A closed society
has no friends, but it has an infinite number of enemies.

Nis was Serbia's second city. It seemed to be in mourning. Death notices were pinned to the trees: black crosses on
white paper, grainy photographs of the recently deceased
gazing down imploringly at passers-by. Nis had known so
much about death. In its long history the town had been
torn apart by Romans, Turks and Germans. The marble
head of the Emperor Constantine had been retrieved from
the debris of what had been his holiday villa outside town.
The Emperor's painted blue eyes still shone sixteen hundred
years after he lost his head. The few remaining columns that
marked the courtyard of his house were snapped like
pencils. Long ago, when Constantine's empire collapsed,
the streets of Nis were full of soldiers. Then, in the Middle
Ages, when the Serbs went down before the Turks, the
defenders of Nis found refuge in the ammunition store. As
the invaders closed in on the town, the Serb defenders blew
up the store, and themselves, in one almighty bomb, taking
many of the Turks with them in a final act of defiance. The
triumphant Pasha swept into town, but did not leave it at
that. He decreed that a tower be built of Serbian skulls. And
some of these remained, cemented into place. The triumphant Pasha had these heads scalped and then packed the
scalps in cotton wool and sent them home to Istanbul.

In the early 1940s the Germans arrived and built a

concentration camp outside Nis. Its dank dormitories announced the departure of Serbs, gypsies, and Jews. They were bound for that final place, Auschwitz. Pencilled on the walls the messages tell you that 'Dragan' and 'Arkan' have been 'taken in 1941 and 1942 – to Germany'. Standing in a quiet corner of the camp I watched the wind, bit by bit, blowing dandelion heads away.

In the spring of '92 the streets of Nis were full of soldiers once again. This time they were Serbs, remnants of the mainly Serbian Yugoslav National Army that had been pulled back from Slovenia, Croatia, Macedonia – the provinces of Belgrade's old empire, outposts of Tito's dream.

When I got back to Belgrade they asked me what it had been like 'on the other side'. In Yugoslavia, everyone now lived 'on the other side'. In Serbia, the Leader was in search of a 'pure' Serb blood-nationhood. What that meant was achingly familiar. A Television Producer told me: 'I keep my Moslem name, that's how they know. They phoned my thirteen-year-old son the other night and told him that they knew where to find us. This week or next. So we're getting out. Slovenia for us. And yet, I love Belgrade. I'd rather live here than anywhere else. But they're wild men.'

Ethnic anxieties, dangerous impurities – 'I worry about my brother-in-law,' the Teacher told me. 'He's a Serb married to a Moslem. He lives somewhere in Croatia, but we never hear from the other side. He changed his name often. From this to that to this. What will happen next? Will he have to wear a yellow star?'

When the questions became hard to answer, I read the

graffiti on the walls. Terrorized countries, totalitarian states are, in a sense, visual and not literate – you learn more by studying their dances or their pictures or their graffiti from the gravestones, the way people laugh, than you will ever do from newspapers or edicts. The graffiti listed heavy metal bands – 'Guns n' Roses', 'Sperm Birds', 'Wicked Uncles' – but heavy metal had taken on a new meaning in Serbia. You could have written entire stories around those titles. The young of Belgrade were fighting out their wars on the walls of their city.

When a society closes in on itself only the police are happy. It is as if the country is in thrall; it is as if what takes place between the tyrant and his country is a kind of tragic love affair – professions of love interspersed with violent beatings, and, often, murder. Disloyalty is punished. In 1992 in Belgrade there were marches against the way that Milosovic ran the country: very brave marches that happened long before the wars were at their worst and long before the killings reached the ecstasy of murder that was to come later. The marchers were routed by the police, and some were badly beaten for their disloyalty. These protests were a failure; they had ended in recriminations, jail terms and arguments about who loved Serbia more. The shadows were lengthening.

I was back in Serbia a year later and headed down towards Kosovo. In the little town of Usce, in Western Serbia, a muddy river turns abruptly to the right and flows beneath an old iron bridge. There were graffiti on the walls: Mortuus and Amadeus, death and music. Well observed. In 1993, the wars in the Balkans flared and the army convoys rattling through Usce on their way into Bosnia were death on wheels. For music I would have chosen the great Serbian lament from the Kosovo song cycle that recalls the defeat of the Serbian armies by the Turks that the monks at Hopovo had been commemorating. The great curse from the epic was more or less what most people felt at the time in Serbia, as war loomed: 'Whoever is a Serb and shares Serbian blood and does not come to fight at Kosovo, may he have no children, may his crops fail, his wheat, his vines . . . Let him wither into oblivion'.

I'd stopped, really, to look at the bridge across the river in Usce. It was a rarity because it carried a hammer and sickle and a red star, symbols of socialism, remnants of the old religion. When Tito went, inside what felt like five minutes, all these holy signs had been stripped away, amnesia set in, and no one talked of Osip Broz, or his times. The all-pervasive presence that animated the country suddenly disappeared, though here and there there were a few pathetic signals from the grave. I looked at the stars, my friends took pictures, and that was when the police carted us off.

The Station Commander was suspicious. The area was rife with arms smugglers running guns between Serbia and Bosnia. Why were we photographing bridges?

I explained I was on my way to spend Easter with the Bishop of Zica. I may as well have told the police I was on my way to Mars – these men, tall, lots of hair, like basketball players with six-guns, had been token communists and now they were token nationalists. Either way, they were good atheists who believed in the Party-as-God when Tito ran it; now they believed in blood and ethnic cleansing and Slobodan Milosovic. The Orthodox Serbian Church had been emasculated by Tito. The monks and nuns saw their great monasteries confiscated and turned into 'cultural monuments', motels for travelling ecclesiastical enthusiasts.

Where, I wondered aloud, were all the red stars that once adorned every important piece of architecture in Yugoslavia? Where was Tito? The Station Commander thought I was mad. Were we spies or gun-runners or cranks ? What had Tito to do with Yugoslavia? Or his stars or his beliefs? Anyway, Tito had been a Croat, hadn't he? And now he was gone. Tito was yesterday. What stars was I talking about? Calls were made to Belgrade and we were released into the safe-keeping of the Bishop of Zica.

As the long Lenten season drew to its close, preparations were being made for Easter. In the monastery garden at Zica a young novice had been set to cracking walnuts. She swung her hammer and the nut exploded and shards of shell landed among the flowers.

There was bread and nettle soup for lunch, Ash Wednesday fare, and then Mother Superior showed us to our cells. Later she reported our presence to the police. It was not a hostile gesture. On the contrary, it would be seen as a hostile gesture by the authorities if she had not reported us.

On the road the next day the royal-blue Yugos the cops drove outnumbered all others. Some had pictures of the Leader stuck in the back window – Slobodan Milosovic, the new dictator, a communist turned tribalist. Nothing better qualified him for joining the band of brothers who ran much of the world for much of the twentieth century. The nationalists and right-wingers, the Hitlers, the Mussolinis, the Pinochets and the Verwoerds exalted race, tribe, blood and purity. On the other side of the political fence, left-

wing despots talked of 'internationalism' and 'solidarity'
and 'multi-nationalism'. But the difference turned out to
be skin deep. When communism died, red turned brown,
and socialists declared themselves born again, ethnically
immaculate sons of their native soil. The Stalin two-step;
they did it without pause or apology, as easily as winking
across ex-Yugoslavia, in Slovenia, Croatia, Montenegro,
Macedonia, Bosnia-Herzegovina, but it was the Serbs and
Slobodan Milosovic who showed the way. When Milosovic
said that he wanted no more than to defend the Serbian
people, by 'Serbian' he meant separation and ethnic hatred
– tribalism is the first and last refuge of a tyrant – and
'defend' meant the rule of the police. In Serbia they were
everywhere, servants of an invisible but ever-present master,
palace-guard of the despot, you hit them every few
kilometres on the roads, with a little round signboard, ready
to yank you over and search you for guns or drugs.
Travellers became enemies of the prevailing power, and the
police had their eyes open, they suspected the worst. But
they were happy – where else but a police-state would
policemen be so happy?

In Pec, in the heart of Kosovo, I listened to politicians of the
Kosovo Democratic League tell me what they wanted.
Independence? Not quite. Autonomy? Something like that.
But what would happen then to the Serbs of Kosovo?

'Talking to Serbs is difficult,' said the Chairman of the
Democratic League. 'They always break their promises. That
is their style of life. It is one of their Asian characteristics.'

He produced two thick dossiers of colour photographs.
A man showed bruises from his neck to his knees. A woman

with bloody eyes showed parallel red weals running across her breasts.

As I walked down the shabby stairs, the muezzin was calling the faithful to prayer. A man was watching me from the gate of the Mosque. 'I see you have brought your shadow,' says the interpreter. 'That officer arrived when you did and has waited patiently.' Up to thirty-five police agents circulated in the market of Pec, and each had watchers of his own.

In Pristina, the capital of Kosovo, the tailors hung Tito's photograph above their sewing machines. It served as an insult to the present Leader. It reminded him, that Tito gave them autonomy but Slobodan Milosovic revoked it, and gave them instead tanks and roadblocks and troops and more secret police than you could shake a stick at. Pristina was a very spooky city.

In the old Turkish market huddled guinea fowl lay on their sides in the dust, strong twine twirled around their feet. Only the occasional blink of their eyes told you that they were still alive. On the tables were paper bags full of eggs, still speckled with barnyard dirt. The Marriage Gown Salesman was lining up mannequins outside his shop; the gowns were peach, maroon, magenta. The Salesman took each rigid petrified bride in his arms and turned her like a dancer does his partner. In his forge the Blacksmith spat on his palms and began pumping his bellows until his fire surged from red to rose. The Candlemaker said to me: 'We are very unhappy. The police are everywhere. My brother works in Belsize Park. We want our own country in Kosovo.' As I left town I passed a field with a scarecrow in one corner. The scarecrow toted a gun.

The plains of Kosovo run up against the mountains of

Montenegro and you are in them before you know it. Mountains, monasteries and anger. Just outside Podgorica, or Titograd, as it had been until a few months before, capital of Montenegro, stood the Monastery of Moraca. It began in the middle ages as a monastery, then it became a mosque when the Turks took over Montenegro, and now it was a monastery again. The monks of Moraca sat in their garden sipping plum brandy and eating jam, and saying: 'We, the Serbs of today, are under attack.'

Who precisely was attacking the Serbs, I wondered.

Many enemies, the monks told me. There was the western world, the American-Catholic-World Alliance, the New World Order. Just as the Serbs had withstood the attacks by Turks, and then by Nazi Germany, it would fight back. I looked at the flaking fresco in the porch of the church. It showed St George slaying a scaly dragon with a particularly Moorish head. I asked the Abbot as we sat in the monastery garden and the brandy went round and birds sang in the trees: 'As a Christian, is it right to live with hatred in your heart?' The Abbot considered my question. 'No', he did not believe that, but – 'The other side is worse!'

When I went back to Belgrade in 1996, after the uneasy peace signed between Serbs and Bosnians at Dayton, Ohio, I found lethargy, self-laceration, leaden despair. Sanctions began to hurt, isolation increased, the wars that had torn the Federation to pieces haunted the Serbs. Older people mourned the old Yugoslavia. Young people dreamed of migration. Things were stuck. Then came the awakening, seemingly, from nowhere.

It grew out of something rather small. Elections had been

held in Belgrade and other cities, the opposition had won, so the Milosovic regime cancelled the results. Suddenly something happened. On icy nights, through the winter of 1996/97, small groups began marching in Belgrade. The marches were 'about' 'stolen' elections, but they were more crucially about something inside Serbs themselves. Our 'democratic marathon', some called the marches, or the 'Big Walks'. It wasn't a demonstration or a riot or a protest, though it had elements of all these things; at heart it was a jubilation, a party, a wild and passionate fling by people with nothing very much to celebrate and no permission to be doing so. Their weapons were kitchen pots and pans, whistles, funny hats and fireworks. At seven o'clock each evening most of the citizens of Belgrade banged away on pots or pans, just as the official nightly television news came on and announced, as usual, that nothing much had happened that day. The street music sounded, said a perceptive Theatre Director, 'like a mass exorcism, as if we were trying to drive out the demons who possessed us'.

The Big Walks went on through the bitter winter, night after night, week after week, in weather so cold the fingers froze and whistles stuck to their lips. More and more people began showing up: there were teachers, lovers, tramps, grannies, children, aunts, dogs, ballet dancers, pianists, models, actors, rock singers, workers, families with babies; there were revellers and there were solitary curmudgeons who had never marched in their lives. The riot police carried guns, the marchers carried condoms. If the police set up a cordon the students replied with an 'anti-cordon'. If the police did not beat them up, they inflated their condoms and, using them like jesters' bladders, they beat themselves up. There were nightly rituals, like the unfurling of the flags of the countries to which young Yugoslav men had emigrated in order to dodge the draft. The mascot of the marathon was seventy-year-old Aunt Olga, who waited on her balcony with her Serbian flag. The walkers would pause below and then call for her elevation: 'Olga for Minister!' And Olga would wave benignly from her window. There was the man who would lower a bottle of Johnny Walker from his flat to warm the freezing cohorts below. There was the stop outside the offices of State Television, loathed for its propaganda and its mediocrity, for the ceremonial hurling of the eggs.

A former producer of the television service saw things clearly:

'We're ruled by semi-dictators, amateur despots, a State without law or constitution, one big black market. What we endure is the ideology of kitsch; we have no heroes any longer, only criminals. I was head of TV drama for a quarter of a century and now I cannot even enter the building, but they did me a favour. I see my colleagues there now, ashamed of what they do.'

In the Big Walks, the police were everywhere – and they were nowhere. They looked on, sometimes they made ineffectual efforts to repulse the human tide, but their hearts were not in it, and, more importantly still, their guns were not in it. They were like the border guards in East Germany who looked on while young people scaled the Wall and began chipping away at it, the same border guards who the week before had been willing to shoot people who tried to cross that Wall. Something had happened to those police in Belgrade, and the students were very clever: they did not fight the police, they fondled them. Let the police marshal the people in droves and shake their truncheons – and women planted kisses on the Perspex riot shields, and brought them flowers. Let the regime announce that the behaviour of crowds would lead to bloodshed – and the next morning students queued at the blood transfusion services and demanded to shed their blood for their country. I talked to one of the student leaders soon after I arrived in Belgrade and he told me what they had tried to do was to appreciate the police, to jolly them along. The marchers were invited to vote in a variety of competitions. There was 'The Policeman with the Largest Moustache', and the contest to choose 'The Most Beautiful Cop'. The clandestine radio stations ran the results for all the city to hear. This whimsical subversion bore fruit. Another of the leaders on those walks told me, 'On one famous night, three of them even smiled!'

There is something so admirable and so unexpected in finding sense and sanity in places where really it has no right to exist any longer. The cities of Nis and Krajuvac had been in the regime's grip for decades, they were shamed by all the usual idiocies of power, they were filled with dispirited and helpless people who should have long ago given up. Perhaps for a time they had given up. Suddenly, it changed and people in these places showed they were neither lackeys, nor sleep-walkers nor ghosts. They said things so cogent, so sharply observed, so withering it knocked me sideways.

The Mayor of Nis, newly installed, looked at things calmly:

'They're like small children,' he said of the ruling gang in Belgrade, 'children who think they cannot be seen when they behave badly. We see them very well. They have been lying and stealing for so long they have forgotten how to blush. And the opposition is trying, for the first time, to ask for an alternative. Someone else for whom to vote. We wish to make a government that can feel shame, a government that remembers how to blush. We have a ruler who presides like a medieval king and runs things by decree. The courts, electoral institutions, the parliament, these are all no more than Party institutions. Milosovic needs the world today because he cannot rely on his own people. He needs the world for one purpose, money. Money buys survival. He is prepared to do anything to stay in power. Thus the flexibility of his programmes: in 1990 he told us we would follow the Swedish model and now that is gone. In 1992 we had Greater Serbia and the war. Now the war is lost and Serbia is not great and so, in 1996, we have the politics of peace. The warmongers were peacemakers and no one was supposed to remember, or to express surprise. Now we learn: there is no world conspiracy; there is no German master plan for the humiliation of Serbia; there is no American plot.'

These were small victories, however. It was not revolution, it was not what we have learnt to call 'regime change'. The Big Walks did not do what many of us felt sure they would – bring down the government. It took several years, Nato bombs, ruined towns, and something close to a civil war before Milosovic went. When things in a police-state become unspeakable it is natural to think it can't last, it isn't tenable any longer, but that is a mistake; you can't put a term on modern tyranny. Tyrannies are indefinitely sustainable – until they aren't. Put another way, tyrannies are not sustainable, but that doesn't mean they can't last. They last until external forces and internal dissension, acting together over time, push the despot out. But they need something else, a withdrawal of belief, a feeling of embarrassment in the people who have suffered most. It is a perversion of the star system. When you terrify the crowds, you're in business; when they groan and look away, you're gone.

In Moscow in the late Eighties, when you walked around the streets you knew what you were seeing – defeat and despair. The Party, and its dead hand, still ran everything, but it was worse than a joke, it was shaming to contemplate. Muscovites did not quake, they cringed. And in Rhodesia, Ian Smith became insupportable, even to his allies, the South Africans. It was not just that it was too costly to go on supporting him, it was embarrassing. If the Big Walks did not bring down Milosovic, they exposed his police for posturing bullies, and they rendered the Leader ridiculous. There is, in the end, something preposterous about total power. You could die laughing.

THIRTEEN

CYCLOPS SPEAKS

I'd first heard Ian Smith's voice, that reedy clarinet, on 11 November 1965, when he broadcast Rhodesia's Unilateral Declaration of Independence. It was a voice unlike any I'd known. I remember, his accent seemed far too 'English'; it was a thin voice that kept dropping its 'Gs', and it spoke of things that I found pretty puzzling. The man behind the voice seemed to be impersonating the sorts of sentiments made famous by people like Thomas Jefferson because what I heard coming out of the radio in the student café that day in 1965 was a kind of pastiche of the American Declaration of Independence. This was pretty shocking. The speech was fat with phrases such as, 'life, liberty and the pursuit of happiness'. What made it shocking was not the largeness of the ambition, but that anybody saying these sorts of things out loud in South Africa was almost certain to be locked up. The radio, which was our premier form of official communication (television had been forbidden), was reserved for our own politicians who never spoke of things like justice, or freedom or happiness, but used the radio as a bully pulpit to threaten opponents with arrest. We knew our rulers would never have allowed the man near a studio if he had not been sound on the matter of black and white relations. In other words his basic position would have to be

'white rule forever'. So what was this Rhodesian doing with
his words like 'democracy'? On the *radio*? It was very
puzzling.

More than twenty-five years later, in 1992, I went to see
him at his house in the suburb of Harare called Belgravia.
He lived near the golf course, once the Salisbury Country
Club, a lush place where sun-bronzed men and women
tapped golf balls across dance-floor-smooth greens, attended
by faithful black caddies. It was very strange to be in Harare,
strange to think that Robert Mugabe had been leading
Zimbabwe for over a decade with limitless power to do as
he wished. It was said by many to have been the greatest
change ever to sweep across Africa.

That was the sort of thing people were always saying in
those days. More nonsense. What struck the visitor who
returned to Zimbabwe, as I did, after a decade of independence, was the degree to which nothing had changed at
all. The regime that succeeded Ian Smith's government had
reproduced in almost every detail the cruelty and the folly
of its predecessor. There was a fierce drought, many black
people were hungry and jobless. The number of whites had
shrunk significantly, down from about a quarter of a million
at independence to about ninety thousand. Those still there
were getting older or getting out, though someone who
showed no signs of departing was Ian Smith. I had the
impression then and on later visits that he was intent on
seeing the great grim play through to the end. Surviving was
his revenge.

He lived next door to the Cuban Ambassador. The
Ambassador's house was ringed with razor wire and ever-
alert closed-circuit cameras, and armed sentries. Mr Smith's
house was open, his car was in the drive, there were no

guards. He was seventy-three then; tall, lean, rangy, moving perhaps a little slowly, but still had the voice with its nasal twang, as recognizable as ever. Smith had a distinguished record flying Spitfires – 'the most beautiful aircraft ever made' – in the Second World War and he still had the morals, I felt, of a fighter pilot. His squadron gave daylight protection to a wing of light bombers known as Mitchell's Boston Marauders. They had been on a train-busting sortie over the Po valley in Italy when, Smith says, he broke the fighter pilot's cardinal rule: 'Hit your target, but don't go back a second time for a look.' He took another look, and was shot down. He baled out of the flaming plane, and spent five months behind enemy lines, in the Ligurian Alps. He lost an eye, and the plastic surgery that repaired his face had also given him that curiously frozen grimace that made some people take him for a cold, hard man.

I think that was a mistaken impression. He always struck me as a passionate, vituperative, rebellious man whose war years, as was the case for so many young men in the Second World War, seemed to have been the finest of his life. Judging by the affection with which he recalled them, and the passion with which he spoke of his attachment to Britain, you might have said that Ian Smith was a romantic. He was more reticent when I asked him about his second war, the white/black settler war, the catastrophe that claimed so many lives in the old Rhodesia and destroyed any reasonable hope of reconciliation between white and black Zimbabweans, but he spoke with passion and his opinions were volatile, in great contrast to his flat, calm, frozen face.

He told me he preferred Harold Wilson to the Tory colleagues of Mrs Thatcher. 'At least you knew where you were with socialists like Harold Wilson, but that man Lord

Carrington . . .' Even Ian Smith's gift for political insult
failed him when he remembered the perfidy of Lord
Carrington. He talked easily about UDI, the Bush War, the
fruitless meetings with Harold Wilson in British frigates
when he was offered settlement terms he would never get
again, the Lancaster House talks that led to open elections
and Mugabe's victory. He talked without pause or remorse
of every step of that tragic dance towards disaster.

He told me that back in 1979 when the warring parties,
the white Rhodesians and the black Zimbabwean liberation
fighters, met in London at Lancaster House and agreed on
the country's petition to independence, he had been prepared to work with the new leaders. At those first elections
in 1980, Robert Mugabe's party, ZANU, won handsomely,
taking fifty-five out of one hundred seats in the new
Parliament. At the time Ian Smith had done his best to calm
the fears of his fellow whites who were terrified at the
prospect that such gangsters were soon to rule over them.

'Mugabe asked me to come and see him. He was living
in those days in the suburb of Mount Pleasant. He was very
excited and said to me he had inherited this jewel of Africa,
this breadbasket of southern Africa, and he planned to keep
it that way. I got home and I said to my wife and friends that
I was very impressed. We spoke a couple of times after that,
and he asked me for the benefit of my experience.'

Ian Smith leaned back in his chair and stretched out his
long legs. He had been a first-class runner at school, Victor
Ludorum year after year. His political opponents had liked
to call him 'Slippery Smith', but I think 'Swifty Smith'
might have been a better name. He served in the governments which dreamt of liaisons between southern Rhodesia
and northern Rhodesia, between Tanganyika and Nyasaland.

Hard to pin down, shrewd, Ian Smith managed always to show his opponents a clean pair of heels. He was still very much a target: ZANU-PF and Mugabe loathed him, he was constantly threatened. The new rulers prided themselves on leaving the old despot alone, but hated themselves for doing so.

I asked him if he thought his life was in danger and he said he'd chosen not to think about it. Instead, he recalled the brief honeymoon that he and Mugabe had enjoyed. Very soon after Mugabe came to power he did what he'd always said he would do, he began making his government in the image of those Marxist regimes from Hanoi to North Korea which he always admired and emulated. He made no secret of it; though, being Robert Mugabe, he continued to pour placatory oils on the waters he so troubled. Eventually Smith went to see him and told him that investors were taking fright at his plans for marching steadily towards a one-party State.

'I said to him – look, what's all this talk about Marxist-Leninism? I haven't criticized you up until now, and I've asked my backbenchers not to do so. I've tried on the whole to be moderate, but what you are doing now is going to damage our nation. And anyway, what's the point? [In talking about a one-party State] Under the Lancaster House Constitution you can't do anything like that for at least seven years. Why start talking about it now? I'm afraid if you go on like this, I'm going to have to oppose you in public.'

Twelve years have passed since that conversation and Robert Mugabe has never spoken to Ian Smith again.

'I could see that he was angry. I could see it in his face.'

That there had been a honeymoon at all was surprising. Years before, Ian Smith had been described by Robert

Mugabe as 'a sadistic killer, who tortures, kills and massacres not to survive, but because he can no longer survive.'

Looking across the room at Ian Smith, I had the old sense of rich unreality. He seemed to be an actor playing the role of Ian Douglas Smith. Theatricality with lethal repercussions – it could serve as another definition of modern tyranny. The flat voice began to swell as he was recalling Mugabe's rejection of his advice. It began to throb as he recalled the injustice and the stupidity of Mugabe's behaviour. It was as if too much power was being pumped into a material that was a very bad conductor of electricity. The ceramic stillness of Smith's face seemed to vibrate under the tension. There was an overheating of the nasal cavities, which had the effect of sharpening still further his reedy voice and his words came out in machine-gun bursts. The Mugabe government was a one-party disaster run by a Politburo which was really no more than the mouthpiece of the Great Leader. 'Complain that people are starving and the Politburo calls you a traitor.' In the silence that followed this remark the only sound in the room was Ian Smith's breathing.

I listened to his descriptions delivered with such vehemence. It was very accurate, the picture certainly fitted Robert Mugabe, but it also fitted Ian Smith. I told him so and he denied it furiously. There was, he said, no comparison. Dissent and protest were stifled under Mugabe, but they had always been permitted under his Rhodesian Front Government.

It was breathtaking stuff. Tell me again, I asked him. He told me again. I sat back and I remembered liberal opponents of the Smith government locked away in jail. I remembered the white spaces in Rhodesian newspapers, which were such a feature throughout the war years. The papers were forbidden to carry reports that had not been censored and they refused to carry censored reports, so they left glaring white spaces where the stories had been banned. The Rhodesian censors banned the stage play *Hair* and Havelock Ellis, the books of Martin Luther King and collections of Irish rugby songs. I remembered a government of second-rate political desperadoes. Some had double-barrelled names and some had double-barrelled shotguns, and they lorded it over people, they preened and postured, they were a disaster.

Smith was having none of it. White Rhodesians were, to the man, good chaps, keen on a spot of golf and loyal to the Queen. 'No country in the world, with the exception of New Zealand, gave as many troops, proportionately, to the war effort as did Rhodesia. Rhodesia has always done its duty.'

Smith's vehemence was full of those sustaining certainties which are the bread and butter of African politics. There had been no apartheid in Rhodesia, neither had there been discrimination. 'The government [of Mugabe] likes to call us white racists, living in the past. They say we're hankering after our colonial status as masters.' The corners of his thin mouth turned upward a fraction. Land was a word that caused Mr Smith some pain. 'The Mugabe government uses land as a potent weapon to buy votes.'

It was true, it was all perfectly true, but it was not new. After all, who had been the instigators of the land-for-votes scam? Who had kept white Rhodesian farmers sweet by ensuring that they stayed the owners of the best land in the country? Mr Smith was looking down the tunnel of time at the end of which was a wonderland where everything had been stood on its head. 'They say to their people – you fought for the land and you should have it, but that's nonsense. They never fought for land. They fought for power.' It was a very strange thing to hear comments that had behind them the force of fact, and to know that their fact and their truth was vitiated by the very man who was speaking them.

We took a drive downtown. Mr Smith swung his ancient Golf out of the driveway. Jacaranda trees flamed purple on the sidewalks. When we were held up in the traffic and some black pedestrians recognized Smith they would come across to the car and tap on the window and shake his hand. Ian Smith appreciated this ironic reversal of fortune. He read into this friendliness signs of imminent revolt, though to me it looked more like the sort of gesture of insolence directed against the incumbent government which had failed the people of Zimbabwe.

'When I walk down the streets of Harare and I hear people say, "It was better with Smithy," well, I know they wouldn't have said that a year ago. They would have had their throats slit.'

In 1992 the repression Smith pointed to was pretty much apparent to anyone with half an eye. The Zimbabwean police, the army, the CIO were all in the service of the Party. The newspapers were so supine that they uncannily resembled the government lickspittle South African press at the height of the apartheid period. Reading the local newspapers, and they were at that time all but one of them official, was to realize that they made *Pravda* look positively outspoken. They were full of expressions of a slavish devotion to the Party and its ministers and its Leader. There was no official censorship in Zimbabwe, but, seeing what the papers were prepared to do about it, there was no need.

Ian Smith had lost none of his taste for invective: 'They're all stooges. All of them. Prepared to blame the problems of this country upon Smith and the white races. But the reality is that Zimbabwe is the victim of one man, Mugabe.'

The autocrat turned freedom fighter piloted his Golf with increasingly savage stabs on the accelerator until we had to stop at a failed traffic light, another victim of the frequent and haphazard power cuts hitting Harare at that time. 'Even their own newspaper, the *Herald*, would criticize some minister or other from time to time. They like to point at this and say, "Well, there you are, we can't be dictatorial. Because, you see, people criticize us." That's where the cleverness comes in. You are allowed to attack the structure, but never Mugabe.'

As we started up again and eased our way into the traffic a black pedestrian saw Smith and his face in a flash became so incredulous with delighted recognition it was really rather touching. Ian Smith was oblivious, wrestling the gears in much the same way as those pinball wizards used to ride the tables back in the University café twenty-seven years before, when I first heard the thin metallic tones of the man beside me. The pedestrian came to the driver's window and shook Ian Smith's hand: 'Mr Smith! Do you recognize me?'

'Of course I don't,' said Ian Smith in happy exasperation, 'I can't recognize everyone, can I?'

Harare in 1992 was a world turned upside down. Ian Smith was a guest at a political meeting, in the Jamieson Hall, of what was to be a new black opposition party. The audience cheered him – the white devil, the man with horns, their former enemy. It was a measure of their own desperation. Mr Smith had been an oppressor, said one elderly black politician who had fought Smith tooth and nail, 'But at least he was a fair oppressor.'

After the meeting, we drove back to the house in Belgravia, Mr Smith and I. It was amazing to be sitting beside him in the little Golf; it was rather like meeting one of the extinct species of Africa, like the elephant bird of Madagascar, someone you had thought had long since ceased to be. But there he was, wrestling the wheel, cursing the gears, enunciating a kind of frantic patriotism. 'I don't want to say, I told you so. Recrimination is sterile. It's no good looking back. I have my family in this country. Friends, children, grandchildren. We have to work to return a little bit of sanity to the country. Before it goes down the drain.'

But the impression he left me with was that he truly believed the corruption was so deeply embedded it could not be rooted out. It was, he said, the disease that always afflicted Africa. White farmers were leaving. They were going to Zambia and Mozambique, and the Mugabe government had found a new villain to blame – the drought.

'In just the same way they used to blame it on white colonial races, but it's not the drought, and it's not the whites. Do you know why we have no food? It's because we're not planting the crops. Cotton, groundnuts, maize, these are our basic foods. They always have been. We managed to feed ourselves ten years ago and we could do so now. What we cannot deal with is this government, with its nepotism, its fraud, its incompetence.'

The tirade went on. Even the question of the other great scourge, Aids, extracted not compassion, but the same furious assault:

'Look at the rate of reproduction. It must be something

like four per cent. One of the highest population rates of increase in Africa. Aids may take away some of those people, but it's a drop in the ocean. They can't go on reproducing by the million.'

It was for Robert Mugabe, however, that Ian Smith reserved his final bombing run. I asked him, 'What is Robert Mugabe?' The answer came back quickly: 'A megalomaniac surrounded by psychopaths.'

I thought about his answer, as we sat in that very English drawing room, somewhere in Belgravia, next door to the Cuban Embassy, and down the road from the Harare golf course. There's no question that the description fitted, but what I was left wondering was – exactly who were we talking about? There was Robert Mugabe and his secret police, his youth brigades, his hitmen and his swaggering Ministers; and there was once Ian Smith, and his secret police, his government of bullies and bigots. Certainly this strangely frozen man saw things clearly; but then again, he had only one eye.

FOURTEEN

MRS THATCHER'S BALLS

Robert Mugabe never minced his words about the whites of Rhodesia – he called them 'settler vermin'. By the early Nineties, the 'vermin' were much reduced, down from about a quarter of a million, when Ian Smith launched his UDI in 1967, to around ninety thousand. Many had left for South Africa, 'taking the gap' as it was called, but those who hadn't 'gapped it' returned to their old lives, and their old ways. It was natural, but not sensible. Everything had altered with the arrival of the new black government, but nothing had changed. Some six thousand commercial farmers owned one third of the land. Eight million peasant farmers owned another third. Yet those who had fought Robert Mugabe settled back into the old life, succumbing to the attractions of sun and space and servants. Fear of the man had dissipated, the sharpness of thought which the war had induced had been blunted in the peace that followed when nothing, it seemed, was going to change. It was bizarre to note the difference between old Rhodesians and new Zimbabweans. A dozen years after Independence very few black Zimbabweans had any illusion about their government, yet the whites were full of timidity on the one hand, and a strange aggressive confidence on the other. They had regained their old complacency which allowed you to tolerate blacks without respecting them, to patronize them without supporting them; an easy life where you contentedly, happily, sleepily enjoyed the rewards of being where you were because of being who you were.

'Bob's all right, and as long as he's there, we're all right,' a farmer told me.

But the war was not over. Independence had merely seen the suspension of hostilities. Robert Mugabe made it plain that he despised his white compatriots; he saw them, at very best, as a necessary evil whom he would tolerate for as long as he had to, and whom he would then destroy, or drive out. Indeed, it was the whites of Zimbabwe who inspired Mugabe to the single instance of poetic insight in his wartime speeches. These little-read harangues were thick with the abstractions of old-style Stalinism, but they held revealing clues to the meaning of the man. Composed during the years when Robert Mugabe and his guerrilla armies were fighting in the bush, they appeared in the revolutionary Party paper, the *Zimbabwe News*, or had been broadcast by clandestine radio stations, between 1976 and 1979. I have a rare collection of them, brought together under the title: 'Our War of Liberation'.

You'd expect them to be lethally dull, and so they are, but Mugabe's feelings towards whites, settlers, Rhodesians, colonials, are clear in these sombre, repetitious tracts, energized, now and then, by blood-thirsty war cries: 'Once upon a time, the Rhodesian white settler held himself immortal and invincible. But now he has become our cannon fodder.' The poetry came when Mugabe, remembering the English teacher he used to be, quoted Tennyson's 'The Lotos-Eaters'. The whites who settled Rhodesia he compared to those superior beings who lived 'On the hills like Gods together, careless of mankind'. They were Sunstruck wastrels in a land where it was 'always afternoon', for whom slumber was more sweet than toil – especially when the toil was being done in the hot African sun by someone else. It was a way of life which could be characterized as superior and stupid inertia shot through with intolerable self-righteousness.

Was it true? Uncannily so. Anyone who thought honestly about white settlers at the foot of the African continent would have to agree. Indeed, travelling through Zimbabwe in the early Nineties and meeting whites was to find yourself amongst somnambulists in shorts, afternoon men in safari suits, astonishing in their complacency, in their plump and self-satisfied inertia and, even more surprisingly, in their shrill blind patriotism for the 'new' Zimbabwe, and their devotion to a man who loathed them. The whites seemed drugged, high on tobacco prices, or golf, or bowls, or comfortably drowsy on their absurdly rich ranches that seemed to run forever. If Mugabe threatened them, they turned over in their sleep and told themselves he didn't mean it. They reminded me of the shades of the dead in Virgil's Underworld – squeaking, pallid, impotent ghosts. Perhaps you couldn't blame them – it's never easy being a hate object.

Robert Mugabe had never hidden the way he felt about the 'settlers', yet he'd not found the effective means of getting rid of them. At the Lancaster House talks in London, in 1979, he was very plain about what he had been fighting for: 'Land is the main reason we went to war. To gain what was taken eighty-nine years ago. There are six thousand [white farmers] owning seven million black people's rights . . . As good revolutionaries we have already liberated fifty per cent of the country. Already sixty-five per cent of white farms are vacant. We have a right to pass that land on to the people. It is a life or death matter.'

But they didn't believe him. White farmers, Asians, Jews, and much of the rest of the world, talked of a Zimbabwean miracle. Following his landslide victory and Independence in 1980, Robert Mugabe had preferred to postpone Apocalypse and that was good enough to be going on with. Whether greed or fear or caution had stayed his hand was never clear. Africa seemed to be showing a reasonable man leading a reasonable country and no one wanted to rain on the parade.

In 1992, the parade was over. All was drift and dream. People seemed cocooned, black and white, each in their own world. Even the ruling Party seemed in the business of talking to itself. The slogans, the paraphernalia of control were everywhere, yet no one appeared to be in charge. Again I encountered the paradox I had seen in other throttled societies: the Leader was everywhere – and nowhere. People talked but the talk meant nothing, they used phases again and again – independence, freedom – and yet Zimbabwe was closed, fearful. No one appeared to know what was going on, but no one was saying so. Whites kept telling you that things were fine, and black people shook their heads; and thousands went hungry.

If Mugabe was right in his detestation of the dreamy superiority of whites, he was wrong to lump them all together. Not all whites were the same, but pretending they were was the means by which you unleashed a war, or a pogrom. Mugabe made no secret of his desire to launch both: but people preferred not to believe him. The campaign to rid Zimbabwe of its white people was apparent even in 1992, though no one would have used those terms. In fact, one might even have said that the only discernible political ambition of the Mugabe regime and his ruling Party was to dispossess white farmers and to redistribute their land to black farmers. Moreover, this was to be done, sooner or later, whether they liked it or not, for reasons that were borne out of the bitterness of Mugabe's war which had now become in his mind the whole of the struggle waged against the old Smith regime, and he had become its only conqueror. Whites had to be stripped of what Mugabe regarded as their ill-gotten gains, not because blacks were to be rewarded, but in order that whites might be punished. Farms had been changing hands since Independence, sometimes willingly, sometimes reluctantly, but nobody talked about it openly. It was retribution – not redistribution but that was not spoken of either. What passed for talk was just party slogans and public murmurs – none of it was really worth listening to. It was better to see for myself.

One day in June I travelled with Andrew Huck to an old farm he had once owned, north of Harare. The farm had been sold to the government after Independence and had been turned into a co-operative. What made the afternoon special was that this farm had been sold voluntarily, and in ten years Andrew Huck had never been back to his old house, had never wanted to go back. What added to the interesting awkwardness of that afternoon was that he had fought with the Rhodesian forces against the guerrilla armies of Robert Mugabe. Losing this farm after the war had been painful and, as we drew close to the place, I could see that this was a hard thing for Huck to be doing. He had grown up on the farm; memories of his youth and the way things had been were entwined in the place.

The original farmhouse had been abandoned. The families who now owned the co-op farm lived in other buildings on the property and they were not having a good time of it. The old house was one of those typical settler dwellings with a wide *stoep* and corrugated-iron roof; and it was cracking up, untouched since the Hucks had left, a ship marooned in the bush with cobwebs growing over the windowpanes and plaster falling off the walls. When Andrew Huck's family owned the property there had been a farm school, shops and a workforce of about five hundred people, together with their families. Twelve years on it was all a mess. The plan had been to turn such commercial farms into co-operatives – by splitting up these large ranches between several families, peasant farmers would be encouraged to take the land – but it hadn't gone that way. The drought made things very bad: no money had been invested in the place since there was none to invest – and the government in faraway Harare could not, or would not, send replacement machinery or answer requests for assistance. Worst of all, on the morning we arrived, the old pump Huck's father had installed to pull up water from the bore-hole had broken down.

For much of the day Andrew Huck and the co-op farmers worked on rigging up a replacement, using what-ever bits and pieces they could scrounge. It was moving to see the new black inheritors of the farm and the former white owner struggling to make water flow again. Ordinary farmers facing ordinary problems.

It left Andrew Huck feeling sad. He didn't believe that the repair was going to hold for very long, and then, he said, the co-op farmers would not be able to fix the pump again. Next time he would not be around to help. He said this without rancour and he kept his voice down.

I had noticed that most whites in Zimbabwe were keeping their voices down – or their mouths shut altogether. Many seemed almost poignantly grateful to be allowed somehow, miraculously, to go on living the good life. Even when the insults came, they smiled and said it didn't matter, it was just one of Bob's little lapses.

Robert Mugabe had had one of his little lapses earlier that year when he declared that commercial farmers were hard-hearted people. 'You would think they were Jews.' That had been too much for the Jewish community who protested, but no sooner had they done so than they drew back, astonished and rather perturbed by their own temerity. If Robert Mugabe had had a little anti-Semitic tirade, nobody should on any account dwell on it. Rabbi Ben Isaacson of Bulawayo put it this way: 'Jews have lived in Zimbabwe for a long time. With no trouble. That's more than one can say for many other parts of Africa.' The statement was very interesting. It read like an epitaph.

Zimbabwe had been reduced to that strange monologue which tyranny invariably creates, a one-way traffic of windy rhetoric which emanates from the Leader and blasts across the country. That is why there are seldom any open conversations in totalitarian countries. Conversation is a to and fro movement and that is not possible when the wind blows one way in a blistering man-made gale. In a tyranny one cannot hear oneself speak. No one but the tyrant speaks in public; everyone else keeps what they have to say for secret conversations in the privacy of the kitchen or the bedroom. Rabbi Ben Isaacson's words often came back to me. How long was a long time? How long did you have to live in Zimbabwe to cease to be a Lotos-Eater? Or vermin? Was everybody black a genuine Zimbabwean or were some Zimbabweans more genuine than others?

I thought about that as I followed a man called Stavros Georgiou down Camperdown Road, in the little town north of Harare called Mount Darwin. We were on our way to the brothel. It hadn't always been the brothel, it had once been the Mount Darwin Country Club. It had survived as the Club until the early Eighties and then it was taken over by the Party, and designated a 'recreation centre'. At some point it had been transformed into a brothel and the Party was embarrassed about it. They said we might visit it, but we should have to take some official minders along.

Stavros was the last white man in Mount Darwin. Garage owner, trader, political fixer, member of the ruling ZANU-PF and sometimes even, he liked to say, Comrade-Mayor of Mount Darwin. Stavros had arrived in Zimbabwe from Cyprus when he was still a teenager, back in the early Fifties. As a boy he had been under the impression that he was actually heading for Darwin, Australia – the postmaster in his Cypriot village had looked it up and said it must be Australia, who else had a Darwin? And who had ever heard of Rhodesia?

Stavros arrived in Africa without money, or a home, or much English. He stayed on and prospered; he stayed on and adapted. He spoke beautiful Shona and he took the continent and his new home to his heart. He was one of the most perfectly assimilated settlers I've ever known. A vast and turbulent and comic man, he lived through the evening of the British Empire in Africa, and he remembered when Mount Darwin could claim to have a District Commissioner, an Assistant Commissioner, three white policemen, a postmaster and eleven Greek families running the trading stores. Stavros had survived UDI when Rhodesia broke from Britain, and the civil war that followed. He had welcomed the coming of Independence and he had watched the white population of Mount Darwin dwindle as the first expropriations of the white farmers began. Darwin was at the centre of the early seizures of farms.

Stavros was a huge man, he overflowed, he exuded a warmth, rather like a benign volcano. Everyone who knew Mount Darwin knew Stravros. Even Margaret Thatcher knew Stavros. On an official visit to the new Zimbabwe of Robert Mugabe, Mrs Thatcher had stopped off in Mount Darwin and met Stavros and donated a bunch of footballs to the local community. She had no sooner handed them over than they went missing. Stavros turned to the Nyanga, the local witchdoctor, who laid a spell on the missing footballs: he let it be known that the loot was dangerous stuff and those who had taken them would die. It worked. The next morning Mrs Thatcher's balls were back. 'A miracle', Stavros liked to say. He was very fond of that word, but then he was something of a miracle himself.

He had a big heart. He recalled the Cuban doctor who came to work in Mount Darwin hospital when all the other doctors left and the Mugabe government and the Castro regime entered into a deal to deploy Cuban medical staff in rural areas. The doctor went down to Harare once a month and handed over her hard currency money at the Cuban Embassy, that large house surrounded by razor wire and electronic cameras, next to Ian Smith's place in Belgravia.

'Then they sent her back on the bus. She didn't even have a decent pair of shoes,' said Stavros. 'I liked her, and my wife and I, we sort of adopted her, but when the Cuban people thought she was getting too friendly, they sent her back to Cuba – the bastards!'

The doctor was succeeded by another, a young man this time. He was also taken into the Stavros home. 'He used to tell me that in Havana he would be obliged to attend all the rallies for the Leader, Fidel Castro. And that, along with all the crowd, he lifted his fist and shouted, "Viva Castro!" – but that in his heart he said, "Die, you bastard!"'

Stavros looked at Mount Darwin, and grieved. He supplied a running commentary on its landmarks and was a vital guide to what had gone. He not only knew his geography, he was unbeatable at detecting the ironies of history. Over there was the house where the last vet once lived, he'd been killed by guerrillas in the Seventies. Over there was the home of the drunken doctor who ran the new hospital, a gift from the Canadians. The hospital was down to its last couple of oxygen bottles in the operating theatre, and had quite run out of thermometers. Stavros remembered the Chinese workers who were brought in to build the tobacco co-op nearby, but knowing nothing of the town or the people or of Africa, being themselves freshly arrived from Beijing, they had erected the kitchen directly above the single well which supplied the only water for several miles. Stavros had shaken his head: 'The bastards!'

He led me down Camperdown Road with a single warning as we approached the small and rather pretty house at the end of a rutty, sandy track: 'Leave the talking to me.'

A couple of heavies from Party Headquarters met the Comrade-Mayor at the door. Stavros pointed to me, winked, and chatted away for a while in Shona. Then we were given the keys and allowed to begin our tour. Stavros had won over the men from the Party. 'I said you were a wealthy foreigner with a mind to restoring the club. You're lucky they didn't ask you for a cheque.'

We wandered from the empty billiard room, through the hall with its bare stage where they'd once put on Christmas shows, out to the squash court which was piled high with bags of cement. There was tough grass sprouting through the cracks of the empty swimming pool. Where the girls had gone I could not say, but I didn't see them. Every so often our two uneasy minders would reappear and Stavros would reassure them. What struck me about the clubhouse was its emptiness; the members' bar had served its last Scotch soon after Independence in April 1980. Its former members had long ago decamped, down to South Africa, or they'd left their farms, sold up and settled in some other corner of Zimbabwe. Only the ghosts were left. Stavros knew his way round the Club – but then, he'd built it.

Father Niederberger, at the Serima Mission, sipped his tea and sighed a long, Swiss sigh. He had been in Zimbabwe for forty years and had never seen his people so dispirited. His church lay at the end of a dirt road about an hour and a half from the town of Masvingo and it had been built by another Swiss, Father Groeber, who had believed that 'sweat is sweet'. Begun in 1955 and completed in 1960, the Serima Mission was one of the great artistic triumphs of southern Africa. Working with sculptors, all schoolboys, some still in primary school, Father Groeber and the people of those communal lands had between them constructed, carved and painted a church in Serima so authentically African, so subtle, delicate and beautiful, that Evelyn Waugh's prediction in *A Tourist in Africa*, that it would one day come to be seen with the same loving reverence that Europeans had for their medieval cathedrals, seemed perfectly appropriate.

But Father Niederberger did not want to talk about art. He turned to me and said that, considering we had reached the year of 1992, it was time to be open about things. The coffin makers were always busy. People were dying around him and no one wanted to name the disease that killed them. They called it everything but what it was.

'Of the people I have been burying lately, at least eighty per cent have died of Aids.'

But openness was not possible. Life was not opening up but closing in. In Bulawayo, Zimbabwe's second city, Joshua Nkomo was ridiculed for failing to answer questions about the bodies that were turning up in the countryside. Nkomo, people said with bitter resignation, was now Vice President, but he had been 'bought'.

I asked him about that. He looked pained and refused to answer. He frowned a lot instead and told me I wouldn't understand. I asked him what I wouldn't understand.

'History.'

'What history?'

'Our history.'

'Then you tell me.'

He shrugged again, but he said nothing.

★

When you compared the lives of black Zimbabweans with those of whites it was depressing beyond measure. Whites lived better, but it was more than that, they also lived in a world that neither knew nor cared about its neighbours. They lived out of Africa. Robert Mugabe repeated tirelessly that he intended to dispossess whites at the earliest opportunity and that those who opposed him would be crushed and driven from the country. Whites behaved as if the man could not possibly mean what he said. Yet Zimbabwean 'whites' (what a grim, lumping term it was; equalled in its horrible meagreness only by the term 'blacks') confronted a vital question that lay ahead of all people of European origin who regarded Africa as their home. The question was this: were they not perhaps fatally mistaken? It was the question faced to some degree by all-powerful minorities who lived within a larger, more or less homogenous, majority: were you at home – or were you always, at best, a tolerated stranger?

I had grown up in a system that said that to tolerate the presence of other races, tribes, groups, was wrong – even suicidal. I had come to reject and attack that doctrine as wrong. Bad science, bad sense, bad politics. I still hold to this belief – you are not condemned to separation and rejection because of race or colour.

Dr Verwoerd said I was wrong: not only was racial mixing wrong, it was a delusion. He went further, he maintained that if you allowed smaller groups to mingle freely with larger groups, the big would repress the small and, eventually, extinguish them. Sometimes I wondered whether, far from being wrong, he had been ahead of his time. Perhaps racial hatred was the motor that made a successful 'people'. It distinguished them; it set them, in a word, 'apart'. This led me to consider some interesting anomalies in the history of colonialism, or conquest or, if you like to use a far better word for these things, 'massacres'.

It was apparent to anyone that the white man's record in Zimbabwe was lamentable, but here one of the paradoxes of power came into play. The price the whites were paying in Zimbabwe was not for being bad – it was, rather, for not being bad enough. The success of a colonial people in territories that once belonged to others required the extinction or the neutralization of those indigenous others. In short, Australia, or America, or Canada, were places where 'nations' had been built on aboriginal graveyards.

I never liked this way of thinking, but there it was. It faced me at almost every turn in Zimbabwe. Perhaps it had something to do with going in short notice from Belgrade to Bulawayo. Perhaps it had to do also with the extreme languor of the whites I met in Zimbabwe, the dreamy blindness, but whatever I felt, the view from Bulawayo, and from Belgrade did look dismayingly like the view of Hendrik Verwoerd. Aspects of the Verwoerdian vision were being bloodily confirmed all the way from the Balkans to Zimbabwe. Ethnic liberalism was dead. Racial tolerance had gone out of the window. Tribalism was the future. In effect, apartheid was triumphant from Sarajevo to Split, and what had begun to happen in Zimbabwe looked astonishingly like the African version of ethnic cleansing.

I often thought of Stavros, a big, warm man, chortling and cursing and steaming, like a Dutch oven on legs, as he guided me through the corridors of the country club that had become a brothel, and for which the ruling Party might have touched me for a dollar or six, to repair what Stavros had built and it had ruined. Africa was a strange and compelling place and Stavros, however you measured him, was one of its great sons, a man more naturally and easily at home there than almost anyone I've met, but a man who stood out and was thus damned, set apart, simply by the colour of his skin. The last white man in Mount Darwin. If Stavros was not 'African' – then who was?

A shrunken and deluded people incapable of serious reflection, the whites of Zimbabwe did not consider that question – they didn't seem to know there was one. Lotos-Eaters were at it again, stoked out of their skulls on sun and space, golf and the good life, adrift in 'a land where all things always seem'd the same'.

In July 1992, twelve farmers in the Mutare district were listed for expropriation by the government – with little or no compensation. These farmers were not the descendants of the original Rhodes' settlers; there were very few of those left. These people were, most of them, Britons, who had settled in what was Rhodesia after the war, thinking it was a little like Kenya, only cheaper and not as class-ridden. People in Kenya, they used to say, went 'home' once a year. Rhodesians went home every night. Now the government wanted their farms. The usual shock and outrage followed the announcement of this land grab. There was pompous and vapid argument decorated with all the old clichés of bygone times, as if this was a debate around the bar of some home-counties village pub, a debate that was full of words like 'legitimacy' and 'courts' and 'appeal' – voodoo words, the modest magic of some marginal people who simply did not understand where they were or who they were: it was as if some small tribe on some small desert island lit the devotional fires and danced to old gods who were dying and could not save them.

FIFTEEN

THE COLOUR OF BLOOD

I went back to Zimbabwe in 1996, sixteen years into the reign of Robert Gabriel Mugabe. I flew one Sunday morning into Harare and as I was driving through the familiar suburbs, I had again that strange feeling I knew from other closed places, a feeling that lives were led in tunnels, and the tunnel-lives ran parallel to one another and so never met. No easy communication was possible, there was only the journey, each to his own, with occasional stops along the way where you might, briefly, swap information with a fellow traveller.

I knew where I was in suburban Harare; nearby was State House where Robert Mugabe lived. It was dangerous to be anywhere near the place because soldiers had a habit of blazing away at motorists who got lost in the vicinity. Not far away was Ian Smith's house, and the house of the Cuban Ambassador, where they shook down Cuban doctors once a month and relieved them of their hard currency and sent them back to the bush on a bus.

God was clearly still more or less in his heaven for down the fairway of the Royal Harare Club ambled an early-morning golfer. He looked like an actor parodying, cruelly but accurately, that extinct creature, the white Rhodesian settler in his prime, when this club was the Royal Salisbury and everything the eye fell upon belonged to him. There he was, his spacious shorts billowing above moon-pale knees. His drive down the fairway was determined, his stride purposeful, his black caddie struggled to keep up with him. Arriving for the first time in Zimbabwe, a Martian visitor might have concluded that little had changed since the days of Cecil John Rhodes, when Heaven was rather like the Royal Salisbury, a tendered oasis of playable greens, advanced whites and obedient blacks, where anyone who was anyone was English. That was quite wrong.

'Anyone listening to what whites say about blacks,' Mugabe told his people, 'will realize that we are insulted every day.'

Was it true? In the main, I think it was. White and black Zimbabweans were two separate people in a single land and they did not understand one another and they did not get on. To say that, of course was heresy, and to suggest that the whites who remained in Zimbabwe were unselfconsciously, easily, and irredeemably racist was something that brought cries of anger down upon your head. However, when Robert Mugabe said so, white people did what they had been doing for years when he said anything clear and unequivocal, they pretended not to hear, they hoped he meant something else, they refused to take him seriously. When the whites of Zimbabwe were confronted by their Leader, they reached for the Lotos.

By 1996 Mugabe had been building his power for years, he was unchallenged ruler of what was really a one-party state. Yet the country was a mess and, worse, the detestable white settlers, seventeen years after Independence, still controlled the best farming land and the biggest business firms. There were a lot less of them. They were down in numbers from ninety thousand a few years earlier to around eighty thousand, little more than a remnant amidst the majority of black Zimbabweans who numbered some ten million. Whites were fading away, keeping their heads down, but they were still there. It was intolerable for black Zimbabweans to feel themselves held hostage by their former masters. How real the grievance was, how accurately Mugabe measured it I can't say, but in the mid-Nineties the feeling was palpable.

Years before, Ian Smith had spoken for most white Zimbabweans when he boasted that 'our blacks' were the happiest in Africa. Now, in a strange and chilling mirror image, black Zimbabweans were saying to me that 'our whites' were the worst in Africa. Reviled from public platforms, depicted as greedy in business, clueless in the ways of Africa, rich but incompetent, lazy, hateful, foolish and dull – yet somehow they were still far more powerful than their numbers suggested. So it was open season on settlers. Whites were to be harried, chased away, they were to be depicted as less than human, they deserved no mercy. The white farmers of Zimbabwe were on the way to becoming what he had said they were – Mugabe's jews, or his *kulaks*.

Once this dread parallel had been invoked, the logic of racism and revenge proceeded along its iron course. Whites, it was said, owned the best land, the finest farms, the largest fortunes, they controlled the economy and plotted in secret cabals to impoverish and destroy the black man, the true children of Africa. The pure inheritors of the African ideal were being undermined and betrayed by this vermin in their midst.

'Whites', declared the *Financial Gazette*, one of the few

independent newspapers in the country where the press and news media were slavishly devoted to the ruling Party, 'are a coterie with a stranglehold on the economy.' Blacks did not die in their thousands in the liberation struggle to preserve white interests, the newspaper added. The *Sunday Mail*, a fervent supporter of the government, warned of a 'Rhodesian' invasion by whites who had left the country after Independence and who were plotting to return 'in their hundreds of thousands'. The whiff of hatred was everywhere. It was called by a new and ugly name, 'indigenization', but it was really no more than a dream of revenge, a desire to destroy those who did not belong.

In Zimbabwe, little by little, as it had been in South Africa when racial obsession reached its high point, the mood of homicidal stupidity was everywhere apparent. Verwoerd, in his determination to stamp out any form of adulteration of the pure and holy blood of the elected Afrikaners, did not simply drive out black Africans from his laager of paradise. That would have been inconsistent and tyranny deplores inconsistency. Verwoerd systematically and suicidally set out to alienate, and then to expel from the holy circle, all his natural allies. He expelled South African Asians for being – Asian. He expelled the Chinese for being – Chinese. He then turned to the people who were actually Afrikaner both by blood and language, the mixed race people of the Cape Province who had come into being because early settlers slept with the local Khoi and Hottentot people who in turn mixed with Malays and others. By summoning up his skin police, he would delve down into the very genes of his people, then into the chromosomes, into the mitochondria, into the atoms from which their beings were constituted, to ensure that only the purest passed muster, only the racially saved would see the Kingdom of God. Nothing and no one would be spared. The law of racial segregation was as real and as weighty to Dr Verwoerd and his fellows – who made up the majority of whites – as the law of gravity. He tolerated English-speaking Europeans because they were white, but he excluded them from the Party of God because they were not truly 'Afrikaans'; they were not genuinely indigenous. This was the test Mugabe applied – black or white? White Zimbabweans were a contradiction in terms. It interested me profoundly this form of distinction, it made me very homesick for South Africa, and that is why I went to Zimbabwe and listened to what people had to say about a 'new' wave that seemed a pretty old, very familiar wave to me.

The first attacks in 1996 were sudden and ugly. An Italian nightclub called Sandro's, in downtown Harare, owned by the patrician Mr Bernardini, was invaded by a group of students from the University of Zimbabwe in order, they said, to voice their disgust at his élitist and racist establishment. The demonstrators trashed the place, barracked black diners, harassed women and, having made their point, moved on to stone a few lesser places around town.

Down in Bulawayo, Maxi who ran the best Italian pasta joint, had no doubt what it meant. The invasion of Sandro's and the stones lobbed through windows of other white-owned establishments reminded him of just one thing: 'Kristallnacht,' said Maxi. It was shocking to hear him invoke the destruction of Jewish businesses in Berlin in 1938 by the Nazis. What was happening in places like Harare and

Bulawayo was on a much smaller scale, but then of course Zimbabwe was a much smaller place. The principle, however, was about the same size. It was Maxi who put that principle rather well. White Zimbabweans in the main, said Maxi, might not be known for their sensibilities – they flaunted their four-wheel drives and their money in the streets of Bulawayo where many people had nothing – but stupidity was not a capital offence and the moment you started talking of people leaching on 'black blood' then you were talking progroms. If they attacked him, he'd be heading back to Florence, just another of the thousands who planned to leave.

I soon found out that there was something in the hearts of many whites, still unreconciled since the bush wars of the 1960s: who were the 'good' Zimbabwean whites and who were the rogue Rhodesians? It was an enmity not unlike that which showed between assimilated 'German' Jews and Jews from Eastern Europe, when the Nazis began their persecutions. White people responded that they were not the problem, it was 'other' whites who caused the trouble. The attack on Sandro's nightclub united the whites I spoke to, right and left, in one belief – he had probably deserved it. Ian Smith put it all down to natural, youthful exuberance. The wife of a leading liberal lawyer detected 'Sicilian tendencies', and declared that the Mafia was probably behind Sandro's Restaurant. A civil rights activist with a notable record in race relations regretted the students had missed the chance of hitting a couple of dyed-in-the-wool 'Rhodie' restaurant buyers, patronized by the sort of people who never got over black independence – and he offered to give the students directions next time they went white-bashing.

At a rally in Bulawayo the Vice President, Joshua Nkomo, peered into the audience and demanded to know why none of 'our whites' were present. When the writer and long-time antagonist of the Smith regime, Judith Todd, pointed out that she was in the audience, Nkomo replied with a backhanded compliment: 'You're not white,' he said, 'you're semi-white.'

A local white doctor went on trial for manslaughter. He had allegedly administered epidural injections of morphine to patients, some of whom had died. When the trial opened the atmosphere was already electric with charges by politicians against unnamed white doctors who were said to be plotting to infect blacks with Aids and heart disease. The ghoulish portrait of a white doctor conducting Nazi experiments on black patients raised the temperature higher still. During the trial, a man called Comrade Obey Mudzwingwa led protesters into the streets and warned that if the verdict of the trial was not to his liking, whites would be attacked and subjected to similar epidural injections and 'amputations'.

The more closely I looked at things, the more I had to ask myself whether I had not perhaps been wrong all my life: that the tolerance of aliens was possible only when the dynamics of power favoured such a thing, but if not – then not. The white invasion of Africa, the arrival in Africa of Europeans, apart from breeding ignorance and cruelty, had committed a sin even more grievous when judged from the steely perspectives of power. The white invasion had failed to make itself strong enough and awful enough to prevail.

If that were the case, then what was being played out in Zimbabwe was a Greek tragedy. The whites in Africa would be seen to have failed, not because they had been murderous

– they had certainly tried their best on this score – but because they had not been murderous enough. They could never quite bring themselves to recognize the humanity of their serfs, thus they took them insufficiently seriously to exterminate them in the tradition of more successful occupations in the United States or Australia. Now, they found themselves, at the end of history, marooned amongst an indigenous population who felt for them nothing but loathing and contempt.

It was difficult to square this bleak view with what I knew about many white Zimbabweans who, by any measure, could be said to have fought and struggled to bring the Mugabe regime to power, and who had identified passionately with the new Zimbabwe. What about Stavros whose identification with the country was so deep it was impossible to see him anywhere else, and who blended into the land like some large and perfectly adapted great tree? What of Judith Todd, or her father Garfield Todd? Both had been to jail for supporting majority rights in Zimbabwe, both had backed democracy all the way. In 1996, however, people like these were beginning to feel the heat. Their crime, it seemed, was to do what they had always done, to say what they had always said, to be what they always were – African liberals who believed in tolerance, consistency and fairness. These turned out not to be advantages, and the sign of their crime was the shade of their skin.

I hoped to see Stavros again but I got there too late; the last white man in Mount Darwin, the Comrade-Mayor, died shortly before I arrived. Stavros, who was known as 'this controversial Greek', and wasn't a Greek at all, who wasn't any longer a Cypriot, who had become a Zimbab-wean; who spoke as he felt and was at home in his town.

Stavros who had always said exactly what he felt and sometimes had to be reprimanded for it: 'Would you please
refrain from shaking your finger at the Minister.' Stavros
who had saved Mrs Thatcher's balls. Stavros who had
refused to sit as an MP. He wasn't after a seat – anywhere,
said Stavros; sitting was not what he did. What he did, and
the thousands who came to pay their respects at his funeral
knew it, from the Salvation Army to the school choirs, to
the chiefs from miles around, to the four blind families
whom, it turned out, Stavros had been supporting for years;
the Aids orphans, and the crowds who came simply because
they knew and liked the man – dozens were there because
they liked the man – and they all knew that what Stavros did
was one sure thing – he belonged. He had arrived from
nowhere and become an African.

Judith Todd told a meeting of writers that 'Whites,
Indians and Coloureds are being detached from the living,
breathing body of Zimbabwe.' It was a statement that
anyone in Zimbabwe would have found very hard to fault.
She went on to say that she had expected 'a wave of anti-
white feeling immediately after Independence. I didn't
expect it now, so many years later.' Her surprise seemed
entirely understandable, yet in 1996 her remarks drew down
on the Todds, father and daughter, a storm of abuse. Her
comments were a cheap trick, the *Sunday Mail* declared,
designed to disguise, 'the liberal dilemma.' Although people
such as the Todds might once have supported freedom for
the black majority they were, at heart, champions of white
privilege. Like whites everywhere, they fixed things to suit
themselves. Black people, declared the *Mail*, had been
deliberately handicapped. Therefore whites deserved similar
treatment: shackles should be 'fastened to their legs and

hands' so that those who were lagging behind could 'catch up with them'.

This reverse racism undermined all the old pieties. It questioned the very notion that people of different back-grounds or skin colours could live together in any kind of amity. Large groups would not tolerate anything but very small, impotent minorities, who should keep their heads down, their mouths shut. It strengthened the view that separation, partition or oblivion was the destiny of people who did not conform to the ways of the rulers. It suggested that Hobbes was right and morality or fairness grew out of power; that those in power set the meaning of those words; and it said, finally, that any other way of looking at things was sentimental cant. It was a luxury available in the warm spells that cropped up between the ice ages of absolute rule, when real power need not show its hand – but it was self-delusion all the same.

I looked hard at Zimbabwe and I didn't like what I saw – not because it was out of the ordinary but because it was pretty normal. If similar circumstances were to prevail in any country, no matter how liberal it liked to consider itself, then the State, the Power, the Leadership, would not hesitate to act in exactly the same way: it would censor the press, jail its opponents and attack all who opposed it as enemies of the people.

Whites in Zimbabwe seemed to be seen, increasingly, in much the way Asians had been seen under the rule of Idi Amin: rich, oppressive and removable. One man who had given serious thought to resolving the problem was Philip Chiyangwa. He had an office in downtown Harare where he held open court. Chiyangwa was in his thirties, ambitious, said to be rich, and said to be related to Robert Mugabe – but then rumours were legion in Harare of all sorts of family connections with the President. Chiyangwa was a good-looking man and his photographs were to be seen all over the walls of his office. He was pictured in various guises: the businessman, the artist, the aloof vision-ary, the impresario. His interests over the years had been varied: he had promoted wrestlers, he had sold musical shows, and now he was interested in commerce. He dressed in a kind of zebra chic, and so did all his young staff: they wore white shirts on which two carved fighting forms confronted each other across a row of buttons which ran between these antagonists like the Berlin Wall. Chiyangwa had started something called the Affirmative Action Group. It was staffed by young men devoted to the cause and to their Leader.

Chiyangwa wanted whites out. It was a cleansing pro-gramme to which he gave the ugly name of 'indigenization'.

'Or else what?' I asked.

He didn't mess around. 'Or else – Rwanda.'

The massacres by the Hutus of Tutsis in Rwanda, a few years earlier, were still vivid, and his answer had all the degree of pugnacious overkill, as well as the violent vul-garity, that marked out Chiyangwa as a man destined to succeed in politics in a country where force was always first, and where threats, boots, sticks and bullets were customarily used to cow your opponents. It was also, given the scale of killing in Rwanda, an obscene reference. More than that, it was not accurate. How was the small white group of business people in Harare to be despatched? Machetes?

A bank of telephones at Chiyangwa's elbow rang two at

a time like unfed infants crying for attention and he answered them simultaneously, murmuring into the squalling receivers until, one by one, they were soothed, fell silent, and could be returned to their cradles.

'Our whites,' said Philip Chiyangwa, 'are no good. Put them in London and they wouldn't be able to cross the road.'

That was an interesting remark. For decades, indeed for centuries, whites in Africa considered themselves to be natural aristocrats. Here at last was somebody who contested that, someone who didn't just think very little of the whites, whom he had, as it were, inherited. He didn't want them in any shape or form; he would have traded them for just about anyone else.

I asked Chiyangwa what he'd like to do with his whites.

'Ship them out,' he said. 'Get in a new lot. Short-term contracts.' He'd settle for South Africans, if he had to, anyone at all except 'our whites'.

On the wall behind him an old fading poster advertised a wrestling match between Pistol Pez Whatley and Hercules. Their arms outstretched, the two wrestlers reached for each other's throats.

The conversation had become really interesting. The question was – to what degree was Chiyangwa bluffing? How much of this talk was exactly that – hot air? I thought back to the lessons we had learnt in my boarding hostel, when death was the ultimate player and came in various guises, some of which had their uses. If one began with death as it were, and worked back from there, how serious was Chiyangwa? Clearly the talk of Rwanda was bluff. He didn't have the means or, I suspected, the rage required to begin full-scale butchery of his fellow Zimbabweans on anything like the Rwandan level. So what then? A war? A guerrilla struggle? But Zimbabwe had had its war, and won its war. The once mighty oppressor had been reduced to a small group of frightened citizens getting older and more confused with each year that passed. Besides, a white overlord who has trouble crossing the road is not much of a danger.

So what then, in place of bloody apocalypse, did Chiyangwa want?

He showed me a letter he had sent to white-owned firms, to banks and insurance companies, warning them that unless black people were given a part to play in their companies they were in dead trouble. I said that the letter looked to me not so much a political demand, but more like an old-fashioned extortion racket: demanding money with menaces. Chiyangwa disagreed. The Affirmative Action Group was merely asking for its money back, money whites had stolen from black Zimbabweans, money whites had grown fat upon over the years, 'black money'. The time had come to make them disgorge.

Well, that was not what Robert Mugabe's politics pointed towards, the kind of Maoist great leap forward with the wholesale nationalization of industry and the liquidation of the 'bourgeoisie'. It wasn't to be forced collectivization as Stalin had done it. It wasn't to be the mass dispersal of whites from their comfortable bungalows and farms in the leafy suburbs out into the countryside in the manner of Pol Pot and the Khmer Rouge. If Philip Chiyangwa was the future, it was to be death by a thousand cuts. It was also – and this was very interesting – about money, and that meant it was also about modernity. Philip Chiyangwa wasn't after the sort of rural revolution for the masses and public ownership of farms and industries of the sort Robert Mugabe had always hinted at but never quite managed to carry out. Chiyangwa's was a much more familiar revolution, a war of the market place. He was a modernizer. Whites were bad because basically they were anachronistic, old-fashioned, slow, and on their way out. People like Philip Chiyangwa wanted not the past, but the future; he was not on the side of the serfs, he was one of the suits.

There was also in him another characteristic that distinguishes modern power from forms previously deployed by other tyrannical states. It is in a sense the characteristic of power at the end of the second millennium that it is interwoven with professional commerce, that it is a willing accomplice of the political movements and particularly of dictatorships. In tyrannies politics is always, sooner or later, indistinguishable from commerce. Everyone, eventually, is on the take. Where Roman tyrants took an interest or a pleasure in spilling blood for its own sake, in our times murder is really an aspect of marketing. The death camps might have been run by armed guards, but they were subsidized by business and supported by investment bankers. You could be taken in by Chiyangwa's rhetoric – you might have had the impression that you were talking politics with a serious politician because he used terms like justice and peace and nationhood – but in fact you were talking loot.

There was also an interesting aesthetic argument made against whites. It went like this. Europeans suffered from a kind of aesthetic deficiency in their looks, in the way they walked, in the way they dressed, they simply didn't look good, they were alien and old-fashioned. There was a certain truth in this. You had only to walk through the streets of Bulawayo to see that the dress sense of many whites was as lamentable as their racial insensitivities. The effect was that everything about these individuals – what they earned, what they owned, how they lived, what they thought, the food they ate and the clothes they wore – now began to conspire to condemn them.

What struck me about this was how very close the disparagement was to the sorts of things that white South Africans once held to be true when they thought of black people, and the way in which it had justified their relentless persecution of these insignificant others. The white citizens of Zimbabwe had now come close to reaching the stage that preceded the final action taken by the executioner as much to relieve his rage and frustration as to destroy the victim. Blank refusal to comprehend that they are doomed inspires exasperation in the executioner. These silly creatures persist in continuing with their pretence at a normal life and wilfully fail to recognize that someone seriously wishes them gone forever from the face of the earth – they make themselves responsible for what is going to happen to them because they have driven their reasonable tormentors mad by their culpable failure to understand how hated they are.

Foreign backers of the Mugabe regime also weighed in. The whites of Zimbabwe deserved extinction one British left-wing devotee of Mugabe claimed; not only were they racists, but their furnishings were lousy, they had a reprehensible fondness for Dralon, they knew nothing of the music of Bach, they suffered from damaged psyches and an impoverished gene-pool, and she predicted the collapse of what she called 'settler-stock'.

This was tyranny as we knew it in our times: good reasons were being found for doing bad things to small groups of people who were said to wield influence far beyond their numbers. These scapegoats were being marked out for destruction, but they would also continue to be useful as scapegoats even after their destruction. It was possible to argue that the white minority in Zimbabwe in its small and incoherent and frightened nature had already been destroyed, but it was possible for a vengeful clique of hate-mongers to continue to target the scapegoats long after they had all been killed. After all, the Jews of Poland continued to be hated long after they had been liquidated.

Still there was my unanswered question as to what degree of force would be applied to get rid of the whites. Would people like Chiyangwa have the courage to make a revolution and live with the revolutionary results: the bones and bodies and mass graves, the children crying in the streets? I asked Philip Chiyangwa what would happen if he got his way, if the next day all whites handed over their businesses and packed up and left. Would that solve the problem?

That would go a long way, but it was not all he wanted. 'Then we go after the Asians,' he said. 'I have a bone to pick with them.'

My account of this visit ran in a British paper and provoked some anger. The Ministry of Information in Harare called me 'hysterical' and went on: 'The assertion that black Zimbabweans are waging an unholy war (anti-white crusade) through indigenization is absolute folly. It is quite clear that Mr Hope does not understand what affirmative action is all about. His allegation that Zimbabwean whites are an endangered species is ludicrous as it is a known fact that there are numerous former Rhodesians begging to be allowed to come back and settle in Zimbabwe again. It is not true that white Zimbabweans are a timid, defenceless people who keep their heads down fearing for their lives in the face of accusations by blacks of incompetence, laziness and racism, while they maintain a stranglehold on the economy. One only needs to visit the commercial farms owned by whites to see who is timid and defenceless. The white man's world reigns supreme and is usually delivered with such godly finality as to brook no argument.'

The cheerfully unrepentant Stalinist *Sunday Mail* renamed me 'Christian Hopeless' and found me guilty of 'monumental falsehoods'. I was 'in intimate cahoots with all the colonial and racist forces that have depended for their viability and wealth on subjugating and humiliating black people'. Had I not, after all, confessed myself to be the neighbour of Dr Verwoerd?

Before I left Harare, I came across a little satire, written in the Sixties, and circulated anonymously during the years of UDI. It lampoons the crudity, ridiculous self-importance and the terrible want of imagination of the old Smith regime. Its author turned out to be Judith Todd. The play contains an uncannily prescient speech by a black MP in the old Rhodesian parliament, who looks into the future, and whose words ring down the years:

'Many of you will leave this land eventually. Some of your children will stay. And you will leave with us the final burden of pleading for justice for your children and your children's children. I fear that when that day comes my brothers will say: "What knew we of justice?" And in the evening the sun will turn red with blood. Our blood. Your blood. No one discriminates against the colour of blood.'

SIXTEEN

PREACHING FROGS

I spent time, in the next years, between ex-Yugoslavia and Zimbabwe, and one reflected the other. Both could be horribly funny at times; the modern police-state is tragedy shot through with bloody farce, tedium fractured by hilarity: so many laws, so many crooks, such self-importance, and so much loot. What do you find in a country that has locked itself in and thrown away the key? You find how well the rulers live – victims on one side, investment bankers on the other, gaol and golf. When people are starving it is amazing how many people are making money hand over fist. Terror is good for business. These people were absurd – but they were in charge, and that's what counted. If they said it, they meant it – because they said it. Something of their Leader's pneumaticism clung to them, they inflated, they tended to moralize a good deal. They were successful crusading bores, free of guilt or conscience or chagrin, and you knew (this was the worst of it) they would stay that way when their world was turned on its head, and a new order replaced the old. Then they would simply become 'something in business'. It was in police-states that you saw the real relation of these lackeys to the Leader: they represented the corrupt class of preachers.

★

One day, in the shaky sunshine of a Belgrade spring, soon after the Big Walks, I visited a beautiful house in the central city. The woman who owned it had declared it a kind of political detoxification clinic and called it The Centre for Cultural Contamination. 'Ours is an Orwellian universe come true,' she told me. In Britain they had mad cow disease, in Belgrade they had 'mad Serb' disease. She described the peculiar claptrap the lordlings who batten on a despotic state tirelessly dish out to their victims: 'It's like living amongst preaching frogs,' she said. 'Everything they touch, they steal. Everything they steal becomes useless. Including our values. We have none.'

Not long after that, I was back in Zimbabwe, sitting over lunch with some big-wigs of the ruling party who seemed to have forgotten the transgressions of 'Christian Hopeless' (perhaps they never read the Party newspapers). They were on good form – servants at play at the lunch table of the Lord – but men who seemed fairly normal much of the time had fatally inhaled the perfume wafting from the Leader. Every now and then they suddenly showed themselves as they were; deeply disturbed. As a matter of course, they were detached from anything like reality, but in a very genuine, wide-eyed way.

I'd experienced something of the sort in Belgrade, among followers of Slobodan Milosovic: after talking good sense about, say, chess or poetry, the man on your right would suddenly reveal the true secret of the universe – there was an American Jewish Masonic New World Order, closeted in New York, and it controlled the world. The Harare big-shots did something similar. After touching

upon cricket or hunting or South Africa, or lumber concessions, they began talking about powerful groups of ex-
Rhodesians plotting to overthrow the Mugabe government
and restore colonial rule. These conspirators were backed by
coteries of British homosexuals in high places. The news fell
strangely between coffee and dessert. The mind didn't just
boggle, it left the room and collapsed in hysterical laughter.

As things turned out a few years later, that was a mistake.
The elements present in despotism – at once bizarre,
ridiculous, open to parody or laughter – do not render the
tyranny any less serious; quite the contrary. Mugabe, as he
grew older certainly seemed to grow more and more a
parody, a stock cartoon of the local dictator. He was the
quintessential caricature in all the things that make up what
you might call the decor of tyranny: in his facial furniture –
the tiny moustache that visited his upper lip like a fleeting
salute to the men he uncannily resembled, Adolf Hitler and
Joseph Stalin; in the tunic, the fist, in the attitude of brooding
solemnity; in his record for murder; in the elusive malice; in
the madness that swirled around him; and in the fine words
he spoke – the noble sentiments of love and devotion, to
which otherwise apparently sensible people were horribly
susceptible. Mugabe had it all, and maybe that's why people
never saw it. Maybe there was something in his unbridled
power that made it almost impossible to take seriously – until
the killing started – and even then lots of people still could
not see it. Even now, who he is and what he stands for and
what he believes are mysteries. I knew that what I heard
about foreign gay gangs was the talk of the despot's court
because these officials caught the inflexions of the Leader's
voice, they were speaking likenesses of their master.

★

What is known about Mugabe's youth is astonishingly meagre. Robert Gabriel Mugabe was born in the countryside in what was called Rhodesia on 21 February 1924, in a little Mission, west of Salisbury. He came from a Zezutu grouping, allied to the main Shona tribe, who make up the great majority of Zimbabwe's population. He was raised in the Catholic Missions of Africa, as many of us were. He grew up in a village attached to his Jesuit Mission in a place called Katuma, where his father worked as a carpenter. This Nazarene upbringing, together with the spiritual devotion of his Catholic mother, and the devout atmosphere of his home, led his mother to hope that the boy might one day become a priest. Mugabe's father deserted the family early and Robert never forgot or forgave him. The burning need for vengeance began when he was a very small child and never left him.

Something has been made of the fact that Mugabe was schooled by the Jesuits, perhaps because the name, particularly for European writers, has sinister connotations, but this old affectation throws very little light on Mugabe's character or his later career. Much more important was the fact that these were Irish Jesuits and that they ran a Mission School. Many people were educated by Roman Catholic Irish Missionaries in Africa and their education was delivered with a particular stamp. I received something very similar from Irish Christian Brothers, hard men from Cork, and the great emphasis in the schools was on literacy, tight discipline, and the overwhelming certainty which was supplied by the dogmas of the one true Catholic faith. These men, who often relied on the belt to keep order, none the less believed entirely in their faith, and inculcated in their students a lively sense both of fundamental certainties and of

Irish history. Our teachers, in very many cases, were republicans, and told of the struggle against Britain, of the struggle of colonial countries against their masters, of the qualities of political freedom. It is perhaps easier to understand Mugabe's natural truculence and his long memory of slights by keeping the Irish dimension in mind.

At Katuma Mission in the 1930s, Robert Mugabe was taken up by an Irish Jesuit named Father O'Hea, who later recalled that very early he had recognized in the boy qualities of dedication and perseverance. He wrote that, 'An exceptional heart rushed Mugabe ahead . . .' O'Hea believed that education was wider than the official syllabus, and he had a discerning eye for the dictators who were then emerging on the world stage. Mugabe watched the unfolding of the Second World War through Father O'Hea's eyes. O'Hea recalled later that the boy always said very little, but made it quite clear that he did not like Hitler. It is probably not useful to make too much of this tantalizing detail. We have only O'Hea's word for it and, in any event, it would not be the first time that something said with such certainty about Robert Mugabe turned out to have no substance whatever. His life has been ceaseless manoeuvre, he has been one of the great political opportunists of our time. It is perfectly possible that he did not like Hitler, but he has shown a devotion to other dictators, remarkable in its consistency.

None the less, this apparent good sense displayed so early, has given comfort to commentators ever since Mugabe came to power. They like to talk of the 'ascetic', and the 'puritan', the patient idealist who did not drink or smoke, who might occasionally threaten his people or his enemies with destruction, but when he did, was not to be taken too seriously because he didn't really mean it. It has been a career involving an enormous capacity to dupe his public, his Party and his people. No one, it seemed, had ever listened very carefully to Robert Mugabe in what was his natural mode of expression, as the schoolteacher in front of a rather unruly class.

Robert Mugabe left what was then Rhodesia, in 1949, to study at Fort Hare University in South Africa and there he became as passionate a believer in Marxist-Leninism as he once had been in Catholicism. Ever since then he has made a point of referring to the strength of his new faith in evangelical terms. Even so, people have preferred to ignore what he says, and have treated him as some sort of non-violent pupil of Mahatma Gandhi. Robert Mugabe is a good chap at heart, who likes cricket and good tailoring. It is a further indication of how, when a tyranny is in full swing, it survives and prospers by the connivance of the world at large, but also of its victims. The fact that he had abused and murdered many of his people was overlooked for the very cynical reason that they were black, and therefore really could expect no better.

Since 1 January 1988, Robert Mugabe has been Executive President and the Head of State; the boy from the Jesuit Mission has become Lord of all he surveys. He has been in charge for over twenty years. The first half of his reign was soaked in blood, the second half has been sunk in despondency, drought, and corruption. In a way it does not matter. The Leader is not just in the ascendant. He has become the landscape, but he remains a mystery. In the absence of other evidence, people have had to make him up as they go along and the Robert Mugabe you recognize will depend on which version you last listened to.

Modern tyranny is a form of modern storytelling, except that the story is, as it were, carved in the living flesh of its listeners. Tyrannical stories are the opposite of the stories Scheherazade told during the Thousand and One Nights and which she was obliged to keep on telling, and to keep on refreshing, because if she stopped she would be killed.

The extreme scarcity of details about the early life of Robert Gabriel Mugabe allowed for speculation and rumour to fill the void, but all the official stories, like most of the readings, were false. The truth seemed to me that there had been no earlier life, there had only been a kind of creation myth – a story of how the Leader came to be. This sketch had come to be taken as gospel and had hardened into dogma. The curious and ferocious non-being of Robert Mugabe was intolerable to his people and so a tale was made up, because all of us perhaps need to believe if not in a life to come, then in a previous life. People needed to believe there had been the usual nexus of human relationships out of which Robert Mugabe sprang, as there was for most people: interconnected events, a biography, a life. What no one could accept was that, just possibly, in his case there had been no previous existence, there was just this furious vacancy, that he had no existence outside his exercise of power, that he was, truly, a modest, shy, retiring, implacable fatal force, a perfume that was picked up in snatches when the wind wafted it in the right direction, but which vanished again into the nothingness it had always been. The feeling when you wait for Zimbabweans to tell you who they think he is, might be best summed up in that old children's rhyme: 'As I was going up the stair I met a man who wasn't there, he wasn't there again today, how I wish he'd go away!'

From time to time, however, Mugabe has made a mistake, and in his mistakes a glimpse of the man is possible.

Zimbabwe had been a strange place for a long time, a land where elections were regularly held, in the fine expectation of getting the backing the President assumed was his by right. The President's will, power and ambition coincided with the will of the 'broad masses'. Such a situation worked more or less flawlessly: President, Party and People constituted a holy trinity against which no one could prevail – and those who tried were dismissed as eccentrics, traitors, racists, or dreamers and might be ignored or beaten or imprisoned or murdered. Then, as the millennium approached, Robert Mugabe decided to sort out the white farmers. He was going to do it legitimately of course, and he made the usual professions of affection:

'We have not stopped singing to the theme of unity and the theme of love. Even the whites are free to live here. But they must change. Your kind – the British kind – are very difficult to change. We rate them as the most conceited, the most arrogant, the most selfish and the most racist in our situation.'

The big year was to be 2000: Mugabe scripted, and forced upon the voters of Zimbabwe, a question to be answered by a straight yes or no in a referendum: 'Would you like me to take the land away from white farmers?'

There were more declarations of affection, reasonableness, honour: 'We ourselves should not ever ever . . . as government, as a party, as individuals within the party, be seen to be acting in a racist way, blacks against whites, we refuse to do that. The whites wouldn't be here if I was like that. I would have been an [Idi] Amin if I was racist . . . we can't do things like that.'

There was something else however, besides the problem of the white farmers; there was another, new enemy. There was a resurgence of the talk I'd heard some time earlier but now it was official, the President said so – a homosexual Rhodesian-British gang was plotting against him. The mood was perfectly caught in the interview Robert Mugabe gave to the BBC shortly before the 2000 referendum.

'I understand they [the Labour party in Britain] have gays amongst them but that's their own affair. What we do not want and desire is for them to foist their own inhuman tendencies on us . . . It is our criticism of homosexuality here at home that has offended them. I had a meeting with them that lasted two hours – I thought it a very friendly meeting. The following morning he [Foreign Office Minister Peter Hain] had his Mr Tatchell ambush me outside the hotel. I felt I was assaulted but he just managed to put his hand here on this arm. I don't want to bring [Tony] Blair into this but I know Peter Hain is reputed to be gay and to be the wife of Tatchell, that's what the papers say. And so if the following morning the husband ambushed me and the previous night I had had discussions with the wife, the conclusion I come to is that the two had discussed it.'

The cause of this anger was an attempt the year before, by the gay rights activist, Peter Tatchell, to serve a citizen's arrest on Mugabe when the President was staying in a Knightsbridge hotel. Robert Mugabe had been on his way to Harrods when the group ambushed him. It was wrong, they said, for a man who tortured journalists to be shopping at Harrods. The hand laid upon Mugabe was not just any hand, it was the touch of a gay man and gays, Robert Mugabe had said, were lower than pigs and dogs. As sensitive to the touch of a homosexual as the princess was to the pea, Mugabe recoiled and 'tried to wriggle free', the newspapers reported – a phrase to be relished. The Sacred Presence had been assaulted in a public place by a sexual leper. Protests were made to the Foreign Office. Back in Harare, there were demands for the head of the CIO, who had been slow to react to the sacrilege. It was remarkable stuff, demented, sour, hilarious, deeply revealing of the provincialism and the narrowness of politics in Zimbabwe and, like all jokes in terrorized states, deeply dangerous and a warning of what was to come.

Then the voters went to the polls in 2000, and they did the unthinkable, they said no to the President's proposal that white farmers be deprived of their land without compensation.

The shock was pretty much mutual: the country surprised itself by suddenly standing up to the tyrant; the tyrant was deeply angered by this display of ingratitude after all he had done for his people. He felt such thanklessness was unpardonable, it would not be countenanced. He was sending his goon squads, his 'war vets', to hunt down the enemy in his grasp – these 'British', these traitors, these hardhearted racist renegades.

'What is our crime, what have we done?' cried the victims of these raids. They questioned in vain. They were 'British' and that was enough.

If the British government raised any objection to the treatment meted out to whites, Robert Mugabe told it to take its 'settlers' back. He had always behaved with exceptional venom when he was crossed, and his hatred of Britain had grown with each rebuke, each mention of imposing sanctions, each report of another farmer killed. From then it was war. Black dissidents were the white man's 'tea-boys'. Deaths of white farmers were alluded to in gloating terms. This was a new war of liberation, waged against a mighty and wicked enemy by the downtrodden peasants of Zimbabwe, determined to reclaim their country.

The unleashing of that war involved invasions of white-owned farms, killings and torture, and it was led by a man who was, in many ways, a sub-version of Mugabe himself. His name was Hitler Hunzvi.

SEVENTEEN

THE RISE AND RISE OF
HITLER HUNZVI

The story of Comrade Chengerai Hitler Hunzvi is an implausible melodrama of cruelty and unwitting comedy turned bloody, all the more disconcerting for being perfectly usual – under the circumstances. It throws light on Robert Mugabe's way of neutralizing a rival, as well as his nostalgic hankering after the glories of war. Hunzvi was a peculiar amalgam: a preacher who called for blood, a doctor who tortured his patients, a 'liberator' who milked the old soldiers he said he wished to help. He encapsulated the modern henchman's ability to seek and find a semi-divine hero, to fix adoringly upon the Leader's political career the way saints of the Catholic Church once fixed upon the passion of Christ.

Quite how he came to be called Hitler is not clear. He once said that he chose the name himself because the Fuehrer's inner weather appealed to him – 'He was a hard, dry man' – though he pointed out crucial differences between himself and the original Adolf: 'Hitler was anti-everyone but I am not. He was a fascist and I am a progressive communist.' There is some evidence that Hunzvi's father gave his son the name and Hunzvi enjoyed its shock value. The Fuehrer had been a victim of Western propaganda, he once explained, and western Europe was only against him because he lost.

Hunzvi was one of those people of whom no one has heard, until everyone has heard of him. In the Seventies, he was in Poland training as a medical doctor, and there he married a woman named Wieslawa. It was an odd match. He was a supporter of the Polish communist government, but his wife backed Solidarity and reform. Hunzvi's idols were the Stalinist chiefs of East Germany and North Korea. He sat at the feet of Nicolai Ceaucescu in Bucharest, when he studied 'strategy and political administration' at the Romanian Military Academy. The Romanian tyrant, the Carpathian Oak, the Danube of Wisdom, was at the height of his power and Hunzvi came away much braced by their meeting: 'I used to like him. He used to visit us there and was very concerned about "the freedom of Africans".'

The Hunzvis returned to Zimbabwe, where the marriage came apart. 'He treated me worse than a dog,' his wife said later. 'He knelt over me and used his medical training to try to stop the bleeding with a towel. Then he tied the towel around my neck and started to squeeze it tighter and tighter, I realized it could be the end of me.' Eventually, Wieslawa Hunzvi fled back to Poland, where she lives with her two sons from the marriage. She wrote a book about her experiences, and called it *White Slave*.

Though Hunzvi claimed to have fought with the guerrilla armies in the war against Ian Smith's Rhodesian forces, his wife maintained he'd never heard a shot fired in anger. He was of the camp of Joshua Nkomo and, like Mugabe, was imprisoned by the Smith regime. Something of a dandy with a taste for natty suits, Hitler Hunzvi, in Dirk Coetzee's careful use of the term, was a thug, but he was that very particular kind of thug which modern police-states, with their mix of high-sounding civic virtue and relentless kleptomania, seem to produce – thugs yes, but thugs with celestial yearnings, one eye on heaven, the other on the money.

It was when he was practising as a GP in Harare that Hunzvi saw a gap in the market. He took something called the Disability Fund for War Veterans and did with it what traders do with obscure financial instruments: he milked it for all he was worth. It was a wonderful scam, beautifully simple, and highly patriotic: he examined the wartime injuries of former soldiers, estimated their market value and then helped the veterans to claim compensation. His master-stroke came when he examined his own war wounds, declared himself '117% disabled', and drew the appropriate compensation.

In 1997 Hunzvi was suddenly famous, feared, and far too ambitious for Mugabe's taste. He upstaged the regime, he led his war vets on to white farms, he set up noisy demon-strations in the streets of Harare and he made a fuss about official indifference to the old fighters. He demanded war pensions and, at one point, he picketed the High Court. He loathed the judiciary almost as much as Robert Mugabe did. For a time the Leader seemed at a loss as to how to deal with this rabble-rouser. Hunzvi was unrepentant: 'No one can stop the revolution we've started.'

The 'war vets' were nothing of the kind, they were really a rag-tag army of landless people mixed in with Mugabe youth brigades, who went on a rampage and invaded farms around the country. These 'invasions' were forms of armed robbery, led by a man without remorse who liked to turn them into crusades blessed by the Almighty. When the freedom fighters crossed borders to wage a military war against the Rhodesian government, they had no food and water but God provided them with everything along the way, Hunzvi assured his troops. 'Likewise, veterans are going into the farms with nothing but they will get something to eat from the farms.'

Perhaps the older man looked on Hunzvi with a certain pang of envy; he was in many ways an echo of the young Mugabe. There he was, out on the farms, the revolutionary nationalist, shooting settlers – and that had always been Robert Mugabe's role. Without for a moment setting out to mimic each other, they were uncannily alike: Mugabe, the schoolteacher who became a tyrant; Hunzvi, a one-time Methodist Sunday School preacher who became a torturer. However, to take farms away from white settlers was right in principle, but wrong when Hitler did it without consulting the Leader.

So Mugabe did what he has always done when faced by a rival, he moved to neutralize the threat; he embraced him, then planned his downfall. He took over Hitler's fervour for the old fighters, he reminded the country he was Patron of the War Veterans' Association, and that he, Robert Mugabe, was the scourge of the settlers. To show that he and not Hunzvi still ran the show, Mugabe threw money around. He announced that the war vets, who numbered anything from thirty to fifty thousand ex-soldiers, would receive large lump sums, plus monthly pensions that easily exceeded what most Zimbabweans earned in a year. The Zimbabwean currency nose-dived, but Mugabe was back in the driving seat. Next, he went after the upstart who'd challenged him.

Hunzvi was hauled into court, charged with defrauding

the War Veterans Association, and, for a while, he seemed headed for jail. Then came Mugabe's defeat in the referendum in 2000, and suddenly Hunzvi was back in business. The charges against him were dropped, Hitler pledged his loyalty to the Leader and the Leader gave Hitler his head.

In February 2000, Comrade Hunzvi, again at the head of thousands of war veterans, cut through the white farmers and their black labourers like the arrow of God he believed himself to be. When the first farmers died he remarked that revolution was always bloody and no one 'should raise eyebrows over the death of four white farmers'. Within weeks, thirty people were dead, more were raped or tortured, and thousands of farm-workers were dispossessed of their homes and their jobs. The ex-Sunday School teacher increasingly portrayed himself as a black Christ at the head of a band of disciples wielding guns and knives: 'Jesus said to his disciples go and preach the word of God to the people so that whosoever believeth in the Son, the Holy Spirit and the Father will get eternal life,' Hunzvi said. As blood flowed the rhetoric grew more flamboyant: 'When they asked God about the resources, Jesus said that the birds of the sky are flying and there are animals in the forest for you to eat. We are no different from that. God will always provide those that have a just cause with something to eat.'

Food came not from heaven but from Party Head-quarters. It was not clear from which government coffers millions of dollars were being siphoned to feed the thirty thousand war veterans on the commercial farms, but few doubted where the battle-plans for Hunzvi's invasions were formulated. I always got the impression that in the mind of Hitler Hunzvi, God and Robert Mugabe were closely related. Of God he said: 'He told us to take the farms.' Robert Mugabe, he prophesied, was the 'Messiah', destined to rule for ever. Hunzvi said his own role was to lead his people out of bondage and into the promised land. It's worth remembering that Hitler's wife, always sensitive about her husband's name when they lived in Poland, called him 'Moses' – she was more accurate than she knew.

Dr Hunzvi's surgery in the Budiriro neighbourhood of Harare, was a rather ugly, low building, with a blue tin roof and his name starkly lettered across the front wall, but it no longer served its patients. Instead it became the headquarters of the farm-invasions. A series of hand-written documents were later made public by some disaffected mole in the security services. These documents, some on Dr Hunzvi's headed notepaper – 'We Care For Your Health' – detail how and why the whites were to be driven from their farms: 'Since white farmers are resisting African freedom, and are now engaging in para-military tendencies to counter back economic advancement – the War Veterans were obliged to respond.'

These secret Hunzvi memos echo orders from on high, they are spiny with the unhinged logic and speckled with the hatred that Mugabe made his trademark. The white farmers were 'the enemy', this was 'war', the 'nation' would fight back. A mobile 'National Reaction Force' was to be formed by Hunzvi: 'The nation is faced with a politically motivated uprising promoted by the former colonial masters. The colonial masters want Zimbabwe to be a neo-colony.' The best method of defence was frontal assault on the enemy, and they were identified, and doomed: 'Zimbabweans under the guidance of the War Veterans have taken a stand to occupy white-owned farms . . .'

Dr Hunzvi's surgery was also used as a torture centre. Gangs of men would comb the neighbourhoods of Harare and bring back to the surgery those suspected of being supporters of the opposition parties. Victims were beaten or given electric shocks. Survivors lucky enough to reach the casualty ward of Harare hospital showed bruises, welts, burst ear drums and burns. One man told how a rubber strip had been bound tightly around the tip of his penis; two other men, naked and bruised lay on the floor beside him. He had been beaten 'with electric cables and wooden poles like table legs'. Police reports implicated Hunzvi as the man behind the kidnappings and torture but the state declined to prosecute.

The forms of torture were reminiscent of the Matabele-land campaign, and indeed, there were reports that Hitler was just a figure-head and the campaign was really led by the old commander of Five Brigade during the Gukura-hundi, Perence Shiri. Other secret documents which have emerged, record meetings of high ranking military officers. The minutes of one of these secret meetings, held in Harare on 2 February 2001, suggest how Hunzvi was seen by those who really ran things. Asked to sum up his feelings, a 'Comrade Mudehwe' responds that, in his opinion, Hunzvi is not so much a leader, but he is more like 'a condom' . . . For the moment he fitted the need – 'He gets used, then disposed of immediately. If he reacts we deal with him personally.'

As things turned out, 'disposal' was not necessary. Hitler Hunzvi exited with a fine sense of timing. His end was as murky as his beginning: swathed in lies and propaganda. He'd been admitted to hospital for various complaints and was said to be recovering when he collapsed suddenly in a

Bulawayo hotel, and he died on 4 June 2001 in Harare's Parirenyatwa Hospital. Though he died in the Coronary Care Unit from what was later said to have been cerebral malaria, he almost certainly died from Aids. He was fifty-two.

It was the beginning of another career for him as hero. Mugabe's affection for his rivals has always increased in direct proportion to the length of time they have been dead. Hitler Hunzvi was solemnly laid to rest in Heroes' Acre, a patch of earth that one day will give a new Zimbabwe as much trouble as Lenin's tomb gives the new Russians. At his graveside, the Leader reached for rough poetry to sing the martyr to his rest: 'Go well, son of the soil . . .' As the tyrant's victims have their unmarked graves, their burial pits, their execution ditches, their funeral pyres, so the tyrant's helpers have their Valhalla.

Not many foreigners get to see Heroes' Acre, not many Zimbabweans see it either, since the place is off limits. It is one of the weirdest burial grounds anywhere in southern Africa, a haunted place where war is raised to the condition of a holy sacrament, and a fitting resting place for Hitler Hunzvi. The North Koreans, the ideological godfathers of the Mugabe revolution, built Heroes' Acre in their own image. It covers fifty-seven acres and is guarded by soldiers with fixed bayonets. A giant sword stood over it and at night was visible for miles and miles, tipped with a five-metre illuminated point of light, flashing the national colours of yellow, green and red. It was switched on at precisely eleven minutes past six each evening, even when other parts of Harare were experiencing power cuts, and at the same time each morning it was switched off. It was an independent entity, unaffected by the real events of the rest of the country: hunger, unhappiness, repression, a cruel drought and the deepest recession for sixty years. Heroes' Acre was self-serving, self-referring and self-perpetuating. It was a tabernacle, a temple, a holy of holies, a shrine to all Robert Mugabe believed to be most precious: soldiers, banners, and symbols of the party, ZANU-PF, which was personified and became the mystical consort of the Saviour of Zimbabwe, much as the Roman Catholic Church described itself as the bride of Christ. In its propaganda, the Party pledged devotion to the being who sanctified, justified, and animated the country, the 'Authentic' and 'Consistent Leader'.

I was once taken on a tour of inspection of Heroes' Acre by a man assigned to guard the graveyard: Corporal Romio. Here, in this giant empty place, lay the soldiers who fell fighting for the guerrilla armies in the war against Ian Smith. Here, depicted in bronze with the freezes edged in granite, was the election triumph of 1980 and the striding bespectacled figure of Robert Mugabe leading the troops of his guerrilla army out of the trenches, on to the ballot box, and onward again to final victory. The triumphal sculptures had that gigantic strained realism, beloved of tyrannical regimes from Nuremberg to Red Square. In its studied air of sacrilegious sanctity which is really the glorification of bloodshed, Heroes' Acre was rather like that great monument built to the Afrikaner Voortrekkers on a hill near Pretoria – an aggressive, smouldering memory of wrong, and the adoration of death.

Corporal Romio marched me from tomb to tomb, regretting the ravages of time. He traced with his finger the bronze panels which had tarnished in the African sun. The North Koreans had given their own peculiar stamp to the marching figures on the walls, they had turned

Zimbabwean soldiers into a kind of Asian-African peasant army, brandishing bazookas and AK47s. A black granite plinth awaited the casket of the next fallen hero. The graves of generals and fighters ascended in concentric rings. The place looked like an upmarket Asian funeral parlour catering to superior socialist corpses. I was in the graveyard dream of a boy who had wanted to be Joseph Stalin when he grew up, and Kim Chong Il when he died.

It was notable how often it was not the battlefield that had claimed a hero but death on the roads. The mysterious car-crash has a long history in Zimbabwe. The accident, in 1979, that killed the popular Defence Chief, Josiah Tongogara, and robbed Zimbabwe of its most accomplished and popular wartime leader, still haunts the country. His heavy marble gravestone in Heroes' Acre cannot keep Tongogara's shade from stalking the land. Legend has it that he cannot rest – a chiding presence who visits the President nightly, a reproachful Banquo to Mugabe's Macbeth.

It was in this Valhalla, on Heroes Day, 11 August 2001, that the Leader once again invoked the shade of Hitler Hunzvi, elevated now to a great fighter against British Imperialists and white slave-drivers. Mugabe relishes these great state occasions at the National Mausoleum, his heart is engaged by the heroes who lie in the black marble tombs, his passion is almost convincing. Chengerai Hunzvi, he said, was a man who stood for freedom, democracy,

> and the search for sovereignty and control over all our resources, principally the land. We will never lose sight of that goal and remain prepared to die for it! We have

repeatedly told the world that the on-going land reform programme seeks to redress land imbalances deriving from the history of colonialism in this country. It is also meant to transform the agriculture set-up which we inherited from colonial governments. That set-up is not just; it is not fair; it is not productive; it is not environmentally sustainable. There is nothing therefore that justifies it beyond racial imperial dominance which we reject completely . . .

The man speaking had held absolute power for nearly a quarter of a century. It was not 'the British' or the accursed 'Anglo-Saxons' he had ruined, it had been the people in Zimbabwe. But the anger was genuine and in it was something of Africa's pain:

We were the white man's hewers of wood and drawers of water; we worked, sweated blood as we dug deep, deep into the bowels of the earth for them as they pillaged our minerals. We worked the land, not so our children could eat but so we could feed their own children and kind. These Anglo-Saxon bigots glibly use the language and vocabulary of democracy to duck their colonial responsibility so they can prolong their evil control and ownership of our land and natural resources. Today as we stand on the shrine that keeps our heroic dead, we tell them that none of the freedoms we enjoy on this land, not even an iota, came to us from them, from the West. The West brought us colonial oppression, economic deprivation, the illegality and unconstitutionality of UDI; inhumanity and racism. It meted out genocidal deaths, and maimings, robbed us of chunks of our lives through restrictions, detentions, imprisonment and torture. Let them remember what they did to us, appreciate the mayhem their kith and kin caused here in the name of their Queen and Government, their law and Parliament.

But what is pain that kills its own? As anyone who has lived in a police-state will know, this is high-sounding bunk, emotional blackmail, an excuse for tyranny. If you questioned a syllable of it, the police would be round in a flash. The Afrikaner regime, on its high and holy speech days at the Voortrekker Monument, reached the same level of rancorous and unforgiving self-glorification, raised the same phantoms, spoke the same mix of history and hatred, to justify itself and its strange policies. Robert Mugabe would set history right by sacrificing his people. Mugabe's Heroes, like so much of power untrammelled, are a confidence trick.

The very notion of heroism is nonsense in a land where there can be no hero but the Leader, where the ultimate loyalty is to die for the Party. Heroes' Acre is less about courage than obedience. In the end, the only good henchman is a dead henchman.

EIGHTEEN

ONE SIZE FITS ALL

Dr Mohammed Mahathir of Malaysia and Robert Mugabe of Zimbabwe are so close they are sometimes called the 'Terrible Twins'. Long before Mugabe began his drive to cleanse Zimbabwe of whites and Asians, Dr Mahathir enacted special laws favouring native-born Malaysians, the legitimate 'sons of the soil' (the bramaputra) over alien species – Asians and Chinese Malaysians. Real Malays got university places, bank loans, government jobs. Robert Mugabe's drive to clear farms of whites and the economy of whites and Asians and Jews is a belated imitation of Mahathir's version of Asian apartheid.

Dr Mahathir wins all his elections and his party, the United Malays National Organization, has ruled the country since 1957. Robert Mugabe lost an election when his mind was elsewhere, but it was a mistake he planned to set right by redoubling his triumphant victory in the next elections. As the Twins have grown in power, their harassment of opponents has grown fiercer. The greater his security apparatus the more insecure the despot feels. Newspapers are subjected to censorship, violence and threat in Malaysia and Zimbabwe. Robert Mugabe holidays in Malaysia, and calls it his home from home. Both men have been in power for over twenty years, both are blood–nationalists, both are

without successors and to discuss their removal or retirement is treason. The immortality of tyrants, like most things,
is a police matter. So alike are these Leaders that if one took
over the other's regime at short notice, the chances are no
one would notice. All despots grow alike, but the closest
Brothers are interchangeable. One size fits all.

Zimbabwe is one of the rare places left on the planet
where a clutch of dictators may sometimes be glimpsed in
their natural habitat. Perhaps the terrain is conducive: the
national graveyard was built by North Korea, the government palaces by Tito, the medical system by Cuba. I know
no better place for spotting the Big Five in the wild. On
a single day Robert Mugabe may be in residence,
Mohammed Mahathir may be visiting, Colonel Gaddafi
may be brokering oil for influence, Mariam Mengistu is in
hiding and Joseph Kabila may be swopping Congolese
diamonds for Zimbabwean soldiers. Tyrants do not only
inflate and merge, they consort – and more of them consort
in Zimbabwe than anywhere else on earth.

Mahathir and Mugabe once called a joint news conference and demanded that journalists stop picking on them.
The meeting with the journalists was 'a unique occasion in
which the press has to answer questions from its victims'. A
wretched hack from Kuala Lumpur got up and agreed, and
praised the fact that the Malaysian press and the Prime
Minister 'co-operated'; it was what he called 'smart
partnership'.

In Zimbabwe not being 'smart' can be dangerous. In
1999, the *Standard*, one of the few independent papers, ran
a story about the arrest of twenty-three army officers, said
to be planning a coup against Mugabe. The reporter and
his editor were immediately detained and taken to army

headquarters in Harare where, in a blood-stained room, they were stripped, burnt, tortured and half drowned by interrogators demanding to know who had told them about the army plot. The journalists were warned: 'We're briefing the President every hour because he's very disturbed. He has signed your death warrants.'

Mohammed Mahathir runs a xenophobic and nationalist regime which detests not only Jews, homosexuals and Europeans but all non-Malaysians, not least the Chinese of Malaysia – and one in three people in Malaysia is Chinese. Dr Mahathir told the paper *Yazhou Zhoukan*: 'We must accept the fact that the Chinese are not a group which can be assimilated easily. Once the Frenchmen or Germans move to the United States, they speak American English, accept American customs and norms, but not the Chinese. You can see Chinatowns all over the world, but not French or German towns.'

Dr Mahathir nourished and developed his own form of autocracy, holding himself to be not so much a tyrant as a firm headmaster, and he has pointed to the hypocrisy of Western countries which seek to give him lessons in democracy. The difference between a despot and a democrat is only a matter of timing. Your 'democratic' regime is merely your preferable form of oppression. All leaders, in times of peril, lock up opponents, suspend the rule of law, censor the media and destroy those they regard as undesirable or dangerous. In a reference to America, after 11 September 2001, Mahathir said:

'We know if they are under attack, they also took actions ignoring the law and the court, take actions to their whims and fancies against people who they think were involved in violence.'

He is right. Americans sharply curtailed their own freedoms in their 'war against terror'. Mahathir has warned his own people against foolish hankerings after change: 'In fact, it happened in several countries the new government that came to power was more tyrannical to the people than the alleged cruelty perpetrated by the previous administration.'

But it won't do, this argument, because it amounts to no more than the advice to hold on to Nurse for fear of someone worse – though it does point to the essential problem that dogs the dictator, the one that won't go away, the one he dare not mention, the problem he cannot solve: how to imagine the world without himself? Death, succession or exile, retirement, the state of his health, the future – these are nonsensical topics of discussions: the state of his health *is* the future. These conversations are acts of insurrection. Such topics are not open to discussion while the tyrant remains in charge. This does not stop people thinking about an ending, hoping for it or praying for it. It is just that, like so much else in a police-state, no one talks about it out loud. Yet no one thinks about it more than the Leader, and the more powerful he becomes the more it haunts him. The end of his reign, the end of his life, these are matters he takes very personally. Who is to replace the irreplaceable? Perish the thought, and off with the head that thought it.

I happened to be in Kuala Lumpur when the question of Dr Mahathir's successor came up – not in those crude terms, of course, but it had been said, rumoured, whispered that someone might one day succeed the Leader. Not very long after that this disputed someone, Anwar Ibrahim, who had been Deputy Prime Minister, was jailed on charges of sodomy and corruption, and while he was in the cells he was assaulted by his jailers (and later sentenced to a term of fifteen years). There were Malaysians who felt this was wrong and they went into the streets. Protests were almost unheard of in Kuala Lumpur and displeased Dr Mahathir.

I was staying at the old Federal Hotel and, one morning, I walked downtown to have breakfast with a man named Jimmy Li Fu. It's a pretty good coffee shop, the First Cup, close to the heart of Kuala Lumpur in what is known as the Golden Triangle. From the terrace, you can watch the world go by. Jimmy Li Fu was a somewhat mysterious figure – he presided over the bar in the Coliseum Restaurant, which is where I'd met him, but in his youth he'd worked for the Chinese gangs. He still had the secret sign, a red dragon, tattooed on his right forearm. Jimmy was a business-man; he owned hotels and a couple of massage parlours, and he used his mobile to place racing bets with his bookie in Singapore. In the evenings he stood by the bar in the Coliseum Restaurant where he received the plaudits of the faithful like the senior and respected Godfather he was. We got on well, for what I'll call family reasons, and that is how I found myself drinking espresso in the First Cup Café when the riots broke out.

It all happened quickly. One moment we were sitting there reading the newspapers, and the next the cops had sealed off the street and there was nowhere to go and nothing to do. It is surprising what you notice when you're under fire. The metal shutters came down hard at Kwang's, the Authorized Money Changer. The girls from the Heavenly Massage Parlour had stopped working. The blinds were suddenly drawn in the windows of Dr Gigi, and at the Fong and Goh Dental Surgery they locked the doors. The scenes shifted as they would on a stage, and suddenly nothing was what you thought it was. Perhaps more accurately, the sensible, stable world was shown to be a sham, dependent for its appeal on the illusion that things are more or less safe and secure.

They weren't. The police advanced, the street was under fire from a battery of water canon, mounted on big red trucks. The curved roof of the taxi rank across the way made a good deflective shield, but the students were out in the open, and, moving much more slowly, so were groups of tourists in long shorts and waist-wallets. It was pandemonium.

Jimmy Li Fu told me why the students were rioting. The Deputy Prime Minister had been sent to jail and his supporters had taken to the streets. Jimmy was shocked by the riot. He gave the impression that by staying where we were and behaving calmly we would somehow reinforce the authority of the State which was being challenged by these impudent youngsters. Staying put was all we could do anyway. The street in front of us was thick with marchers and police. Behind us in the B & B shopping plaza, the security staff had dropped the steel grilles over the exits, trapping hundreds inside the shops and there was a lot of shrieking. Minutes earlier there'd been customers at Marks and Sparks – now they were prisoners. They stuck their hands through the grilles waving and chirruping, it was like Sing Sing.

The policemen wore black uniforms and carried long canes, and when they lashed out they reminded me of the Irish Christian Brothers who had schooled me. Lifting and bringing down a stick on someone's back or legs was a violent gesture, it distorted the body, starting with the flexing of the calf, and a pivot of the ankle, like a golfer. Then came the rising shoulder and a forward darting downward movement as the bamboo cane came thudding down on the flesh of the victim. You could read, in the twisting body of the policeman, an expression of pleasure. It was good to be beating someone. It had about it a naturalness that suggested that this must have been one of the earliest hominid's most primal pleasures – striking someone, hitting the target repeatedly with a fist, a foot, a stick, until the victim ran away or fell down.

The students ran away. The riot police lacked a target and they were not going to be cheated. The foreign tourists were out in the open. In the season of Asian slump and uncertainty, travel agents had been selling Malaysia hard. It was billed as being hot, cheap, and safe. Best of all went the message, calculated to appeal to British and Australian travellers, Malaysia was just like home: Malaysia had Worcester sauce and Guinness and baked beans, and when you wanted to call the police you dialled 999.

I watched an elderly man in short grey socks and sandals trying to cover his head with his camera case, so the cops began beating him about the buttocks. I saw three women running with their handbags flapping, and the water canon hit them between the shoulders and knocked them down. I could feel the outrage in their gestures. Malaysia wasn't like home any more. Nothing like this had ever happened to them before. They came from countries where these things never happened at all. Suddenly, without warning, they had become overweight, clumsy, pale-skinned prey, ridiculously running here and there in their shorts and their bulging money belts, being chased by sprightly black dervishes with sticks and being doused by a water cannon.

The three women who had been knocked over were now standing quietly outside the café with water streaming from their hair. Jimmy Li Fu shook his head. 'Dearie me. It's best to keep out of the water. That water's got something chemical in it. It sticks to the skin. Get a touch, and you're itching for days.'

Jimmy Li Fu and I dined at the Coliseum that night, a reassuringly shabby restaurant that felt haunted by the ghosts of the British settlers, the old rubber planters who had once eaten there. Big steaks set down on hot griddles sent up such curtains of steam you had to step away from the table and hold your napkin up to your face and the waiters handed you towels. A parade of Jimmy's friends stopped by our table: a Malaysian policeman and his girl-friend – he'd been beating up students and tourists earlier that day, and Jimmy was very warm to him – some Chinese friends, an Indian from Mallaca, called Trevor, who drove a cab. They talked, paid their respects, received Jimmy's crooked smile of benediction, and departed. Jimmy was in high spirits, so pleased, so relieved at the way order had been restored that day.

'May the Prime Minister live a hundred years,' said Jimmy Li Fu.

He must have seen my astonishment.

'What do you think would happen to Chinese like me, if the government fell?'

'Chinese, like me.' It was a most extraordinary phrase, summing up in its plump complacency, in its slightly edgy provincialism, the cry of all small communities who exist, rather as Jimmy's Straits Chinese community did, on suffer-ance, by permission, at the pleasure of a larger, not very friendly, host community that tolerated them provided they did as they were told, kept their heads down and their mouths shut. I understood him then.

We came from the same place, Jimmy and I. We were, precisely, nowhere people – and for that paradoxical reason I knew where I was when we sat and talked. He was a stranger to whom I was intimately related, not by blood or background but by membership of the club, people on the edge, guests on the fringes of larger ethnically 'pure' majorities who tolerate us – if we are lucky, or drive us out if we are not. Someone like Jimmy was not what I would call a friend. He was closer than that. People like Jimmy were family; they were the tribe I came from. In him I saw the fate awaiting the white settlers in Zimbabwe, impotent and emasculated, who might just be allowed to stay on if they emulated the Chinese of Malaysia and, each day, prayed devoutly for their Leader to live a hundred years. And that is exactly what they had done, most of them, ever since Robert Mugabe had come to power. In the topsy-turvy world of power, terror and tyranny, it makes sense to pray for the long life of the Leader, even if he loathes you; and to fear and hate the idea of his passing on, even when it may appear to be in your interest that he does so. Dying is the last thing a Supreme Leader plans to do for his people. Death is what others do for him.

The saint and tyrant are only a prayer apart. The saint sacrifices himself to save souls and the tyrant sacrifices his people to save himself. If the effects of terror have been impressive then the life of the lost one flames in the minds and hearts of his people, they succumb to the urge to worship him. It doesn't matter that the Leader is dead, you can put him in a glass box and he becomes the sentinel keeping watch, he signifies that the State is awake and watchful, and the dead dictator is its sleeping policeman.

When Stalin died in 1953, what broke out could be described as religious riots. The authorities were forced to move in troops and tanks to control the huge and grief-stricken crowds of mourners. Rostislav Dubinsky, first violin of the Borodin quartet, was summoned to the Kremlin to play before Stalin's open coffin, as he lay in state in the Hall of Columns. The dead Leader was attended by the men who had ordered the deaths of so many, and who would themselves soon be facing oblivion: Beria, Molotov, Kaganovich, Malenkov, and Suslov. David Oistrakh, the great violinist, was summoned to play Tchaikovsky's Sérénade Mélancolique, and while he played the hall was filled with hysterical screams. A woman cried out incessantly: 'You didn't stay! Beloved.' Mourners had to be torn away from the coffin. When the violinist Pavel Mirsky made the mistake of stopping to look into the coffin, two plain-clothes policemen tore his fiddle case away from him, pinned his arms behind his back and dragged him off, while a piano continued to play on the far side of the stage.

The Borodin Quartet played for three days, slept in the hall with the coffin, and were not fed. When eventually they were allowed to leave, Dubinsky walked through scenes of devastation left by the hysterical crowds that besieged the Hall of Columns, desperate for a sight of their lost Leader. In their riotous grief they had turned central Moscow into a wasteland of smashed windows, upended trucks, twisted streetlights, and pieces of clothing trampled into the mud – a scene, Dubinsky recalled many years later, that reminded him of a battlefield.

Joseph Stalin lay beside Lenin, in Red Square, for a few weeks – another set of terrifying twins – and then he was removed and secretly buried in the Kremlin wall. But it really didn't matter. The despot lays on his country and people an imprint that lasts for years, that glows in the dark of their dreams, and which they carry like a terrible birthmark. Death may intervene but it is strangely incidental. Death has always been in the forefront of everything, anyway. A tyrant haunts his people long before he dies.

I went to North Vietnam in 1997 and experienced that shock of recognition, the surge of familiar excitement that told me that I knew where I was. It was another of those ex-police-states, newly emerged from the long night of the commissars – like Moscow, East Berlin, Belgrade – where the rules were legion and corruption was rampant, where the level of mendacity was so effortlessly high, the comedy so immediate, the arrogance of officials so preposterous, the greed of foreign merchants so naked, the whiff of corruption so rank, that they really ought to be enjoyed by consenting adults. Judged by these standards, Hanoi was the next best thing to home. It was also one of those places where the (increasingly rare) Red Paradox still survived in its natural habitat. It went like this: everything not expressly permitted was forbidden. The rule was not as chilling as it sounded because it hid in its devious heart its liberating opposite – to wit, everything not expressly forbidden was permitted. Once you grasped that, anything and everything became possible.

Hanoi Airport brought back a surging sense of déjà vu. Here were all the old reassuring sights: the surly passport officers, the passion for small forms and big blue stamps; for doing things very slowly, in duplicate. It was the perfume of the past and Hanoi had it, that inimitable blend of hypocrisy, charm and crookery. Everyone, it seemed, was on the take, on the make, and, increasingly, on the needle. When all the propaganda sheets talk of the public good, people expect to be ripped off. What was clear was that the Party still ran the place and it meant to take everyone for a ride. That was called – what else? – 'democracy'. It meant someone was going to be robbed. The Party was doing it to the people, the people did it to each other, and, sooner or later, Party and people planned to do it to you.

I hadn't been in Hanoi very long before I realized that Ho Chi Minh was not only immortal, he had entered the pantheon of gods long ago. Quite unlike the Western versions of the tyrant preserved, of the god-king, Uncle Ho had been adapted, with a kind of Buddhist tolerance, so that he fitted quite naturally into all aspects of life in Vietnam. He had become a household spirit. Walking through Hanoi you saw his portrait in shop windows beside the Sacred Heart of Jesus; his image was in the window of the snake-wine seller, he was on the banknotes, and on the propaganda posters for family planning.

One Sunday morning I joined a long line of the waiting faithful outside Ho's mausoleum. The wait was expected to be something like three hours. Women removed their hats when they finally got close to the entrance and the police-man who controlled the crowd was seeing off boys who tried to gatecrash, twisting their ears and sending them to the back of the queue. The police then turned from sentries into ushers, gently pushing us down the steps into the semi-darkness. We were grateful for the air-conditioning, watching our own sweat condense on the cool brass letters of the hero's name.

The man himself, small and pale as a blanched prawn, with a wispy beard, lay on a black cushion in the subdued light. He went to Moscow once a year for repairs, they said. You were allowed to circle the glass box in which he lay and then, without pausing, the ushers began drawing you firmly up and on and out again into the huge sunshine.

The Leader does not have to be alive or dead, he may be in that special transitional state between the two: he may be in exile, or 'resting'. Colonel Haile Mariam Mengistu, the former tyrant of Ethiopia has lived for some years in the suburban reaches of Harare, close to the Zimbabwean President. Colonel Mengistu ranks amongst the great killers of our times. He overthrew Haile Selassie in 1974, in a military coup. The 83-year-old emperor, so the story goes, refused to tell Mariam's interrogators what he'd done with the money in his Swiss accounts, and he was suffocated with a pillow and buried outside the palace window, very close to the office taken over by Colonel Mengistu. A tomb with a view. Many of the Emperor's relatives were also murdered, others were chained to the walls of the Palace.

Mengistu built one of the largest armies in Africa; at one time he had two hundred thousand men under arms. His Stalinist regime, the Dergue, began a campaign of annihilation, known as the Red Terror, in which tens of thousands of 'reactionaries' and other enemies of the people perished. When rebels closed in on Addis Ababa in 1991, Mengistu fled. Robert Mugabe took him in, providing 24-hour armed security from the Presidential Guard, and a comfortable villa in the pleasant suburb of Gunhill. The two men were old allies. Mugabe's ZANU-PF party and Mariam's Dergue were sister movements: both saw the liquidation of whole classes of opposition as right and proper, both used food as a weapon, deliberately starving people, Mugabe in Matabeleland, and Mengistu in the provinces of Tigre and Eritrea.

Since settling in Zimbabwe Mengistu has kept his head down. There was a rumour in 1998 that he had fled to North Korea. The *Zimbabwe Independent* newspaper quoted Mengistu relatives and Zimbabwe officials as saying that he is seeking political asylum in Pyongyang and his wife and children were soon to follow him. There was no substance in the reports. In Addis Ababa, the Ethiopian high court sentenced former Mengistu officials to death in absentia for their involvement in acts of genocide during his 'Red Terror' campaign and Mengistu is top of the list of men they want, but Robert Mugabe has refused to extradite him.

He was flushed out briefly when an ambitious Eritrean assassin got close enough to fire a single shot into his heavily guarded house. Mengistu, believing that justice had come for him at last, ran panic-stricken into the street calling for help. Since then the Executioner of Addis has moved to a farm in Mazowe, which his guards may more easily defend.

Ethiopia tried again when Mengistu travelled to South Africa for medical treatment. While he was there, he told a Johannesburg newspaper that, far from being the killer he'd been painted, he was a decent Marxist who had fought a war to defend the peasants of Ethiopia, only to be betrayed by Mikhail Gorbachev. Ethiopia disagreed and asked the South African government to extradite him, but the ANC leaders who govern South Africa were also once fond of Colonel

Mengistu: they had been, he told the BBC, 'my comrades in arms, my friends, my colleagues'. The South Africans returned the old tyrant to Zimbabwe, where he has lived happily ever since.

NINETEEN

THE BORN-AGAIN

When people in Zimbabwe try to describe the man who rules over them, they fall into puzzlement and despair. Someone is clearly 'there' – but then, again, there is nothing there. Power and vacuity. Terror and nullity. The Bulawayo lawyer, Washington Sansole, suggested that Shakespeare was as good a guide as you were going to find, and pointed to Caesar, and to the perplexity the tyrant feels when faced by some apparently ludicrous group or faction who call into question the unfettered exercise of executive power. Julius Caesar, like Robert Mugabe, was a blending of the victorious warrior, autocrat and messiah. When Mugabe looked at himself he could, quite literally, see his singularity, and say, like Caesar, with sober megalomania, that he had 'no fellow in the firmament'. Other stars 'move and flare and die' says Caesar, but only one of those blazing suns is 'unalterable, eternal, fixed forever', the all-seeing heavenly 'eye', sun of God and sun in heaven – and 'that I am he . . .' Or, as Mugabe put it long ago, when some white farmer threatened legal action: 'I, Robert Mugabe, cannot be dragged to court by a mere settler.'

However, Mugabe, like Caesar, has made enemies of men who once backed him to the hilt. There might be some use then, I thought, in looking at Robert Mugabe through the eyes of a man who perhaps knew him better than anyone, who had been a political ally, a godfather, a mentor, a minister, a servant, and an executioner. So, during the elections of 2002, I went to see Enos Nkala at his home in the suburbs of Bulawayo. He had been Mugabe's Minister for Police in the early Eighties, and he had been given the job of putting down the rebellion which Mugabe feared might well be brewing amongst supporters of Joshua Nkomo.

Enos Nkala was a perfect instrument of terror. Though he came from Matabeland himself, and from the Ndebele people, he had been the architect of the Gukurahundi. In his view there was one government, one party and one ruler and, 'anyone who disputed that was a dissident and should be dealt with.' He was loyal, ruthless, and terrifyingly effective. He brought an end to any question of 'dissidence' in Matabeleland. He never faltered in pursuing a man he detested and whom he once memorably called, 'public enemy number one' – Mugabe's rival, Joshua Nkomo. He was to Mugabe what Yezhov had been to Stalin, his chosen, loyal and energetic instrument and he did his master's bidding unswervingly and never minced words: 'We want to wipe out the ZAPU leadership.'

It was Enos Nkala who set up the Special Police Intelligence and Security Unit known as PISI – a mob of thugs more feared even than the Central Intelligence Organization. I remember an exemplary performance when he was being interviewed by a television reporter while the turbulence in Matabeleland was at its height. Enos Nkala swivelled his big round eyes in the way he has when he is thinking hard, they seem to take on an extra brightness and revolve like Catherine-wheels. If there was a problem with 'dissidents', Nkala said to the interviewer, then the solution was obvious – no more dissidents, no more problem. Everyone who has met Nkala remembers the eyes.

Under Nkala's zealous tutelage, the army, the forces of Five Brigade, the CIO, the PISI, and the police, systematically terrorized people until so many were dead or starving that all rebellion in Matabeleland was over. Zimbabwe now also had its killing fields. The human remains dredged from the mine-shafts of Kesi were mute witnesses to Robert Mugabe's desire for 'peace' in Matabeleland, and to Enos Nkala's determination to enforce that peace.

Nkala was living in quiet retirement in sleepy suburban Bulawayo. I let myself in the gate, ignored the large dog in the backyard, admired the black Mercedes parked beneath the wash-line, and found Nkala nursing a heavy cold, stretched out in a chair in the living room. His own background made him so notorious and so feared that very few ventured to see him. I knew he had never before spoken before about his life and times, but there was a softening in retirement, and perhaps a certain melancholy in his conversation. There was also an edge of anger against his former protégé and Leader, which led him to speak freely and openly, and with a passion that warmed the room even if it chilled the blood.

We drank milky tea and talked about death, God and Robert Mugabe. Nkala had pledged his faith and his life to the Lord, he had embraced Pentecostal Christianity. He was, he told me, happily and imperturbably, a convert: 'I am a serious born-again Pentecostal Christian. I'm doing a degree in Theology. Mugabe almost made me reject God – he doesn't believe in the existence of God, he doesn't believe in the life hereafter, he is an atheist, he preferred Karl Marx.'

The portrait of Mugabe that emerged was of a man who got his way by skilful manipulation, by stealth, a man of the shadows, a man who, if challenged, would instantly withdraw. Nkala also portrayed him as unscrupulous and irreligious, something he found hard to forgive. Why, he had almost caused Nkala to lose his faith! There was something incongruous about Enos Nkala as the born-again Christian – though I had the feeling that, perhaps, he had turned to religion with as much fierce loyalty as he had once pledged to Robert Mugabe.

It had been at Nkala's house, in Highfield Township, in Harare, on 8 August 1963, that the ruling Party – the Zimbabwe African National Union – had been founded by a Minister, cleric and teacher, Ndabaningi Sithole. It had been Nkala and his friends who transformed ZANU when they ditched Sithole in a palace coup, and replaced him with a young teacher named Robert Gabriel Mugabe. Nkala had been with Mugabe since the early Sixties, and spent years with him in Smith's jails, when they had shared a cell. He had been with him in 1980 when Mugabe became Prime Minister of the new Zimbabwe. He had served him loyally as the Minister of Finance, and as Defence Minister. He had watched him grow.

Mugabe was 'our baby' said Nkala, and he talked with parental pride of the brilliant boy who grew up to lop off the heads of those who'd raised him.

'He was a very convincing speaker, brilliant. With him we were able to move much faster, it speeded up our fight, but we were always looking for ways to impose checks and balances. He didn't like that, so he had to find ways of ditching some of his very loyal colleagues. He had to push some of us out to play the game he's playing.'

Recalling their time in the communal cells, back in Salisbury nearly forty years before, he remembered Mugabe as impressive, quick, highly determined, always reading, always studying; he took degree after degree by correspondence. Nkala confirmed, again, that the man continually dissimulated his ambition and his desire to rule. 'Terribly modest' was a phrase Nkala used. He also spoke of him as being 'meek' and even 'timid'. He portrayed Mugabe as the earnest swot, the eternal teacher, the headmaster who had been overpromoted. 'He is a very reserved person. I was very close to him, but I did not detect in him a love of power when I was with him in detention.'

In the late Eighties, when Enos Nkala was Defence Minister, things began to go wrong for him. There had been a scandal that became known as 'Willowgate'. It was a scam that worked by buying cars from State factories and selling them at market prices. Enos Nkala bought and sold a car or two. Questions were asked in the press and Nkala, in a typical flourish, wanted to arrest the editor of the paper for insolence. However, for reasons that are still not at all clear, he resisted his natural instincts. He went further and did the decent thing, he fell on his sword, and resigned.

He needn't have bothered. Robert Mugabe later got rid of the offending editor anyway, and no government newspaper has broken a scandal ever since. Willowgate ended badly for everybody except Robert Mugabe. Of the other ministers charged with Nkala and taken to court, one committed suicide and the other was sent to jail for nine months for perjury – though, in fact, the perjured Minister spent only one night in prison when Robert Mugabe pardoned him with these words: 'Who amongst us has not lied? Yesterday you were with your girlfriend and you told your wife you were with the President. Should you get nine months for that?'

There is much more to this speech than the usual attempt to denigrate the courts and disparage the rule of law. Robert Mugabe has never shown any compunction about doing either. It is the language in which the speech is couched that makes it interesting. Again, there is this quasi-biblical tone – 'Who amongst us has not lied?' – which has interesting echoes of Christ's injunction to those who wished to stone the woman taken in adultery: 'Whosoever is without sin amongst you, let him cast the first stone.' And then there is the nature of the alibi. The man taken in adultery tells his wife, not that he has been down at the pub, or seeing his accountant, but absolves himself by claiming to have been with 'the President', and he becomes the object of all understanding and forgiveness. The increasing tendency of Robert Mugabe to see himself as the redeemer of his country, as the font of all power, even of salvation, has become more marked over the years.

Nkala was still sore about the affair: he was a proud man and I got the feeling he hadn't wanted to jump, he'd been pushed. At any rate he felt he had been humiliated. He had gone to see Mugabe and told him he was resigning as Minister – and he was also leaving the Party.

Mugabe had been shocked. 'Leave the government, yes,' he said, 'but you – leaving the Party!'

Shocked he may have been, but perhaps Robert Mugabe is not without wit: when he could not talk Nkala out of resigning, he said, 'Well, keep your Merc.' After all the service Nkala had loyally given the Party over the years, it was the very least Mugabe could do. That was the big car under the wash-line, it had once been Nkala's Ministerial limousine.

When I asked him if he could say what had gone wrong with Mugabe he began to speculate on what I might call the mysteries of his person, the secrets he had hidden away beneath his constant collar and tie and his good grey suits. Nkala pointed out that despite his detestation for all things European, Mugabe was the most European of African leaders, in his dress, his education, his inflexions, but, as with everything else about the man, his secrets were concealed.

'This man has had a few tragedies in his life. When he was in Ghana, he was working as a teacher in Ghana; I don't know what he did to his employees. He had an employee in his house. This man threw boiling water over Mugabe, and that's why you'll never see him in a short-sleeved shirt.'

The burn, or birthmark, or sign of Cain that Nkala believes Mugabe hides beneath his carefully tailored veneer grew large in the conversation, but it really only underlined how, in the face of the mystery, one was obliged to seek for explanations for a man who was as bizarre as any you will find in fairytales. Enos Nkala described the reasons behind Mugabe's prim attitude whenever he sits. He mimicked the knees touched carefully together, the girlish modesty it conveyed. This was something that those who have seen Mugabe on the platform will confirm and it added to the impression of a strange and mincing gentility.

'When we were forming ZANU he developed cancer on his private part. That's why he has developed a way of sitting as if he is a frightened man.'

Nkala went on to suggest that although Mugabe was operated upon for this cancer, the malignancy had never been entirely eradicated and had now come to infect his body and had made its way to his brain. It was another flamboyant theory. There were so many floating around Zimbabwe, all of them yet further symptoms of an inability to explain the phenomenon who was their Leader and who had, through his own efforts, laid his country low. All rational explanations had failed. As it had been in the Rome of Caesar, so it is in the wild atmosphere of Zimbabwe today; the court of Mugabe and his cronies are shot through with supernatural omens, and magical signs. Because the man remains a mystery, even to those close to him, it is perhaps inevitable that people look for spiritual or fantastical explanations to explain to themselves the phenomenon that has them in thrall. Signs, soothsayers, spells, plots, agues and fevers grip the state and its divine 'he' – rumours of fateful malfunctions that seize the tyrant: syphilis, Aids, albinism, or scarifying burns, penile malfunction, or brain cancer.

The effect of these stories or legends or rumours has been to buttress the myths of Mugabe's semi-divine power. He has become, as Shakespeare's Cassius said of Caesar, a colossus, 'and we petty men walk under his huge legs, and peep about to find ourselves dishonourable graves.'

Nkala had a way of cocking his head, and then the Catherine-wheels of his eyes began to spin and he talked with complete sincerity of unspeakable things. Not since I'd met Dirk Coetzee, who had confessed to murdering opponents of his political masters, had I been so impressed by the modern functionary's capacity to combine open and honest sincerity of purpose and honesty of demeanour with a considerable ability to plan wide-scale homicide. Maybe this was always the case, you split things in your head, but what I believe is new, what truly deserves to be called modern, is the way moral authority is also the prerogative of the executioner. Of course, the two men had different jobs.

Dirk Coetzee was a foot-soldier employed to do the dirty work. There was no indication that Enos Nkala had ever personally killed anyone. But he was the political commissar under whose stern direction the war to extirpate all bandits and dissidents in Matabeleland had been waged and, at the end of that campaign, thousands of people were dead.

The years he had spent in contemplation of his lost Leader had deepened and darkened Enos Nkala's view of Mugabe, his power and his personality. Nkala was preparing himself for the next world, and in doing so he had taken precautions lest he find himself too closely associated with some of Robert Mugabe's colleagues, even in death. Nkala had said that on no account would he consent to be buried in Heroes' Acre in Harare. In that place there were people he had no wish to spend eternity with.

'I'm going to go to my lawyer to write a document to say: I don't want to go to Heroes' Acre. I am a Christian, a Born-Again, and I don't want to mix with certain people there. And I don't want anybody standing around speechifying over my body.'

I had the sense that Nkala felt something of the frustration felt by Cassius and other conspirators, when the intolerable arrogance of Caesar began to plague them – that urge to remove him from the world, or at least to cut him down to size, that wish that the conspirator Flavius confesses as he plunges his knife into the body of Caesar, to clip his wings and destroy forever the tyrants urge 'to soar above the view of men'.

So now Enos Nkala, once the hammer of the dissidents, the Butcher of Bulawayo, had decided to give the opposition Party, the Movement for Democratic Change, some advice. There had been suggestions of peace talks between

Robert Mugabe and his opponents. Enos Nkala thought that would be rather like pygmies talking to giants:

'I went to the deputy President of the MDC and I said to him – look – don't be foolish. The ultimate result is that you are going to be swallowed, just as ZAPU was swallowed. If you say yes to the principle of unity, working together or whatever . . . You are going to be giving up positions, he'll give you everything and then he'll swallow you up . . . That's what happened to Nkomo. I said to them – be courageous: if he arrests you, or jails you, don't agree to anything. Why go into the leadership if you have no courage of your convictions? They [the opposition] must die for what they think wrong. If he puts them in prison they must go. In this spirit of compromising with the devil, you never win.'

I asked if he worried about Mugabe's reaction, were I to publish the things he was saying to me.

'When I issue statements about Mugabe now, he doesn't answer. I am not frightened, my friend, of a creature that is crazy.'

I wondered how long he thought Mugabe might last.

'I don't think this man will go through this year, that's my humble instinctive prediction. Zimbabweans are angry; they have no mealie meal, no sugar, no cooking oil, no washing soap. On the economic front, he's a Jesuit. The economy is collapsing. We have no buyers except Chinese and Egyptians. The western buyers have gone. Mining has almost collapsed. Industry is closing down. Unemployment is massive, agriculture collapsed with the farming invasions. The war vets come and steal your cattle in the night, marauding over the farms, destroying the economy. Mugabe wanted to maintain power, he called on the war vets to sustain his powers, and now you have two parallel governments; his government and the war vets' government. There is no place where the war vets are not. They need a strong man, a man they have to know who will tell them to stop the nonsense; the only way to stop them is to demonstrate power beyond any reasonable doubt.'

But whatever force is going to bring Mugabe down, it is not the opposition. He thought very little of those trying to topple Caesar:

'You can't create a leader or go shopping for leaders. Leaders are born with the instinctive courage and determination. You don't create them overnight. These people make stupid statements. They don't know who Mugabe is. He will not be frightened by their threats. Mugabe is of a higher order than these little men who walk the streets.'

He had brooded, it was clear, on the exceptionally devious nature of his old comrade and he had drawn several conclusions, few of them flattering:

'Now some of those he has around him – them, I wouldn't employ to look after my chickens because my chickens would die without water. He has put around him political idiots. He was our baby. Some of us would say, 'No, no, no!' This is how dictators crop up; dictators are by their nature cowards. They haven't the courage to stand face to face with someone who will tell them, 'Nonsense!' They are always frightened of you, so they look for subtle means of removing you. When you stand up to them with courage and determination, they give in. Like them, he is a coward.'

I thought about the words people had chosen to describe Robert Mugabe: meek, mild, modest. Nkala had used perhaps the best. He had said to me during the afternoon: 'He can kill surreptitiously. I know many people he has killed.'

Then the minister from Nkala's Pentecostal church arrived, as he always did on Sunday afternoons, a quiet and gentle young man with a scrubbed and earnest look. Enos Nkala was very solicitous; he took his faith with great seriousness, but before he devoted his heart and soul to God, he had a few last words about Mugabe's appeal, his attraction, and his treachery:

'Robert has created a vacuum because he is frightened. He destroys. He only takes people who can't say no. A Mugabe Minister is like a prostitute, he can't say no. When Mugabe sees a crowd he sees a classroom. He is a teacher who never became a headmaster. He gives generously to those who kneel. He is a man who likes to ruin good people.'

In the late afternoon when I left the house, the sky was high and blue. Bulawayo was a town edgy with fear, dark with the foreboding that accompanied the elections of 2002. The black Mercedes, the parting gift of the man who liked to ruin good people, was in the car-port beneath the washing lines and, inside the house, the Born-Again and his Pentecostal Prayer Group began offering prayers to the Lord.

TWENTY

I, ROBERT MUGABE ...

On that February afternoon in Lupane, after watching the President vanish into the heavens, my police minders walked me back to my car and warned me about wild animals, particularly the elephants, many of whom had been seen crossing the road. I drove on through the late afternoon towards Victoria Falls. I took care to watch out for the elephants, but I wasn't particularly worried. Generally, they are shy and benign creatures, they do not mount roadblocks, or drop the bodies of their victims down mine-shafts, or promise them heaven and send them home hungry. Besides, now that the official presidential caravan had moved on, the road was free.

Victoria Falls is one of the most exciting places on earth. As you drive over the rise that stands behind the town you look down towards the column of spray from the Falls, standing straight up in the sky, like a strong right arm. But the Victoria Falls I drove into, a couple of days before the election of 2002, was a ghost town. Nothing moved, the hotels were empty and only the beggars and the money-lenders walked the streets, pursuing any foreigner they saw with great wads of Zimbabwean dollars or small soapstone statues, running after you and hurriedly polishing these souvenirs on their shirts and dropping their prices with every step. There were no tourists; governments had warned their nationals not to travel to Zimbabwe. I had the Falls to myself.

Because of the cloud of spray that hangs permanently over the Falls, the borderland of the water canyons is always lush and green, a little rain forest in a thirsty sunburnt brown land, a wetland fat with grass, ferns, creepers. In this marvellous place it was still possible to feel something of the trembling excitement David Livingstone must have felt as he stood on the lip of these canyons a hundred years before. He had found what he had been looking for, even if he had little idea of where he was. I always thought it was one of the most endearing things about this dour Scot, that his real talent was for getting lost. He had an iron vision; somewhere he knew this wonder was to be found and he stumbled on towards it with terrible courage and he found what he dreamt of before he died. The Victoria Falls was vision rewarded.

Then again, Livingstone didn't really discover the Falls. They'd been known to local people for a very long time – Mosi-oa-Tunya they called them, 'the smoke that thunders' – but in Livingstone's universe only Scotland and London were 'local'; everywhere else was lion country, wild stretches of nowhere, places that did not exist until he found the words to describe them. So Livingstone named the Falls again, in that rather daffy way of Victorian explorers who were quite certain the world was run and ruled and named from Kensington, where the headquarters of the Royal Geographical Society were to be found. The great explorers did this around the world; there was nothing unusual about it. They trespassed on other people's mountains and lakes; they walked into places that already owned perfectly good names, and re-baptized them. Such places did not exist until they had been 'seen', and they could not be grasped until they were named, and they could not be real until they were mapped. For Livingstone, Speke, Stanley, Africa was an orgy of naming: names they took from their wives, children, the rain-swept towns in faraway Britain, and their own tribal totem goddess, Victoria.

There is a statue of Livingstone beside the Falls. It stands tall on its plinth, and shows this weary overjoyed man gazing towards the great torrents of creamy tawny water that pitch over the many cliffs that make the falls. There were signs of scuffing or scratching on the statue, and I knew what had caused these. The year before, Robert Mugabe's ruling Party had held its conference at Victoria Falls and a group of men, 'war veterans', marched down the winding road that crossed the railway line and ends at the Falls. Once there, they began to stone the statue. The idea was to tear it from its plinth and toss it into the Falls. They were stopped by the police, but there was a series of rocks at the base of the statue engraved with the history of Livingstone's discovery, and these they broke up, one stone after another, and threw the bits over the edge of the canyon, down into the water.

In unforetold ways, Livingstone's discoveries were to prove a disaster for Africa. Behind the Scots missionary came the traders, peddling a miraculous form of snake-oil. Bishop Desmond Tutu's succinct summation of the hundred-year scam, the continental con-trick, is worth repeating: when the missionaries came to Africa, Tutu observed, we had the land and they had the Bible. When they left, we had the Bible and they had the land.

The day of the stoning of Livingstone, 6 December 2001, was in many ways as important as the day when Livingstone

first saw the brown and white waters of the Zambezi toppling into the deep gorges, from which point on Africa was
to be seen through the prism of his discoveries, his maps, his
journeys, his language, and the commerce that followed
him. He had renamed and re-invented the southern subcontinent of Africa. After Livingstone everything was
different for Africa. After the stoning of Livingstone everything was utterly different for whites. The war of attrition
was over. From now on they were to be targeted, intimidated, invaded, kidnapped, driven off their farms and,
where it was deemed necessary by the planner of this
pogrom, they were to be murdered.

In the run-up to the elections of February 2002, land
invasions were a well-established fact. Robert Mugabe took
the view then that white-bashing was good for his image as
a strong black man. At the height of the election campaign,
he told a television journalist, who had suggested that the
land invasions had harmed his standing overseas: 'I suppose
it depends on who looks at you. If the perception is that of
Europeans, well, I suppose you are right to say my reputation has gone down. But in terms of Africa, go anywhere in
Africa and I am a hero.'

The newspapers at election time made strange reading;
the government press predicted victory. The independent
papers predicted victory. It was all babble. There were no
foreign reporters in the country, there were only some
international observers from the Commonwealth and
Southern African states who drove here and there in
important vehicles. On the pages of the papers were tales of
violence, hysterical praise for the President, and then the
lists: pages of compulsory acquisitions, column after dense
column in which the thefts were summarily announced:

'Notice is hereby given . . . that the President intends to acquire compulsorily the land described in the Schedule for resettlement purposes.' There followed farm after farm, owned by Murray, Biffen, Curtis, Smith, Gifford, Forrester. The announcements were called 'Preliminary Notices to Compulsorily Acquire Land'; but they were in fact announcements that daylight robbery was planned.

Since my last visit in 1996, the numbers of whites had fallen again, down now to fifty thousand said some, others said thirty thousand, but no one knew for certain because no one was counting. The white farmers of Zimbabwe, down to about four thousand, had become a species of game to be hunted down. The lists of those to be dispossessed appeared in the official press, in a crust of legal jargon, in much the same way as the various Land Acts were invented by the white settlers of Rhodesia to rob blacks of their land. The instrument used to drive whites from their farms began with what was known as a Section 8 Order, which operated under the Provisions of the Land Acquisitions Bill and its effects were these:

Full ownership rights are invested in the State imme-
    diately upon service of a Section 8 Order;
the landowner is restricted to the homestead with
    immediate effect;
the landowner may continue farming operations with the
    permission in writing of the acquiring authority;
the Section 8 Order is a 90-day eviction notice.

Behind all the talk of law came the predators: local Party men, the youth 'militia', and Hitler Hunzvi's 'war veterans'. There was some uncertainty about the degree to which

Robert Mugabe was pressed by genuine grievances felt by ex-soldiers who had fought in the war against Ian Smith. As with every challenge to his power, he managed to harness, and then emasculate, the threat by embracing the aims of the war veterans and presenting them as his own. Even so, it was impossible to see the mixture of cruelty and farce that accompanied the forced removals of whites from their farms as anything but a smash and grab raid on a broken tribe.

To travel in Zimbabwe in the spring of 2002 was to travel backwards in time, into a universe governed by a deep hatred of the civic virtues – tolerance, liberality, the sanctity of the courts, an unfettered press. It was a place where the rulers preached a religion of racial hatred, whose binding agent was the proud, mystical stupidity of its followers who believed that the way down was the way up, the way back was the way forward, and who would seriously damage those who disagreed or questioned this belief. The ghost of my old neighbour Dr Verwoerd smiled over Zimbabwe, where the specious argument in defence of racial clearances went like this: when whites practised mass removals of blacks, it was because they were innately racist, but when a black government in Zimbabwe cleared whole regions of whites – as has been done in Stavros's old home of Mount Darwin, now referred to in party parlance as 'a liberated area' – that was not 'racism', it was justice long overdue.

Maybe it was. The question remained: why should these settlers be singled out for special condemnation? I had first seen the farmer I shall call Patricia on television, in the days before the elections. She was hiding in what looked like a field of maize and her eyes were red from weeping. She'd been driven off her farm, arrested and assaulted, and she was now in fear of her life. Patricia sent a message to her children, telling them that she was safe, and asked what it was that farmers like her were supposed to have done? Why was she being hunted? All that people like her wished to do was to farm, to grow crops, to feed people, to get on with their lives. The questions were good, the questions were understandable, and the picture of the weeping woman in the maize field was unforgettable, but somehow such good sense seemed to miss the point; the trouble lay in its very reasonableness. Such questions failed to take account of a world from which all sense had been drained.

I later sat with Patricia in a tea garden outside Harare and she told me about her last few weeks. She farmed alone, one of the few women who did. She grew tobacco, she employed three hundred and forty people and it looked as if she was close to the end of her tether. She had been abducted in 2000, attacked in 2001, and then, in the run up to the elections, at about the time I had seen her hiding in the maize fields, she had been assaulted. A few days earlier there had been another arrest. Thirty-two armed policemen had marched into her house and carted her off to jail. 'It was free accommodation in a government hotel, and a pit latrine . . .' The CIO officers who came to her farm had asked her, 'Aren't you bitter? They are going to take everything from you, your house, your farm, everything.'

Patricia was a woman of considerable religious faith. It was, she said, part of God's plan. Life was a game – providing the game didn't get too dangerous. Sitting in that garden, as women parked their Japanese sedans and headed off in search of cacti and roses, and the sun shone in a rich blue sky, it was hard to think that things could get much worse for Patricia – but of course that was to fall into much the same trap as everyone else, of thinking that what had been happening in Zimbabwe was merely a temporary aberration, that on the other side of madness lay the old world, undisturbed, rational, normal. In the air was the perfume.

A few weeks later, when she'd been back to court to get an order preventing her eviction, Patricia was informed by her local Member of Parliament that she was to be removed from her farm by ZANU youth brigades, who would work together with local war vets in her eviction. For good measure, the MP, an industrious man, had also threatened to send in the local paramilitary police, the 'blackboots', to beat up her staff if they tried to prevent their employer from being thrown off her farm. In tandem with these eviction orders, went the usual orders forbidding her to plant or harvest crops, to remove livestock or equipment, or in any way damage the property or the equipment on the farm, all of which was to become the property of the State.

The reason behind her MP's sudden haste to get her off her farm, after three previous attempts, after a beating, attempted abductions, and arrest had failed to do so, was evident from an item in the government newspaper which listed in its columns not only the farms to be seized but sometimes the people to whom those farms had been allocated. Patricia read that her farm had been allocated to Party men, and its new owners were anxious to take possession. She remained defiant. She had won a court order against her tormentors, they were in contempt of court – surely this would not be allowed to pass uncensured?

Patricia was determined in her belief that she had law on her side. She was furious about the way her MP was able to show contempt of court and get away with it, that the Minister himself could do the same. She wrote to one of the leaders of the Opposition: 'I plead for your help in bringing this issue to a just conclusion and to help me ensure that my three hundred and forty staff, myself and our families, are allowed to keep our jobs, our homes, and our lives intact.'

It was admirable but eerie. Those who ran the country had long since placed themselves above the law. Farmers had died to underline the lofty divinity of the Ruler. 'I, Robert Mugabe' could not be dragged to court by a settler. It was astonishing to see with what tenacity white farmers continued to cling to notions of civility, to the law, and seemed to place what looked like inordinate hope on reason and discussion. When a farm was taken, or one of their number was beaten, or a house was burnt down, or cattle slaughtered or maimed, machinery destroyed, someone shot, they called the police, and the police more or less ignored them. They went to court, and the courts sometimes ruled in their favour, but this was not the success it might have seemed. Robert Mugabe made it plain what he thought of courts of law, and he warned the judges of his own Supreme Court that should they question his decisions, they might well suffer the same fate as the white farmers. In the inimitable words of Hitler Hunzvi, the judges were simply stupid and he told them to go to hell. 'They are part of the system that hanged us when we fought for independence. They think they are above even the country's executive President. Who do they think they are?' Several Supreme Court Judges got the message, left their jobs and, even, in one or two cases, the country.

Mugabe's incessant invocation of 'the land' and his unwearying repetition of the dubious proposition that

Zimbabwe is in Africa, Africa is black, and the black African is superior to all other people, and whites are second-class citizens, apart from its fatuity, partakes of the same sort of overheated mysticism that was at once so onerous and so damaging under Dr Verwoerd. These two terrible messiahs have come, like their beliefs, to echo each other.

Truth in dictatorships is accompanied by great garlands of lies that no one believes but everyone accommodates. Everyone is expected to believe the absurd. That is natural. To do otherwise is to be unreliable, unpatriotic, untrustworthy. It seems to me that at least the rulers can be looked at, their words recorded, their methods of execution noted. I have great difficulty with the way the powerful present themselves with such certainty when in power, and with such modesty, with such charming fits of forgetfulness, when their power is gone. They may kill, destroy, corrupt with open enthusiasm and with backing from those they appoint, but when they must give up power, or are brought to book, they protest that all they have done was for the good of their people; that it was not they but, 'others' who were responsible. In the aftermath of evil there is seldom justice. There never is remorse – there is only forgetfulness and denial and blankness. Worse, there is the appallingly smooth line taken by those who would like to call themselves 'realists', and who reckon that barbarism was no more than 'a stage through which these countries pass'; or that the victims brought it upon themselves; or, even more cynically, that what had been done was what any ruler would have done in the tyrant's place, and that to question or condemn such self-exculpation is unrealistic, naïve and childish.

★

To travel through Zimbabwe at election time was one of the eeriest and most thrilling things I have ever done; it was a journey into absurdity, cruelty and great courage, into a wonderland, a terrible fairytale about dragons and dark angels. Zimbabwe was the purest example of a police-state I had known: it compared with Serbia, with Vietnam, with the old East Germany, and outdid them in palpable fear and the paralysis of its citizens, weakened by hunger and the ever-present officers of the state. Its only free agents were lackeys and functionaries who served the all-powerful ruling party, which was directed by a politburo of servile place-men, all of which ponderous apparatus meant nothing at all, actually, because it was controlled at every point by a tyrant whose whim was law. His name and image were every-where: His Excellency, the President, Comrade Robert Gabriel Mugabe. There was his face again, blossoming and blooming, a cloud of small pellets of colour that became a face, a dangerous cluster, like grapeshot or shrapnel, wired to the roadside fences, constellations of the Leader.

The days of the election in 2002 were some of the strangest I had ever lived through. I watched the campaign as it unfolded. So much in Zimbabwe then seemed to be touched by State-run insanity. There were peerless examples of the big lie, with various new elements thrown into the mix. Land-reform was the key element in the nightly hallucination that was local television news. There was no way, when watching this, to distinguish between news, advertisements and lies. They married so tightly and were presented with the brazen effrontery that Goebbels would have admired. We were shown each night a dream farm, newly liberated from the greedy whites, being worked by grateful Zimbabweans, young 'peasants' in baseball caps, wearing cell phones the continuity man had apparently forgotten to remove still clipped at their waists, dancing their gratitude amid ears of fat green maize in lush fields. From this adulation of the sons of the soil we slid naturally and easily and bizarrely into advertisements for soap powder, and we watched the purveyors of Surf inviting customers to vote for their brand, and doing so in a language that was neatly spliced into the prevailing mood: 'Remember – your opinion, and only your opinion, will decide . . .' – a promise that was as unreliable about soap as it was about the votes that people were preparing to cast in the election. The power of detergents to remove stains shifted to the power of God to shrive souls, the programme went from politics to soap powder to a religious revivalist campaign that promised health, wealth and miracles to those who came together in a spirit of peace. 'Peace' was a word used in Zimbabwe as a form of code. What it really meant was 'Vote for the party, or you get your head kicked in'. It was shameless, riveting, surreal stuff. It was praise for the leader and damnation for his enemies, with copious infusions of commerce and religion thrown in for good measure. It was a kind of triptych made up of soil, soap powder and salvation.

And it got better. The next morning, 21 February, the government television service began the day by showing pictures of the Leader, in his customary grey suit, now for some reason also wearing a red boy-scout's scarf, running across a meadow holding a big bunch of red and white balloons. Behind him, on the sound track, Stevie Wonder sang a little Happy Birthday song in his enthusiastic fashion. As he sang, the President went skipping through the field, releasing his balloons. I was watching the opening celebrations of Robert Gabriel Mugabe's seventy-eighth birthday. It was dictators in clover. This was happy hour in the Great Leap Forward Disco. This was Mao mixed with Mary Poppins, here was the skipping Emperor serenaded by his blind minstrel.

For the rest of his birthday the President ate cake. He ate cake in State House, his official residence, in the company of visiting executives from Lever Brothers who sometimes appeared to have become co-sponsors of his election. He ate cake on the campaign trail for the television cameras, he ate cake on podiums and on platforms. His generals ate cake, and his wife ate cake. It seemed to me there'd been no more mistimed consumption of cake in a hungry country since the day that Marie Antoinette had made the mistake of recommending it to starving Parisians. The newspapers were full of grovelling party pieces – 'May the Almighty grant you many more years and may your wisdom to empower the masses remain steadfast'. There were dozens of similar adulatory notices from a variety of people who judged it wise to join in the huge birthday praise poem.

Mugabe's revolution seemed to be like a spool of film endlessly spinning backwards, a succession of mirror images of worlds that were long gone. In the run-up to the election, white critics of the regime like Judith Todd were detained, just as once she had been by the Smith authorities back in the good old 'bad' old days over thirty years before. She had been taken to Harare for questioning and had an attack of déjà vu when she found herself being carted off in a police Landrover. 'The only difference was that then the police were all white. This time they were all black.' Her father, Garfield Todd, former Prime Minister of Rhodesia, had been deprived of his citizenship and his right to vote, and had issued a remarkable challenge to Robert Mugabe: 'I have been a citizen of this country for sixty-seven years. Today I must shoulder the responsibility of totally rejecting the disenfranchisement of Zimbabweans by ZANU-PF. I totally reject the theft of our citizenship [approximately two million Zimbabweans are affected] by ZANU-PF. I am horrified by the destruction of our economy, the starving of our people, the undermining of our constitution, the torture and humiliation of our nation by ZANU-PF.'

Torture and humiliation were set to continue. It had been Garfield Todd, then a young missionary in Katuma, who gave a bright young teacher named Robert Mugabe his first job, and docked a few shillings from his salary to cover the fees of students whose parents couldn't afford them. Mugabe was very angry. He challenged Todd to box him: 'I raised a hell of a row,' Mugabe remembered years later. He was still doing it and his single-handed destruction of his country was well advanced.

Yet, in February 2002, it was a measure of how disturbed the place had become that many opposition black voters were convinced victory was within their grasp. The mood in Matabeleland, deep in the heart of the country in a little place called Kamativi, where I spent the night that the polls closed, was not depressed at all, on the contrary, it was euphoric. Voters had walked miles on the two days of polling to cast their ballots and as I would drive through the long evenings, I saw them walking towards me, holding their open hands in what looked like a salute but was in fact the sign of the opposition Party, an open hand versus the ruling Party symbol, the clenched fist. The spirit amongst the walking people was one of fiesta. People were convinced that a great day was dawning. Mugabe had lost, there was no way he could have won, no way he could have fiddled the figures or cooked the books or stuffed the ballot boxes. 'Mugabe has gone,' said a man who ran a petrol filling station on the road to Victoria Falls and had just seen it trashed by Mugabe supporters. 'Mugabe's out.'

They wanted to believe better things, who can blame them, but they forgot what Mugabe had said he planned to do; he'd been quite open about it since the drubbing he had taken in the elections the year before, and the humiliation of the rejection in the referendum. 'We were a bit rusty, last time round,' he reflected later, 'we didn't do our homework, we let things slide, we were taken unawares. Next time we won't make the same mistake.' This was the next time. This was the presidential election and Robert Mugabe was seeking another six years in power. He was seeking re-election, but he was also after revenge. The poll was, from beginning to end, an event staged precisely in order that Robert Mugabe should be seen to win. There would be no mistake.

Just before I left Zimbabwe, I drove through Bulawayo. Over at Milton School, where Harold Ferwood, alias Hendrik Verwoerd, had once read the English poets, someone had begun the long process of renaming the 'white schools'. A thick line of paint had been drawn through the name of Milton School and something indecipherable had been scrawled below it. It didn't in the least matter what the name was, because in Zimbabwe names, words, promises, laws, life and death had all become mixed and meaningless.

Even the dead were not safe. If Livingstone could be stoned, then surely Rhodes was not far behind? I went out to the grave where Cecil Rhodes was buried, on a great boulder in the Motopos Hills outside Bulawayo, dark and brooding stone hillocks. Great round boulders lie like loaves baking in the sun. I went out to the grave because I knew I might not see it again. The quaintly named 'Secretary for Projects' of the War Veterans' Association had just made an announcement about the Rhodes grave: 'We cannot find peace when we are keeping a white demon in our midst. It is the very core of our problem. This grave should be returned to the British or just destroyed.'

I climbed up the great rock to where Rhodes lies in a place called World's View. It was characteristic of the man that he should lie, even in death, facing south, eyeing his possessions. What an eye for majestic décor! Unparalleled solitude, splendid isolation, always the best seats in the house, from Table Mountain to the Matopos, that sort of swashbuckling greed was Rhodes all over. It was also the arrogance of his successors. However, the solution was just as bad. The plan was to grub him up and 'purify' the land where he lay. This was a national park of some three hundred and twenty hectares which included herds of buck, San-bushman caves, and some of the most remarkable rock formations in Africa. He was going to be dug up and, once the site was pronounced Rhodes-free, the land was to be parcelled up and handed over to peasant farmers. This was the way to restore pride and prosperity. Perhaps there was something to be said for getting rid of the old rogue, but the question was – why stop there? The tragedy of Africa is that there have been too many colossi and we would have done better to have torn down every one of them, but who will be first and where will you stop?

A walk through the Matopos showed something about the eternal struggle between white and black. It has been an illusion, this long battle for legitimacy, these arguments about who had been in Africa first, who was more indigenous, who was more entitled, who was more virtuous, who was more wicked. All of it was a sham – as a visit to one of the caves in these hills soon showed. On the walls were painted the small and graceful creatures who had lived here thousands of years before black or white came anywhere near this beautiful country. These leaping, hunting people chase after eland, or ostrich. The early San hunters, the bushman – they were the only true possessors of this country. Where were they now? They were extinct, gone, shot out, run to earth, vanished – but they gave the most resounding answer to the futile and familiar racial war that has broken out in this part of southern Africa: the first true Zimbabweans were neither black nor white – they were red.

picador.com

blog
videos
interviews
extracts

www.ingramcontent.com/pod-product-compliance
Ingram Content Group UK Ltd.
Pitfield, Milton Keynes, MK11 3LW, UK
UKHW040640280225
455688UK00002B/41